CW00742185

The Indian Ocean in World History

Throughout history, dominance of the Indian Ocean has been a critical factor in defining a nation's supremacy and power. It is well known that domination of the Indian Ocean played a major part in the success of the Portuguese nation at the start of the sixteenth century. In this innovative text, Milo Kearney shows how the trading and imperial expansionist possibilities offered by the Indian Ocean were exploited by many leading powers from the third millennium BC to the very recent past. Periods covered include:

- The first assertion of Mediterranean European and Chinese influence
- The Arab Golden Age
- The first assertion of North Atlantic influence
- The Cold War period

The Indian Ocean in World History provides a useful synthesis of many of the key issues in world history, such as colonialism, trade, and spread of cultures and religions. It is compulsive reading for all students of world history.

Milo Kearney is Professor of History at the University of Texas at Brownsville. His books include *Boom and Bust: The Historical Cycles of Matamoros and Brownsville* (1991), *Border Cuates: A History of the U.S.–Mexican Twin Cities* (1995), and *Medieval Culture and the Mexican–American Borderlands* (2001).

Themes in World History
Series editor: Peter N. Stearns

The *Themes in World History* series offers focused treatment of a range of human experiences and institutions in the world history context. The purpose is to provide serious, if brief, discussions of important topics as additions to textbook coverage and document collections. The treatments will allow students to probe particular facets of the human story in greater depth than textbook coverage allows, and to gain a fuller sense of historians' analytical methods and debates in the process. Each topic is handled over time – allowing discussions of changes and continuities. Each topic is assessed in terms of a range of different societies and religions – allowing comparisons of relevant similarities and differences. Each book in the series helps readers deal with world history in action, evaluating global contexts as they work through some of the key components of human society and human life.

Gender in World History
Peter N. Stearns

Consumerism in World History:
The Global Transformation of Desire
Peter N. Stearns

Warfare in World History
Michael S. Neiberg

Disease and Medicine in World History
Sheldon Watts

Western Civilization in World History
Peter N. Stearns

The Indian Ocean in World History
Milo Kearney

Asian Democracy in World History
Alan T. Wood

Revolutions in World History
Michael D. Richards

The Indian Ocean in World History

Milo Kearney

Routledge
Taylor & Francis Group

NEW YORK AND LONDON

First published 2004
by Routledge
29 West 35th Street, New York, NY 10001

Simultaneously published in the UK
by Routledge
11 New Fetter Lane, London EC4P 4EE

Routledge is an imprint of the Taylor & Francis Group

© 2004 Milo Kearney

Typeset in Garamond by
Florence Production Ltd, Stoodleigh, Devon
Printed and bound in Great Britain by
TJ International Ltd, Padstow, Cornwall

All rights reserved. No part of this book may be reprinted or
reproduced or utilised in any form or by any electronic, mechanical,
or other means, now known or hereafter invented, including
photocopying and recording, or in any information storage or retrieval
system, without permission in writing from the publishers.

Library of Congress Cataloging in Publication Data
Kearney, Milo.
  The Indian Ocean in world history / Milo Kearney.
    p. cm. – (Themes in world history)
  1. Indian Ocean Region–History. I. Title. II. Series.
  DS340.K36 2003
  909'.09824—dc21   2003008623

British Library Cataloguing in Publication Data
A catalogue record for this book is available from the British Library

ISBN 0–415–31277–9 (hbk)
ISBN 0–415–31278–7 (pbk)

To my dear wife Vivian,
who wrote:

And yet . . .

There is a loveliness,
through all your wondering,
your sense of nothingness,
your moods of tears,
fears of death —

that shows through sorrow —
through emptiness;
a soft whisper,
forming a saddened smile,
saying —

And yet . . .

Contents

Maps

Acknowledgments

I am grateful to the series editor, Professor Peter Stearns, and to Professors Stephen S. Gosch of the University of Wisconsin–Eau Claire and Harry Wade of Texas A & M University for their suggestions on shaping this book, and to Ed Moore, CNN war correspondent in Turkey, and Will and Mimosa Stephenson, all three my friends and colleagues at the University of Texas at Brownsville, for their encouragement and comments. The remaining flaws and shortcomings are entirely my own responsibility. Many thanks are due to my loving family: to my wife Vivian for her constant and many-faceted aid; to our daughter and son-in-law Kathleen and Danny Anzak and to our son and daughter-in-law Sean and Lisa Kearney for their help in finding sources and with computer problems; and to our grandsons Benjamin Edward Anzak, Elijah Daniel Anzak, and Ian Dylan Kearney for their unwitting moral support.

Chapter 1

Introduction

What is the role of the Indian Ocean and its region in world history? The thesis of this book is that significant participation in Indian Ocean trade has always been a major indicator of a state's or region's prominence and leadership from a global perspective. It is conventional wisdom that Indian Ocean trade played a large role in the Portuguese success at the start of the sixteenth century. However, its consistent influence on the rise and fall of other states or regions has either been understated or, most commonly, not acknowledged at all. This is not to say that the Indian Ocean floated the economy of every state or region that reached a top position, but that a major presence in Indian Ocean trade has always indicated a level of economic health essential to world leadership. In presenting this thesis, this book will discuss five different international trading patterns benefiting from the Indian Ocean that have prevailed in succession spanning world history from the beginning to the present. It will be argued that the participating states or regions were those making a prime contribution to world progress and cultural creativity. The reasons for the shifts, and the contributions and results of each trading configuration will be considered in turn.

Because of the highly controversial nature of a possible New World tie-in to these patterns before the fifteenth century (and the relatively sub-ordinate role of Latin America in Indian Ocean trade and world leader-ship), principally Old World trading patterns will be considered. The Western Hemisphere through much of history lagged behind the Eastern Hemisphere's levels of civilization precisely because of its distance from the Indian Ocean and the major trade routes leading from it. Within the Old World, the impact of Indian Ocean trade on the rise and fall of European states and regions is the most unusual and controversial part of the thesis, and thus will require the most detailed attention. The importance of Indian Ocean trade to the nations around its rim is far more obvious and accepted, and its role in the history of China and Japan only slightly less so.

Trade, wealth, power, creativity, and geography

What are the factors that determine which states or regions take a lead in history? Biologists point out that more changes in physical variations in a species tend to occur with an increase in the size of the gene pool. A corollary states that the most change within a particular gene pool tends to occur toward the geographic center of the population, where the greatest contact occurs. Thus, the paleontological record shows a preponderance of new species appearing in the Old World, then spreading gradually first to North America, then to South America, and finally to Australia. Applied to history, this principle suggests that change in general, other factors being constant, should center in the Eastern Hemisphere, with its heavier population concentration. Within the Eastern Hemisphere, change (and thus leadership) should be expected especially in the Middle East, where the Old World's three main continents converge. This is exactly where human history received its initial impetus and long retained its primary focus.

Another principle is that culture grows fastest along the main trade routes. Trade, as emphasized by Fernand Braudel in his study of the Mediterranean in the sixteenth century, follows mainly those waterways that bring together the greatest variety of peoples and lands, along with their products. The protected inland seas and rivers, encouraging commerce, are stimulated all the more. Highly indented coastlines, rich soil, a good climate, and a plentitude of rivers and side seas all enhance trading opportunities. Long-distance trade brings a meeting of different peoples, with an exchange of ideas and the leisure and investment in learning which the trading wealth bestows. The greatest such favorable maritime trade route on earth, by a long shot, is the water route in the very middle of the Old World, stretching from the Indian Ocean through either the Persian Gulf and the Tigris and Euphrates Rivers or through the Red Sea to the Mediterranean, and thence up the Rhone and down the Seine, the Moselle, the Scheldt, the Meuse, or the Rhine to the English Channel, or alternatively through the Strait of Gibraltar and up the Atlantic coast. This is the world's major contact route between West and East.

The Indian Ocean, which forms a central hub of this long trading belt, is also favored by its monsoon wind patterns, which move dependably to the northeast in the summer, and to the southwest in the winter. The hospitable warm climate and waters throughout much of the Indian Ocean coastal region encouraged similar cultural traits to move from one port to another (the arid Arabian and Persian coasts in the far northwest and Australian coasts in the far southeast being the main climatic exceptions). The gigantic bay shape of the Indian Ocean further encouraged trading contacts. In addition, the merchants of the lands lying on the Mediterranean (the world's largest inland sea), particularly those along its northern, better-watered and highly indented coast (good for harbors and trading contacts) which were favored as dominant merchant societies, along with the merchants of China to the east, were consistently drawn into the Indian Ocean trade.

The combination of the above factors of waterways, topography, and wind patterns determined that civilization has been led overwhelmingly by a small number of the regions of the world, as predestined by their locations along these and corollary trade routes. These form one long, continuous belt stretching from China through India, Iran, Iraq, Egypt, Syria, Greece, Italy, France, Spain, and Portugal to England (and its modern extension the United States). Principal 'wannabe' countries lying somewhat off this trade belt that have made what (to date) have been unsuccessful bids for 'top dog' status have included Japan, Russia, and Germany. History has not been egalitarian. This prime world trade route with its Indian Ocean focus has showered its blessings and curses in turn on selected parts of various continents, blind to the claims of any particular race or tongue.

The Indian Ocean factor

Thus, which land (or lands) has (or have) been in the lead in world wealth, power, and creativity at any particular time has been determined to a significant extent by, or been correlated with, control of or significant participation in the trade of the Indian Ocean and the lands of its periphery. This region represents the largest single chunk of exploitable wealth on earth, with such lucrative products as spices, gems, oil, gas, uranium, gold, tin, manganese, nickel, bauxite, and zinc. The Persian Gulf region is believed to hold over half of the world's oil reserves. India still leads in the production and export of spices, which have been sought after through the centuries for flavoring food and as medicines. The forests of the Western Ghats range of mountains along India's southwestern Malabar coast provided ginger and pepper (which was later spread to Sri Lanka, Thailand, Sumatra, and the Lesser Sunda Islands). Here pepper plant vines with aerial roots covered the palms, their tendrils producing peppercorns waiting to be stripped off into bags and dried. The local ginger grass root was ground up, and in part used to produce curry powder (colored yellow by the expensive saffron derived from the turmeric or Indian saffron's dried flower stigmas). These plants require just the right climatic conditions to prosper, and the Western Ghats provide an unbeatable combination of heat with high humidity and high altitude. Cinnamon (from the bark of the cinnamon tree stripped, rolled into sticks, and then dried) grew on the western coast of the island of Sri Lanka. Distillate of cinnamon and ginger was thought to help the complexion and to cure paralysis. Indigo grew along India's southeastern Coromandel coast, as well as in Gujarat and Rajasthan.

The Moluccas (or spice islands) in the Indonesian archipelago supplied cloves, nutmeg, and mace. Clove spice is the dried, unopened flower buds (the 'black rose') of the clove tree (myrtle family) of Ternate, Tidore, Bacan, Motir, and Makian Islands, and is used either whole or ground up as a seasoning. Nutmeg is the dried and ground large seed from inside the fruit of the *Myristica fragrans* tree of the six small Banda Islands; and mace is the dried and ground bright red lacey covering from around the fruit of the same tree.

Diamonds were mined in Golconda and other parts of India, which also exported emeralds and rubies. Onyx and carnelian came from Gujarat in western India. Sri Lanka provided pearls and gems. Gold was found in the rivers of Mozambique. Exportable woods included the teakwood and sandalwood of Malabar, the west coast of India.

In addition to such natural wealth, the Indian Ocean region also holds the world's largest exploitable mass market for buying the goods of any dominant state or region. Its geographic location in the middle of the world's main trading belt has made it eminently accessible. Its peoples (mainly for religious reasons which will be detailed in the sections on Hinduism, Buddhism, and Jainism) have been neither notably militaristic nor especially aggressive traders abroad, but have been eager to trade with foreign merchants coming to their ports. By contrast, China, which also has a dense population, has been less prodigiously showered with trading products, has less of its area and population close to a coast, and does not have a conjunction of so many neighboring states clustered around its China Sea.

Four blocks of would-be exploiter states or regions have been drawn to this beckoning wealth, eager to control it. The lands in these blocks have frequently acted as allies, due to their common interest in emphasizing a particular trade route in and out of the Indian Ocean area. The four blocks, by their major entry route, can be outlined as follows:

1   The Strait of Malacca route. This is the route leading between the Malay Peninsula and the island of Sumatra to China and Japan. China controlled trade through this route most energetically in the Yuan, and early Ming (and possibly already in the Han) Dynasties. Japan tried to establish a similar domination briefly during World War II.

2   The Persian Gulf route. This route has been the most favorable for Iraq, Iran, and Russia. It was the favored trading path in the Copper Age, Iran's periods of prominence, and the Abbasid caliphate.

3   The Red Sea route. This is the route that has been preferred by Egypt, Palestine, Lebanon, Greece, and Italy. It has also been favorable for France. This route has been emphasized through more centuries than

any other, including in the Bronze Age, the Iron Age, the Roman Empire, the early Byzantine Empire, the Umayyad Dynasty, the Fatimid Dynasty, the Ayyubid Dynasty, and the Circassian Mamluk Dynasty.

4   The Cape of Good Hope route. Not developed until the start of the sixteenth century, this route came to be favored by Portugal, Spain, the Netherlands, France, the British Empire, and the United States. It was the favored trading path of early modern times.

In the competition for world leadership between the powers favoring one trading route or the other, certain factors have repeatedly come into play. A shift in technological or military advancement has often allowed a new society to rise to the top. The resulting change is usually sudden, as one society makes use of its new advantage while the innovation is still its monopoly. Social enervation sometimes results from success, as self-indulgence weakens a society that has made its way to the top. Assuming that the power they enjoy will last indefinitely, the people may become lax, allowing an alert and determined rival power to grab control in its turn. States or regions in power are sometimes pushed to overextend their resources in order to consolidate their control even more, with a consequent weakening of their position, allowing other states or regions to defeat them. States or regions out of power may 'gang up' on the state or region at the top to bring it down, underscoring the importance of diplomacy and public relations. The cohesiveness of a state or region, dependent on the unity of its leaders and on harmony between its social classes and ethnic groups, can affect the rise and fall of societies. Religious beliefs can add a fervor that may push a society to the top or destroy it. Religious beliefs have helped or hindered mercantile development, just as trading interests have in turn shaped religious developments. Furthermore, the clash of religions has often gone hand in hand with the conflict of rival commercial and power interests. Those states or regions that allow foreign mercenary elements to take a strong position in their armed forces may risk collapse due to lack of a loyal military. The personalities of the leading figures can have a major impact on developments. An element of chance may be taken into consideration, unless the reader is convinced of the rule of destiny or providence in human affairs. While every historical period builds, to an extent, on the accomplishments of the previous period, the borrowing is more extensive if the previous state or region was still productive at the time of its demise.

These factors are interwoven with a state or region's presence in Indian Ocean trade, and will be considered as the histories of states or regions shifting in and out of power are traced. However, it is argued that significant participation, directly or indirectly, in Indian Ocean trade, is one of the consistent and key factors in explaining a state or region's leading role in history. This book is thus not meant to be strictly a maritime or trade history, but rather a presentation of the thesis that the rise and fall of the leading states and regions of the world through history is linked in important measure to the extent of their participation in Indian Ocean trade.

The trading contacts in and with the Indian Ocean area will be considered for each period, along with a consideration of other factors in the rise, fall, and creativity of states and regions through time. Western scholarship is currently undergoing an adjustment in perspective that for many years has viewed the world through Western eyes, downplaying the role of non-Western nations while highlighting the classical-studies approach that traces the spread of civilization from the Fertile Crescent and eastern Mediterranean to western Europe. Such an approach has left the period from the sixth century to the twelfth century under the rubric of the Dark Ages, rather than the Golden Age, as it will be termed here. This study will point to the importance of South Asia from first to last, emphasize the Chinese contribution in opening the eastern Indian Ocean to world trade, detail the Indian role in the blossoming of Southeast Asia, and underline the Mongol and Ming Chinese role in transforming world trade for many centuries.

On the other hand, it is possible to distort in the opposite direction as well. Europe already in antiquity played a more important role in world history and trade than might be expected, for two main reasons: (1) the Mediterranean's relatively calm seas (in the summer), highly indented coasts, and diverse regions easily attainable by navigable rivers drew ships early to the west; and (2) the disruptive impact of the military destruction and epidemics caused by the thirteenth century Mongol conquests was far more severe for Asia than for Europe, leaving European states for half a millennium as the main competitors for Indian Ocean trade.

Certainly it cannot be a coincidence that each dominant state or region has striven for and obtained a large part of the Indian Ocean trade. Indeed, the period of its significant participation in Indian Ocean trade has coincided with its period of historical prominence. As the American military moves into an increasing confrontation and potential friction with Muslims of the Indian Ocean fringe, an understanding of this pattern of world history has become particularly critical.

This book will look at five successive patterns of suggested world leadership in wealth and power (and usually creativity, as well). These five general periods are:

1 The original monopoly of Indian Ocean trade by lands lying either directly on its shores or on seas leading immediately from it (down to the sixth century BC);

2 The first period of intrusion of Mediterranean European influence from the west and of Chinese influence from the east (from the sixth century BC through the sixth century AD);

3 The receding of the European and Chinese impact in the Arab golden age (seventh century AD through the eleventh century AD);

4 A period of resurgence of Chinese and Mediterranean European influence in Indian Ocean trade (twelfth century through the fifteenth century AD); and

5 A rising dominance of the Indian Ocean and its trade by the lands of the North Atlantic (from the sixteenth through the twentieth century). The last period will be divided into various chapters, in consideration of its greater importance for today.

These are the proposed five turns of history's wheel around the Indian Ocean trading hub.

Further reading

Reading applicable to the book in general include the following. On geographic influences: W. Gordon East, *The Geography Behind History* (New York: W.W. Norton, 1965); and Clark G. Reynolds, *History and the Sea: Essays on Maritime Strategies* (Columbia, South Carolina: University of South Carolina, 1989).

On global interconnections: Jerry H. Bentley, *Old World Encounters: Cross-cultural Contacts and Exchanges in Pre-Modern Times* (New York: Oxford University Press, 1993); Daniel J. Boorstin, *The Discoverers: A History of Man's Search to Know his World and Himself* (New York: Vintage Books, 1983); James Burke, *Connections* (Boston and Toronto: Little, Brown and Company, 1978); Philip D. Curtin, *Cross-cultural Trade in World History* (Cambridge: Cambridge University Press, 1984); Paul Kennedy, *The Rise and Fall of the Great Powers: Economic Change and Military Conflict from 1500 to 2000* (New York: Random House, 2000); John Robert McNeill and William Hardy McNeill, *The Human Web: A Bird's Eye View of World History* (New York: W.W. Norton, 2003); Michael S. Neiberg, *Warfare in World History* (London and New York: Routledge, 2001); Reay Tannahill, *Food In History* (New York: Stein and Day, 1973); and Arnold Toynbee, *War and Civilization* (Oxford: Oxford University Press, 1950).

On the history of the Indian Ocean: G.A. Ballard, *Rulers of the Indian Ocean* (Lahore: Al-Biruni, 1979); Giorgio Borsa (ed.), *Trade and Politics in the*

Indian Ocean: Historical and Contemporary Perspectives (New Delhi: Manohar, 1990); K.N. Chaudhuri, *Trade and Civilisation in the Indian Ocean: An Economic History from the Rise of Islam to 1750* (Cambridge: Cambridge University Press, 1985); S.N. Kohli, *Sea Power and the Indian Ocean, with Special Reference to India* (New Delhi: Tata McGraw-Hill, 1978); K.S. Mathew (ed.), *Shipbuilding and Navigation in the Indian Ocean Region AD 1400–1800* (New Delhi: Munshiram Manoharlal, 1997); Kenneth McPherson, *The Indian Ocean* (Delhi: Oxford University Press, 1998); Rudrangshu Mukherjee and Lakshmi Subramanian (ed.), *Politics and Trade in the Indian Ocean World* (Delhi: Oxford University Press, 1998); and M.N. Pearson (ed.), *Spices in the Indian Ocean World*, vol. 11 of A.J.R. Russell-Wood (ed.), *An Expanding World: The European Impact on World History, 1450–1800* (Aldershot, Hampshire and Brookfield, Vermont: Variorum, 1996).

On India: Robert and Roma Bradnock, *India Handbook* (Bath: Footprint Handbooks, 1998); John Keay, *India: A History* (New York: Atlantic Monthly Press, 2000).

On East Asia: Samuel Adrian Miles Adshead, *Central Asia in World History* (New York: St. Martin's Press, 1993); Samuel Adrian Miles Adshead, *China in World History* (New York: St. Martin's Press, 2000); and J.D. Legge, *Indonesia* (Englewood Cliffs, New Jersey: Prentice-Hall, 1964).

On the Middle Eastern shores of the Indian Ocean: Brian Doe, *Southern Arabia* (New York: McGraw-Hill, 1971); Clément Huart, *Ancient Persia and Iranian Civilization* (New York: Barnes and Noble, 1972); Ira M. Lapidus, *A History of Islamic Societies* (Cambridge: Cambridge University Press, 2002); Bernard Lewis, *The Arabs in History* (Amherst, Massachusetts: Hutchinson, 1964); Sandra Mackey, *The Iranians: Persia, Islam, and the Soul of a Nation* (New York: Dutton, Penguin Books, 1996); Joseph Malone, *The Arab Lands of Western Asia* (Englewood Cliffs, New Jersey: Prentice-Hall, 1973); and Patricia Risso, *Merchants and Faith: Muslim Commerce and Culture in the Indian Ocean* (Boulder, Colorado: Westview Press, 1995).

On the African shores of the Indian Ocean: Joseph E. Harris, *Africans and their History* (New York: New American Library, 1987); Robert M. Maxon, *East Africa: An Introductory History* (Morgantown, West Virginia: West Virginia University Press, 1994); Kevin Shillington, *History of Africa* (New York: St. Martin's Press, 1995); Gideon S. Were and Derek A. Wilson, *East Africa Through a Thousand Years: A History of the Years AD 1000 to the Present Day* (New York: Africana Publishing Company, 1984).

On the Mediterranean trade extension: Fernand Braudel, *The Mediterranean and the Mediterranean World in the Age of Philip II* (New York: Harper and Row, 1973); Peregrine Horden and Nicholas Purcell, *The Corrupting Sea: A Study of Mediterranean History* (Oxford: Blackwell, 2000); and Archibald Lewis and Timothy Runyon, *European Naval and Maritime History, 300–1500* (Bloomington: Indiana University, 1985).

Chapter 2

The earliest leadership in Indian Ocean trade

This chapter will trace the initial development of trade in the Indian Ocean and the resulting patterns of wealth, power, and creativity. The period from the fourth millennium to the sixth century BC will be examined, during which the Indian Ocean trading world with its spices, metals, and gems was the preserve of lands located on its periphery. It will first deal with the period down to the eighteenth century BC in which Mesopotamia was in the forefront, closely followed by the Indus Valley and Egypt. It will then examine the millennium from the sixteenth to the sixth century BC in which Egypt took the limelight, noting Egypt's shifting trading alliances in the Mediterranean extension of the Indian Ocean trade.

India and its ocean were so central to world trade, power, and the march of progress that the very first civilizations on earth emerged in connection with it. Nature dictated where trade would first spark the rise of important civilization, in the western Indian Ocean (also called the Arabian Sea). Here drier climates spurred irrigation with a concomitant advanced social organization supportive of greater trade along major river systems (the Indus, the Tigris and Euphrates, and the Nile). Southeast Asia developed trade, but this commerce did not yet spark the rise of great urban centers. The dichotomy between the eastern and the western halves of the Indian Ocean was made all the more pronounced by the fact that the weather makes it very difficult to round the southern tip of India in any month but January, causing sailing layovers of up to a year. This pattern encouraged an initial emergence of trade and civilization in the western Indian Ocean.

One inducement to the start of sailing in the Persian Gulf was the abundance of fish that beckoned to fishermen who must have developed the ships and the maritime knowledge subsequently applied to trading ventures. Dugout canoes were made fit for the open sea by building up the sides with planks, inserting frames for strengthening, holding the planks together by sewn cords, and adding a square sail. Since the square sail moved the ships with the winds, oars were also used, for moving against the winds when necessary. Such sewn plank boats were used in the Indian Ocean to the end of the fifteenth century, and are still common in India, Ceylon, and East Africa. Lateen (or triangular) sails would eventually prevail in the Arabian Sea (the date of their appearance is disputed). Large double-outriggers (rafts or other vessels with projecting contrivances terminating in a boatlike float, braced to the side to prevent capsizing) would come to dominate the Bay of Bengal in the east. Teakwood from the forests of the Western Ghats made especially the ports of the Malabar coast ship-building centers. The paucity of land foodstuffs on most of the shores of the Persian Gulf would have further encouraged people to harvest the sea. (In contrast, the Mediterranean has a good deal of fertile coastline but a sparser population of fish.)

Once fishermen were working the Persian Gulf, the wind pattern gave another impetus that fostered contact with other lands. In the Indian Ocean, the summer (May to October) monsoon blows dependably and constantly from the southwest (pushing ships to the far coasts through the summer). A winter (November to April) monsoon blows from the north-east (bringing the ships back to India again). These winds are usually below gale force, strong for speed, but not too violent. Only in June and July did the summer monsoon pose a danger to travel. This wind pattern was a natural invitation for the peoples of Iraq to navigate through the Persian Gulf and Indian Ocean to India and back (as it similarly encouraged travel in the Bay of Bengal). Use of sea-going boats for trade dates from before 4000 BC At first trading voyages hugged the coast of Iran, until in a later period ships could be designed powerful enough to hold up under the force of the monsoon winds. While the Red Sea route was not much more remote from India than that of the Persian Gulf, the Red Sea's huge rocks and sharp coral reefs extending out from both coasts allowed sailing only by day. Furthermore, winds blowing from the north year round over the northern half of the sea induced most traders to either land on the Egyptian coast half way up and cross over to Aswan and the Nile, or to land at Jiddah and take the caravan route north to the Fertile Crescent.

How Indian Ocean trade helped the Sumerians rise to prominence

The first people to forge a 'civilization' were, not coincidentally, also the first people to wrestle a trading control over a significant portion of the Indian Ocean. These were the Sumerians of the third millennium BC (with a tentative start reaching back into the fourth millennium BC). There are several reasons that may explain why Sumer should have been the first society to transform itself from a simple farming folk into a mercantile civilization. For one, Mesopotamia's soil was hard and difficult to work. Where Egyptians could make do with a simple digging stick, Mesopotamians by 4000 BC had invented the ox-drawn plow. The plow did such a good job of working the soil that the Sumerians developed a surplus of wheat and barley, which they were then able to trade for other goods.

The need for organization to carry out irrigation projects led to a more advanced social structure useful for launching new projects. This advantage was shared with Egypt, but the extensive flooding mentioned in Mesopotamian records and confirmed by archeologists as occurring from around 4000 BC must have given special urgency to the Sumerian impulse to cooperate in monitoring and controlling the river water: *shumer* (from which we derive the name Sumer) means 'watchman' or 'guard.' Located in an area of geographic overlap (the arid zone extending southward with its desert folk, and a major river system pulling down northern peoples from the Iranian Plateau), Sumer was home to people speaking two languages. This must have made the inhabitants comfortable with cultural differences, encouraged travel and connections in contrasting regions, and stimulated thought. Being poor in natural resources (except for wheat and barley), Mesopotamian people needed to look to trade to import needed goods, including presumably timber from the forests of India.

Thus, located at the juncture of the Tigris and Euphrates Rivers with the Persian Gulf, Sumer accepted the open invitation to begin trading voyages over the waves. The kings (*ensi*) and temple priests provided the organization and support for trading ventures, which were set up as royal monopolies. Most of the ancient cities of Sumer built complex observatories, and this

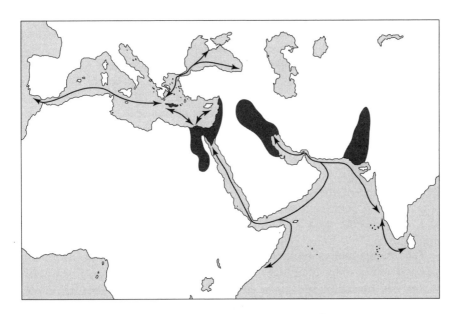

Figure 2.1 Principal lands and sea routes discussed in Chapter 2

development of star study must have facilitated navigation across open stretches of water in the Indian Ocean. Sumerians pushed east along the coast to the Indus Valley. Evidence shows very early trade between Mesopotamia and India. The Sumerian trade of the third millennium BC included shells from the Persian Gulf, copper from Oman, timber from the Zagros Mountains, silver and lead from the Taurus Mountains, carnelian from the Indus Valley, and wood brought in (by sea) from 'Meluhha' (India?). India also supplied ivory. Bahrain was a major port-of-call. Sargon the Great in the late 2300s BC boasted of ships sailing from Oman up the Euphrates River all the way to his capital of Akkad. The trade helped to turn farming villages like Uruk, Ur, Lagash, and Kish into trading towns. Ur and Eridu seem to have developed as port towns. Priest-kings ruled some of these towns, and military kings others, but both types of leaders served to maintain the order and to protect their wealth.

How the Indian Ocean trade stimulated Sumer's inventiveness

The Sumerians' less advanced and envious neighbors (geographically closer than Egypt's neighbors) obliged them to stay on their toes to protect their ingeniously acquired wealth. New inventions appeared, useful for Sumer's budding trade. Writing evolved by the end of the third millennium BC from pictographic hieroglyphics into cuneiform writing. Symbols for words (similar in concept to computer screen icons) were carved with a sharp wedge-shaped stylus on to wet mud tablets, which were then sun-dried to harden them. An arithmetic system was developed, good for keeping track of expenses and profits, with a number system based on units of sixty. Our reckoning of sixty seconds in a minute, sixty minutes in an hour, and twenty-four hours in a day is based on this early approach. So are our twelve-constellation zodiac and our twelve-month calendar, twelve being one-fifth of sixty. The Sumerians themselves introduced that calendar, with twenty-nine and thirty-day months and seven days to the week. There were 354 days to the year, with an intercalary month added occasionally for readjustment. Weights and measures were worked out, important for buying and selling. Maps were produced to guide the merchants on their travels. The invention of the wheel was applied to making pottery as well as to wagons. Iraqi petroleum was already put to use, oil being used for lamps and asphalt being used for calking boats and mixing paints, among other applications.

The Mesopotamian religion reinforced the mercantile ethos. The early pastoral and farming communities had been helped by the ethical teachings of the Creator-and-Savior gods, Anu and Enlil. An emphasis on coopera-tion and sharing, family morality, and simple living had smoothed the hard lot of the farmer. The rise of the city with its industry and trade had found reinforcement in the rebellious teachings of the god of death and the underworld, Ea/Enki, and the goddess of forbidden love, Ishtar. The magic formulae to help oneself and hurt one's enemies gave approval to a spirit of business competition; temples of prostitution encouraged the work incentive (by allowing profits to be spent however one chose); and human sacrifice encouraged a spirit of military ruthlessness to protect new-found wealth. On the other hand, the prosperity of the Sumerian city-states created a society able to introduce reforms like the laws of Uru of Lagash to protect the weak. The wealth and leisure generated also stimulated the Sumerians to develop other elements of civilization. The world's first literature and megalithic architecture were the most spectacular of these contributions. *The Epic of Gilgamesh* in part traces the travel adventures of King Gilgamesh of Uruk in the twenty-ninth century BC. Merchants and sailors in the audience must have listened to the hero's travels with personal interest. The world's first monumental architecture used the most basic forms to adorn the Sumerian city-states, the column, corbel arch, vault, dome, and ziggurat step pyramid.

Early trading contact between India and the Middle East is evidenced by the many shared literary and artistic symbols. Two examples might be mentioned: the Tree of Life and the Tree of Knowledge. Both trees are mentioned in Genesis and elsewhere in early Fertile Crescent lore. The Tree of Life to the Indians is the acacia. Acacia beans are ground into a food available even during droughts as an ever-present life-sustaining nourishment. (The acacia tree also releases a chemical signal into the air that warns other acacias that leaf-eating animals are at work, causing them to release a protective poison to preserve themselves.) The Hebrew cabinet or 'arc' of the covenant (according to Exodus), and (by a later tradition) the 'gopher wood' box or 'ark' of Noah (both English words derived from the Latin *arca* or box) and the Cross of Jesus (by one tradition) were all made of acacia wood. The Tree of Knowledge is said by the Indians to be the *bo* or *bodhi* tree (*Ficus religiosus*, a member of the fig family that bears no figs). A cobra represents the spirit who lives in the tree. The fig is a symbol of sexuality; Adam and Eve wore fig leaves over their private parts in the Garden of Eden once they realized that they were naked.

Sumer's trade and creativity spreads to the Atlantic and to the Pacific

The trade enjoyed by the Sumerians extended to both east and west, following the principal water routes in each direction. Four major new civilizations resulted, two to the east (the Indus Valley and Chinese) and two to the west (Egyptian and Iberian – see page 13). Sumerian traders appeared in both Egypt and the Indus Valley, while the trade to China and Spain went through intermediaries.

The trade stimulus to Indus Valley civilization

To the east, the main trading partner of the Sumerians to emerge into civilization was the society of the Indus Valley in the third millennium BC. A mile-long canal connected docks at the Indus Valley port of Lothal with the Gulf of Cambay on the Indian Ocean. Indus Valley inhabitants inscribed steatite seals (believed to have been used in trade) that have been found in Mesopotamia excavations. The Indus Valley merchants also seem to have traded local cotton goods regularly with other parts of India, obtaining tin, copper, lapis lazuli, jade, turquoise, building stone, ivory, and timber from western India. Mesopotamia provided foodstuffs, silver, and woolen cloth and other manufactured goods. Oman and Bahrain (Dilmun) acted as ports of call, and provided pearls and coral (from Bahrain) and copper (from Oman). The Indus Valley economy and culture centered on the towns of Mohenjo-daro in Sind (southern Pakistan) and Harrappa in Punjab (northern Pakistan). A large citadel, rising from an artificial mound (beside a great bath), stood at the town centers, the location of a ziggurat in a Sumerian city. The town was served with an elaborate water and drainage system, with garbage chutes and drainpipes coming out of the houses.

Sumerian influences merged with local Indus Valley culture. A local Indus Valley script, still undeciphered, appeared. Buildings employed pillars, corbel arches, and vaults. Parallels existed between Sumer's and the Indus Valley's religious systems. Ea/Enki's Indus Valley counterpart as the god of death was a prototype of the later Hindu god Shiva, while Ishtar's equivalent was a goddess of fertility, the prototype of the later Hindu goddess Kali. Just as these deities prefigure developments in later Hindu religion, so other traits typical of later periods of Indian history emerged at this point, including wrap-around saris, nose rings, the urna dot on the forehead of married women, and statues of people in the lotus position practicing the breath control connected with yoga meditation.

The (land) trade stimulus to Chinese society

Sumer's vitality resulting from its trade routes across the Indian Ocean allowed it also to establish a major land route across Central Asia to China. The Sumerian trade contact helped to stimulate China in the second half of the third millennium BC into creating its own civilization as well. While this development came via overland trade, the Chinese society stirred into life would later come to play a major role in the Indian Ocean trade, and thus world history. This was the period of the legendary first dynasty of China, the Xia, based in the Huang Ho (Yellow River) Valley of northern China. The region was called Chung-Kuo ('Central Land'), which is still the name used by Chinese for their country. This area was the part of China that land trade from Sumer would naturally encounter first, by the route across Central Asia and Sinkiang.

The trade stimulus to Egyptian society

After 3500 BC, the Sumerians worked their way up the Euphrates, over to the Mediterranean coast, and then sailed or followed the land route south to Egypt, where a prosperous wheat- and barley-farming society was already in existence. Two artifacts recovered by archeologists, the Gebel al-Arak Knife and the Two Gazelles Palette, show that the Sumerian presence in Egypt was at first violently resisted. The flint knife's decorated handle depicts a sea battle between Sumerian high-prow and high-stern ships and Egyptian reed boats. The palette shows Egyptian soldiers leading off prisoners of war. Despite such initial difficulties, the Sumerians persisted. They became so crucial in Egypt's awakening civilization that the upper class of Copper Age Egypt came to be marked through intermarriage by the brachycephalic skulls and lighter skin of the Sumerians. The Sumerian influence also stimulated unification. The new trading wealth brought by Sumerian merchants into the Nile delta of Lower Egypt acted as a magnet drawing Upper Egypt to conquer the lands downstream about 3000 BC.

The Egyptians joined the Sumerians in seafaring. By at latest the twenty-fifth century BC, Egyptian ships were sailing the Red Sea. By the twenty-fourth century, these ships were bringing manufactured goods to Yemen, Ethiopia, and 'Punt' (probably Somalia) in exchange for slaves, ivory, and gold (from Ethiopia and Somalia), spices (from India via Yemen), and the resins frankincense and myrrh (from Yemen). The civilization that blossomed in Egypt borrowed many Sumerian features, including religious teachings. The Sumerian Ea/Enki's Egyptian equivalent as god of the underworld was Osiris, while Ishtar, the Mesopotamian goddess of illicit love, was mirrored in Isis. The Mesopotamian teaching about Ishtar's role in the return of vegetation in the spring was paralleled by the Egyptian belief that Osiris was put to death, and that Isis gathered his dismembered limbs and magically gave new birth to him as the hawk-god Horus. At the annual Heb-Sed festival, the Pharaoh was (only symbolically) put to death and then reintroduced as having been rejuvenated.

Mesopotamian motifs were adopted into Egyptian art, including serpopards and winged griffins (with eagle head and wings on a lion's body). The most spectacular Mesopotamian influence over Egyptian architecture was the pyramid. The first Egytian pyramid (a step-pyramid like the Mesopotamian ziggurats) was built in the twenty-seventh century BC at Saqqara. The Sumerian-born prime minister Imhotep constructed it as a tomb for Pharaoh Zoser. Aside from his function as minister and architect, Imhotep was a great physician, who introduced trepanning (removing a piece of the skull), for which the Egyptians later worshipped him as the god of medicine.

The trade stimulus to Iberian society

Just as in the case of the rise of Chinese civilization, so it was of the greatest significance to later trading developments in the Indian Ocean and to world history that the main trade route through Egypt led westward through the Mediterranean to Atlantic Europe. Here another civilization was stirred into being, that of the Iberians. The Iberians, native to North Africa from Libya through Morocco, had spread from the Maghreb to populate Atlantic Europe. They mined copper at Río Tinto (Huelva, southwest Spain), and exported it along with furs and other trading items. Fortified walls were built at Los Millares southwest of Valencia to protect the trade. Their most important trading port was Tarshish, located on an island off the Atlantic coast of southern Spain a little to the east of the mouth of the Guadalquivir River. This location was ideal for coordinating an exchange of trade between the Atlantic and Mediterranean. The Iberians picked up many of the elements of civilization already passed from the Sumerians to the Egyptians. They, too, developed a megalithic architecture, although menhirs (erect stones), dolmens (table stones), cromlechs (stone circles), and beehive structures were preferred to pyramids.

The Indian Ocean trade disruption of the mid-third millennium BC

The seeds of collapse of the Sumerian trade ascendency were sown by the envy of its neighbors. Two nearby powers were especially threatening: the peoples of the Zagros Mountains and the Iranian Plateau to the northeast, and the less prosperous upriver city-states of central Mesopotamia. Twice the upriver towns marched under aggressive kings to conquer Sumer. When weaker successors to the conquering kings came to the throne, northern barbarians were encouraged to swoop down on Mesopotamia and conquer it in their turn.

The first time this sequence was put into motion was about 2300 BC. Sumerian wealth stirred King Sargon I of the upriver town of Akkad (or Agade) to conquer Sumer, victoriously dipping his spear in the Persian Gulf as a sign of ownership. The conquest was followed by a disruption of trade. Under the rule of Sargon's grandson, Mesopotamia was hit by drought, seismic activity, and the invasion of the Gudi peoples from the Zagros Mountains to the north. Sargon I was said to have sent his troops to Egypt and Ethiopia, and his actions, followed by a commercial upset, may have played a role in the collapse of Egypt's Old Kingdom at this time. A pessimistic agnosticism appeared, as is seen in the Egyptian *Dialogue of the Despairing Man with His Soul*.

Sumer for a time re-establishes its independence and Indian Ocean trade

The Sumerians soon managed to drive off the Gudi. They returned to their old system of city-states, resuming their overseas trade. Prosperity reached a new height, most notably under the rulers of Lagash about 2250 BC and of Ur in 2094 to 2047 BC. Egyptian unity was likewise restored by Upper Egypt in the so-called Middle Kingdom of the twenty-first through the nineteenth centuries BC. A vigorous foreign trade sprang up again, facilitated by the construction of the first canal between the Red Sea and the Nile. Again, Egyptians ships traded with Punt (Somalia) and probably with the southern Arabians of Yemen. The Egyptian *Story of the Shipwrecked Sailor* tells about a sailor stranded on an island along with a snake who claims to be the Prince of Punt. The *Story of Sinuhe*, an Egyptian travel adventure equivalent to the Mesopotamian *Gilgamesh* epic, was also written at this time.

Why the first trading pattern eventually ended

At the start of the nineteenth century BC, the Amorites of Babel (Babylon) conquered and reunited Sumer. The economic role of the Sumerian kings in trade, brokerage, and moneylending fell with them, and was replaced by independent merchants joining together to share the risks. The sixth Amorite king, Hammurabi, who ruled from 1792 to 1750 BC, is remembered for his severe law code, with such punishments as drowning, mutilation, and impaling. At this point, Indo-European peoples with new and superior bronze weapons invaded south, overrunning civilized societies from Atlantic Europe through the Middle East to the Indus Valley. Shortly after Hammurabi's death, the Hittites raided from Anatolia and left widespread destruction. This devastation allowed the Kassites to move down from the Zagros Mountains and to conquer Mesopotamia. The rule of the primitive Kassites brought an end to Sumer's control of the Indian Ocean trade. The Tanach (the Hebrew form of the Old Testament) tells how Terah and his son Abraham with his wife Sarah left (troubled) Ur to resettle in Haran in Syria at about this time.

At the same time, Celts overran the Iberian areas of Atlantic Europe, Semitic Hyksos took over Lower Egypt, and Aryans poured into the Iranian Plateau and the Indus Valley. An eastern branch of the Celtic-linked peoples, the Aryans were distant relatives of the Irish, whose country Erin/Eire bears a name etymologically related to Iran. Evidence of these early Celts has been identified as far eastward as Sinkiang in westernmost China. The Aryans conquered the more advanced inhabitants and plundered their wealth without being sophisticated enough to continue its trading source. The first major trading pattern to have emerged in world history (that of early

Mesopotamians into the Indian Ocean) was at an end, along with the world's earliest leading states (the Sumerian city-states), which it had made possible. The conquests would be repeated in the thirteenth century BC by a second wave of Indo-European invaders, based this time on the use of iron. The double blow delivered by these two conquests meant that it would be a full millennium before northern India and the Persian Gulf would be able to reassume their original leading roles in the Indian Ocean trade.

The new centers of trade

The conquests of Mesopotamia and the Indus Valley, and the resulting isolation of northern China, left the Egyptians for a time in a relatively stronger position in Indian Ocean trade. The above-mentioned invasions caused a shift of the main trading routes to the south. Now they ran from Crete and Egypt to southern India and down the east coast of Africa, but not so much into the Persian Gulf or to the Indus Valley. The *Vedas* ('Knowledge'), holy Hindu books of this period, give a glimpse into the trading difficulties of the Indus Valley. The *Rig Veda* of the mid-second millennium BC includes a tale entitled 'Bhujyu,' telling about pirates waiting at the Strait of Ormuz (Hormuz) to attack merchant ships sailing with trading goods from the Persian Gulf back to Sind (the southern Indus Valley). Raja Tugra of Sind sends a punitive expedition under his son Bhujyu. The fleet is sunk in a storm, but Bhujyu survives by holding on to a log. When a shark appears and grabs the log, Bhujyu prays. The Ashvin twin gods of light appear and save Bhujyu, returning him to Sind. Bhujyu forms a new fleet that is used to ambush the pirates at the Strait of Ormuz and to recover the stolen wealth. However, the Indus Valley to Persian Gulf trade route was clearly in trouble.

The Aryan conquest may have weakened Indian trading initiative in the Indian Ocean by the subjugation of the Dravidian natives through much of India to the caste system (from *casta*, the word for 'pure' in Portuguese). In Sanskrit, this system is called *varna* ('color') in reference to the distinctions made between the lighter-skinned Aryan conquerors and the swarthy natives. Four main castes or hereditary occupational groups were introduced, each, from the highest down, with declining privileges, but increasing burdens. The top three castes were reserved for the victorious Aryans, the bottom caste for the Dravidians. The highest caste was the Brahmins (the priests), followed by the Kshatriyas (warriors), and Vaisyas (merchants and craftsmen). The fourth caste was the Sudras or serfs. Another even lower group, not officially a caste, was the Pariahs, outcasts who had bucked the system and were given jobs that nobody else wanted, such as garbage collection. The main spiritual and educational center for the new Aryan order was Taxila, in what is now Pakistan's Punjab ('Five Rivers') region.

Justification for the caste system was provided by the new Hindu religion of India, which in its early Brahmanist form emphasized a trilogy of top gods vaguely reminiscent of the Sumerian Anu, Enlil, and Ea/Enki: Brahma, Vishnu, and Shiva. Brahma was the creator god, seen as the nebulous world soul rather than a personal force. Vishnu was the savior or preserver god, who in human avatars or incarnations rescues the world at the end of each cosmic cycle. Shiva as the destroyer, a fierce god of destruction, was imagined whirling in a dance of time with weapons of mass destruction in his multiple arms. Hinduism, like Buddhism and Jainism later, turned the attention of people from struggling for position in this life toward a spiritual ascent and a final escape from the material world. In this orientation may be found part of the explanation for why India's wealth has so often been shared with or exploited by foreigners, Indians rarely dominating their own ocean.

An outpouring of literature reinforced the new teachings of Hinduism. In the eighth and seventh centuries BC, three Indian holy books were written to canonize Hindu doctrines, the *Upanishads*, the *Mahabharata*, and the *Ramayana*. In the final section of the *Mahabharata*, called the *Bhagavad Gita* ('Song Celestial'), the god Krishna (in the disguise of a charioteer) tells the hero Arjuna that he need not worry about sorrows in this world, as his men who are to die will come back through reincarnation or transmigration in another form, to work out their own *karma* ('destiny'). The *Ramayana* ('Rama's Story') tells how the Demon King Ravana abducts Rama's wife Sita and the monkey king and his councilor Hanuman help Rama to recover his wife. Worried that Sita has been defiled by Ravana, Rama sets her on fire in a literary case of the Indian custom of sutee, in which widows and other women no longer considered as an asset to their husbands are burned to death. Even though Sita's innocence prevents the flames from harming her, the tale again induces contempt for concerns of this world.

As to China, the collapse of Mesopotamia and Indus Valley societies in this period undermined the trade that had made its way across Central Asia. The resulting Shang Dynasty Bronze Age (1766–1027 BC) and Chou Dynasty (1027–256) in the Iron Age witnessed the elaboration of the Chinese culture laid down in the Xia period without any notable new ideas introduced from outside stimulus.

The great Indonesian migration

Around this time, Indonesians began to sail in large ocean-going ships, and to settle over great distances. To the east, they began the great migration that founded the Pacific island culture of Polynesia, and added a Malayan component to Japanese language and culture. To the southwest they moved in Indonesian double-outrigger canoes over 4,500 miles of open sea into Madagascar, permanently implanting their speech and culture in that island.

This immigration at the latest occurred before AD 200, when Sanskrit language and culture were introduced to Indonesia. The large Indonesian double-outrigger rafts of this period are said to have been among the first ships in the Indian Ocean area that could have managed such a feat. They must have followed Sharp's Current across the open water of the south Indian Ocean, as there is no evidence (cultural, linguistic, or social) that Indonesians ever touched on the coastal areas between Indonesia and Madagascar before or at this time.

Bananas and coconuts from their homeland were added to the list of East African staple crops, along with new species of yams and cocoyams. The Madagascar pigs are also believed to have originated from Indonesia. A new, if infrequently used, trade route opened up from Timor to Madagascar (either direct or via the Cocos Islands and the Chagos Archipelago south of the Maldives) and thence up the East African coast to Egypt. Most notably, cinnamon (then originating only from southern China and northern Southeast Asia) was transported to Madagascar, from where Arab merchants brought it up the East African coast to Yemen. This was the sharper Chinese cinnamon (called cassia); the production of the true cinnamon of Ceylon had not yet emerged. Cinnamon was used as an element in mummification in Egypt.

The success of the Egyptian merchants

The above-mentioned Bronze and Iron Age invasions brought and kept Egypt to the fore in trade, power, and progress by eliminating the other leading trading states from competition. While the Sumerians were devastated by Kassites, the Indus Valley society wrecked by Aryans, the Iberians driven back by Celts, and the Chinese isolated, Egypt was hit only by a minor spin-off of the conquests. The Semitic Hyksos or Shepherd Kings, displaced by the invasions from their own homeland in the Levant, managed to conquer only Lower Egypt, and were not as destructive as the other Bronze Age invaders. Furthermore, they were soon confronted by a native reaction from Upper Egypt. Pharaoh Ahmosis I in the sixteenth century BC adopted bronze technology, drove out the Hyksos, and reunited Egypt in the New Kingdom. His son Thutmosis I (r. 1536–1520 BC) consolidated the reunification with military campaigns against the Semitic city-states of Canaan.

These military campaigns allowed Egypt to resume trade in the Indian Ocean in the reign of Thutmosis I's daughter and successor, Hatsepshut (r. 1520–1480 BC). A favorite daughter of Thutmosis I, she had been associated with him in his rule in his old age. In gratitude, she had his coffin placed in her own tomb. In accord with tradition, she married her brother, Thutmosis II. However, Hatsepshut kept the government in her own hands. She then sent a five-vessel trading expedition down the Red Sea into the

Indian Ocean. The Egyptians had mastered astronomical skills, as can be seen in the alignment of the entrance gallery of the Pyramid of Kufu with the sighting of Polaris. Avoiding the northern trading partners disrupted by the Bronze Age conquests, the Egyptian ships turned south from the Straits of Aden, reaching 'Punt' (Somalia). The most prized trade item obtained was myrrh (resin from a tropical tree plentiful in Africa but rare in Arabia), used for perfuming and preserving corpses. Frankincense, another aromatic gum resin, and slaves were also obtained in Somalia.

The walls of Hatshepsut's tomb in the Valley of the Kings celebrated the feat in the oldest surviving recorded account of a specific salt-water sea voyage. A frontal structure of two colonnaded levels accessed by ramps represents the myrrh terraces of Punt, and wall carvings depict the trade mission. Since the ships of the expedition depicted there were Nile river-boats, the enterprise was quite risky. Following Mediterranean rather than Indian Ocean tradition, these Egyptian ships used wood joinery rather than the sewn-plank method, with planks set edge to edge rather than lap-strake. Possibly ninety feet long, they held fifteen rowers to a side and had a single square sail.

Hatshepsut's first expedition was important for launching many centuries of Egyptian trade with the Indian Ocean. The Egyptians began to be supplied with Indian spices by the Arabs of the southern Arabian Peninsula, cara-vans crossing back and forth between the Red Sea ports and the Nile. The Egyptians also imported ground bark from the cinnamon tree. Larger ships were developed for its transport. The Arabs tried to protect their part of the cinnamon trade by telling the Egyptians fibs about its place of origin, claiming that the dry sticks were brought from an unknown land by huge *roc* birds (the inspiration for what became the rook piece in chess, originally in the form of a bird) to build their nests with on mountain peaks. The Arabs related how they left huge cuts of oxen, which the birds tried to carry off, only to crash from the weight. The Arabs could then safely gather the cinnamon from their nests. Similar lies were told about their collection of cassia from fierce bats, and their wresting of frankincense from dragons.

Ancient Egypt's Mediterranean partners join in the Indian Ocean trade

In a development significant for the long-term pattern of trade in the Indian Ocean, the Late Kingdom Egyptians still looked to Mediterranean trading partners to handle the trade to their west. Egypt's resulting dependence on Mediterranean trading partners for naval protection and for the carrying trade west would cause the European involvement in that trade to become ever more intense through the centuries. At some point (certainly by the twelfth century BC with the Phoenicians from the shores of what is now Lebanon), Egypt's Mediterranean trading allies would assume a prominent position in trade (purportedly representing Egyptian interests) in the Indian Ocean itself.

Since the Iberians had been hard-hit by the Celtic invasions, Hatsepshut's Egypt cooperated with what might be described as an Iberian offshoot society in the eastern Mediterranean, the Minoans of Crete. Various shared traits (including ritual bull fights and labyrinth construction) linked the Minoans to the Iberians. Trading city-states reminiscent of Iberian Tarshish had arisen on Crete, the most powerful of which, Knossos, on the north coast, was ruled by a king called the Minos. The resulting palace murals and Kamares ware pottery, both drawing on sea imagery for a new level of decorative beauty, again testify to the link between Indian Ocean trade (albeit at one remove, in the Mediterranean) and the advance of civilization. After the death of her brother and nominal husband, Thutmosis II, Hatsepshut officially married his son, her nephew Thutmosis III. This move was a miscalculation, for Thutmosis III toppled his aunt, and mutilated her statues and inscriptions in an attempt to eliminate any memory of her. As pharaoh from 1480 to 1447 BC, he did consolidate Egypt's trade with the Indian Ocean by establishing Egyptian control of the Levant (the eastern shore of the Mediterranean), strategically close to the northern ports of the Red Sea. Winning a victory at Megiddo, he absorbed Canaan, Lebanon, and Syria into his kingdom.

The first crisis of the ancient Egyptian-centered trading cycle

One of the peculiarities of the Egyptian predominance in the Indian Ocean's trading wealth is that it overcame four major crises, succumbing only to the fifth. Each time, Egypt found a new trading ally in the Mediterranean in order to keep the vital trade between the Indian Ocean and points west flowing through it. The first crisis was the result of Amenhotep IV's emphasis on the god Aten as a god of peace and love. Changing his name to Akhenaton to honor Aten, this pharaoh (r. 1375–1358 BC) failed to recognize that rulers must be stern judges if they are also to be merciful. Losing fear of the law, the Levant rebelled and broke away; the Egyptians withheld taxes, and law and order collapsed. Trade was disrupted, weakening Egypt's main trading partner, Minoan Crete.

The Achaean Greeks took advantage of the crisis to raid and plunder Crete. In the breakdown, Akhenaton seems to have been murdered. Two of his daughters and their husbands ruled after him briefly, but were unable to restore stability. Egypt was returned to law and order by a line of army generals become pharaohs, most notably Rameses II, who completed the return to a strong Egypt. Rameses II (r. 1292–1225 BC) reconquered Canaan and part of Syria, restored Egypt's overseas trade control, and redredged the canal from the Red Sea to the Nile. Egypt's main Mediterranean trading partner in the Mediterranean shifted from a weakened Minoan Crete to the Achaean Greeks. The Achaean city of Mycenae, built atop a hill or acropolis in the northeast Peloponnesus, was famous for its 57-foot-thick walls, punctured by the Lion Gate. Mycenae's most famous ruler, the legendary Agamemnon, extended Mycenean trading control to the wheat and gold of the Black Sea, after besieging and burning Troy, the town which had controlled the Hellespont passage from the Aegean Sea to the Black Sea.

The second crisis of the ancient Egyptian-centered trading cycle

The second crisis to hit the Egyptian cycle was that caused by the Iron Age invasions around 1200 BC. Iron weapons (harder and more durable than bronze, and suitable for cutting as well as piercing) gave the Indo-Europeans a new advantage, allowing them once again to invade the richer areas to the south toward the end of the thirteenth century BC. The Dorian Greeks conquered most of Greece from the earlier Achaean Greeks. The Dorians poured down through the Peloponnesian Peninsula over the Dodecanese Islands, Crete, Rhodes, Cyprus, and coastal Canaan, where they intermarried with the natives to form the Philistines. They also attacked the Nile Delta. In the ensuing dilemma, Egypt's Hebrew slaves rebelled and fled to Midia, in the northwest of the Arabian Peninsula, and Canaan. Yet Egypt managed to hold its own in this crisis, too.

Phoenicians move into the Indian Ocean trade

One of the army generals provided the muscle required for keeping Egypt's predominant position by usurping power and founding the twentieth dynasty, taking the name of Rameses III (r. 1198–1167). He employed the Phoenicians to help drive off the Dorian Greeks and to safeguard the trade in the Indian Ocean. The Phoenicians had an improved ship design, which added a sharp prow to their oared and sailed ships, which was used for ramming the Greek ships. They would come from the side at full speed, pierce a hole, and then rapidly back row, leaving the water to gush into the hole and sink the Greek ship. The Phoenicians also derived wealth from two popular new trading products derived from their local beaches and waters: glass and purple dye. The Phoenician use of an alphabet (Punic) greatly facilitated record keeping and thus commerce in general.

Rameses III's acknowledgement of the Phoenicians as his official sailors and merchants facilitated a Phoenician move into the carrying trade in the Indian Ocean. They consolidated their control of that trade by founding a Punic colony among their cousins, the southern Arabians, at Marib in the kingdom of Sheba or Saba (modern Yemen), to control the passage from the Red Sea into the Indian Ocean. The old trade to Punt (Somalia) was restored, and Sinai copper mines were exploited. Sheba's sphere of interest extended into Ethiopia, and southern Arabians (along with migrants from western India) followed the trade route to settle along the east coast of Africa at some point during the first millennium BC. There the Arabians intermarried with the natives, and handled the export of ivory and slaves. Sheba developed camel caravan routes from Yemen through Mecca and Medina to Suez and Damascus, to obviate the dangerous sea passage through the Red Sea. To the luxury goods of India, Africa, and the Far East transported along this route they added southern Arabian frankincense. In Spain, the Phoenicians established a trading control center at Gades (Cádiz), purchasing copper, fur, and silver from the Iberians, gold and ivory from West Africa, tin from Britain, and tuna fish preserved in salt taken from Las Marismas, the swamp at the mouth of Spain's Guadalquivir River.

The Phoenician King Hiram of Tyre (r. 970–936 BC) continued the arrangement with Egypt, first with the twenty-first dynasty and then with Shoshenk (the Shishak of the Bible), founder in 945 BC of the twenty-second or Libyan dynasty. The Philistines were finally eliminated as an independent rival power by an alliance with the rising Hebrews, who were initiated as junior partners into Phoenician trade. The port of Eilat was developed as a base for trade into what the Hebrews called the Yam Suf ('Sea of Reeds'), and the Greeks the Erythraean (or 'Red') Sea, what we would call the Indian Ocean (at least the western part of it known to them), along with its extension the Red Sea. The joint Punic-Hebrew fleet sailed to Ophir (variously identified as southern Arabia and as Supara near the later city of Bombay in India) for gold, silver, jewels, ivory, wood, apes, and (Indian) peacocks. They bartered using copper from Israel's Negev region. The Punic Queen Bilkis of Sheba (Yemen), which was the trade emporium and strategic control point at the southern end of the Red Sea, visited Jerusalem and gave King Shlomo (Solomon) a son named Menelik, the ancestor of the 'Lion of Judah' kings of Ethiopia. Bilkis's Sabaean peoples of southern Arabia settled in Ethiopia in this period, intermarrying with the natives. Ethiopians can still be found who claim descent from 'Arabic' peoples from across the Strait of Aden (or Bab al Mandab). The Ethiopian kingdom of Axum arose, centered on the port of Adulis. The Ethiopians exported gold, iron, slaves, animals, hides, tortoise shells, and rhinoceros horns. In exchange, they imported principally metal tools and weapons, cloth, and wine. The Phoenicians secured the western Mediterranean end of their trade route by founding such colonies as Carthage, in 814 BC.

The work of the Phoenicians in bringing Yemen and Ethiopia into trade prominence stimulated the Sudan as well, filling in the land link between Egypt and Ethiopia. In the eighth century, King Piankhy built up the state of Kush, centered on the capital of Napata on the Sudanese Nile. Piankhy seized Egypt from the Libyan Dynasty. The northern Sudan had been captured by Egypt in the late second millennium BC, and had become Egyptianized in culture. (The Sudanese rulers in the seventh century BC would take to erecting miniature brick pyramids for themselves in their relocated capital of Meroë.) The insertion of the Sudan into the power picture did not disrupt the Indian Ocean–Red Sea–Mediterranean trade route, but drew the Sudanese region more closely into it. Meroë stood at the end of a main caravan route from the Red Sea to the Sudanese Nile, so that the Sudanese added gold, iron (smelted in furnaces fired by acacia tree charcoal), ivory, and (at least by Ptolemaic times) elephants.

The third crisis of the ancient Egyptian-centered trading cycle

The third crisis to challenge Egypt's strong trade position and historical cycle came from the expanding Assyrian Empire. The bloody fighting of the Iron Age invasions had left the ancient world more militarized, bringing greater brutality. The Assyrians now turned the cruelty into a tool of psychological warfare for creating the world's first true empire. In 671 BC, Essarhadon conquered Lower Egypt, and the period of ancient Egyptian ascendancy once again seemed to be at an end. Trade through the Persian Gulf via Bahrain to India picked up again, and the traffic through the Red Sea to East Africa also intensified. The Assyrian elite showed a special passion for the purchase of Indian and African ivory for inlaid furniture, and jewelry. About this time, the Mesopotamian and Persian sailors learned how to sail directly across the Indian Ocean using the monsoon winds, from the Persian Gulf to India to Southeast Asia.

However, a subsequent relaxation of Assyrian military vigilance due to material success from the Indian Ocean trading wealth soon gave the Egyptians a chance to rebel. Since Phoenicia was at this point subject to Assyrian control, Egypt turned back to an alliance with the Greeks, linking up with the Doric Greek city of Corinth. Corinthian trade flourished in this period, allowing the establishment of Greek colonies from the Black Sea to the northwestern Mediterranean, including Corinth's colony at Syracuse in Sicily. Greeks in 652 BC helped Egyptian rebels under Psammetichos, governor of Upper Egypt, to drive the Assyrians out of Egypt. Greek soldiers remained in Egypt as mercenaries to guarantee that the outcome was decisive. This Graeco-Egyptian cooperation allowed Egypt and its allies to maintain their position in trade with Psammetichos as pharaoh presiding over the Saitic Revival of ancient Egyptian culture from its delta capital of Sais. The town of Naucratis in the Nile delta was established as the main Greek trading emporium in Egypt. Corinth became so wealthy that a saying sprang up that ran, 'Not every man has the luck to sail to Corinth.'

The fourth crisis of the ancient Egyptian-centered trading cycle

The fourth challenge to the Egyptian hold on the Indian Ocean trade and historical cycle came from a revived Babylonian (or Chaldean) Empire, the main successor state of the Assyrian Empire in the Fertile Crescent. In 605 BC, Greek mercenaries fighting for Psammetichos' son Necho swept aside and killed King Yosiahu (Josiah) of Judah when he barred the way at Megiddo. Necho moved on north, only to be pushed back by Nebuchadnezzar's army at the battle of Carchemish in Syria. However, the pharaoh's army fought vigorously enough to preserve the borders of Egypt. Necho redredged the canal between the Red Sea and the Nile River to facilitate trade between the Indian Ocean and the Mediterranean. He also sent out two fleets of discovery, manned by Phoenician sailors, to circumnavigate Africa, one sent counter-clockwise via the Mediterranean, and the second sent clockwise via the Red Sea. According to Herodotos, the Phoenicians traveling clockwise managed to circumnavigate Africa. Some controversial writers even feel that the Phoenicians may have called into life the first advanced civilization of America, that of the Olmecs in southern Mexico. If this is true, an Indian Ocean trade stimulus can be linked to the rise of the colorful Amerindian civilizations of Mexico, Peru, Colombia, and elsewhere. Egypt's Greek alliance soon shifted from Doric Corinth to Ionian Athens. Solon led Athens in challenging Corinth for a leading position in trade, a policy continued by his relative Peisistratus. The Ionian Greek merchants traded from Egypt (via the Red Sea) to the Persian Gulf and western India (where the Greeks were called *Yavanas*).

The fifth and final crisis of the ancient Egyptian-centered trading cycle

By this point, the peoples who lived near the Persian Gulf and the northern coast of the Arabian Sea had recovered from the Bronze and Iron Age invasions, and were eager to resume their original central position in the Indian Ocean trade. The stimulus to this trading power shift would be provided by a fifth crisis to hit ancient Egyptian society and trade, consisting of a religious revolution which was about to sweep along the northern coast of the Indian Ocean and exert an impact from the Mediterranean to the Pacific. Mesopotamia, India, and Egypt had led the way in building wealth, power, and creativity on Indian Ocean trade, in essence creating civilization and history. However, their very success finally led to their decline as lands eager to share in it found a means to do so in the religious ferment. The main result would be to allow new lands at a remove from the Indian Ocean to exert a significant if remote impact on Indian Ocean trade. The initial period, in which lands on the Indian Ocean periphery had flourished through a near monopoly of its trade (centered first on Mesopotamia and then on Egypt), was at an end.

Further reading

On early sailing: Lionel Casson, *Ships and Seamanship in the Ancient World* (Princeton, New Jersey: Princeton University Press, 1971).

On Early Dravidian India and the Indus Valley: Bridget and Raymond Allchin, *The Birth of Indian Civilization: India and Pakistan before 500 BC* (Harmondsworth, Middlesex: Penguin Books, 1968); Georg Feuerstein, Subhash Kak, and David Frawley, *In Search of the Cradle of Civilization: New Light on Ancient India* (Wheaton, Illinois: Quest Books, 1995); Karam Narain Kapur, *The Dawn of Indian History* (New Delhi: Sarvadeshik Arya Pralinidhi Sabha, 1990); Jonathan M. Kenoyer, *Ancient Cities of the Indus Valley Civilization* (Karachi: Oxford University Press, 1998); and Shereen Ratnagar, *Encounters: The Western Trade of the Harappan Civilization* (Delhi: Oxford University Press, 1981).

On Iron Age India: Xinru Liu, *Ancient India and Ancient China: Trades and Religious Exchanges* (Delhi: Oxford University Press, 1988); Romila Thapar, *Early India* (Berkeley: University of California Press, 2003); and Romila Thapar, *Interpreting Early India* (Delhi: Oxford University Press, 1992).

On ancient Mesopotamia: J.N. Postgate, *Early Mesopotamia: Society and Economy at the Dawn of History* (London: Routledge, 1991); H.W.F. Saggs, *Babylonians* (London: British Museum Press, 1995); and H.W.F. Saggs, *The Might That Was Assyria* (London: Sidgwick and Jackson, 1984).

On early Egypt and East Africa: Nicolas-Christophe Grimal, *A History of Ancient Egypt*, trans. Ian Shaw (Oxford: Blackwell, 1992); and H. Neville Chittick and Robert I. Rotberg, *East Africa and the Orient: Cultural Synthesis in Pre-Colonial Times* (New York and London: Africana Publishing Company, 1975).

On the Phoenicians and their Hebrew allies: Maria Eugenia Aubet, *The Phoenicians and the West: Politics, Colonies and Trade*, trans. Mary Turton (Cambridge: Cambridge University Press, 1993); and Michael Grant, *The History of Ancient Israel* (New York: Charles Scribner's Sons, 1984).

On the disputed theories of New World crossings: R.A. Jairazbhoy, *Ancient Egyptians and Chinese in America* (Totowa, New Jersey: Rowman and Littlefield, 1974).

Chapter 3

Early northern Mediterranean and Chinese influence

In the millennium from the sixth century BC to the seventh century AD, lands at a distinct remove from the Indian Ocean joined in a significant way in its (mainly spice) trade. These were Mediterranean Europe (specifically Greece and Italy) to the west, and China to the east. The shift resulted from the expansion of trade, and with it of civilization, to Mediterranean Europe and China, causing them to emerge politically and militarily. They then used their new strength to reach out for a controlling share of the trade that had called them into life. India, although still divided into many small states, linked up with the new outside forces to its own commercial benefit. This chapter will trace the aspirations of Persia to lead in this period, its long struggle against Greece for that position, and the final Greek triumph. It will then trace the rise of Rome, with its conquest and domination of the Greeks and their trading success. It will show how, after the decline of Roman power, the Persians would again make a bid for trading and military dominance, only to be thwarted all over again by the Greeks (this time of the Byzantine Empire).

The rise of the Persians

The Persians first rose to imperial power by taking advantage of a universal disillusionment with most of the earlier religions, with their aristocratic priesthoods, and their emphasis on magic. This development would open the door wider to mercantile interests. The Hebrew emphasis on justice and mercy brought by the Jews exiled to Babylon in 587 BC, and upheld most famously by Daniel (as described in the Tanach), provided the model. As important merchants in the Babylonian trading world, especially favored by Nebuchadnezzar's successor Nabonidus (r. 555–538 BC), the Jews spread these values spread far and wide.

Through the sixth century BC, ethical teachings spread throughout the civilized world. Zarathustra (called Zoroaster by the Greeks), perhaps a former student of Daniel in Babylon, founded Zoroastrianism, with its *Avesta* ('Book of Brotherly Love'). The Zarathustrans worshiped the good creator god Ormuz or Ahura Mazda, who was in rivalry with the demon-surrounded Ahriman, god of death, for the possession of people's souls. The Zarathustrians taught that, in the end, Ormuz will triumph, and they called for a king of justice and mercy to reflect the wishes of this god. Pythagoras, perhaps a Greek pupil of Zarathustra, went on to establish a communal cult of vegetarian nonviolence. In China, Kung Fu Tse (Confucius) likewise laid out ethical rules for a peaceful, law-abiding society.

In India, Buddhism and Jainism challenged Hinduism (rooted mainly, despite its assigning the Vaisya merchant to the third of four castes, in the old agricultural and pastoral economy), advocating practical solutions for society, trying to reveal a pragmatic way to salvation, attainable by all without the mediation of priests. Buddhism, founded by Siddharta Gautama (Buddha), who lived 560–480 BC, called for overcoming evil with good, anger with love, selfishness with generosity, and lies with truth, with an abolition of distinctions between castes. Vardhamana (540–468 BC), called Mahavira ('Great Hero'), founder of the Jain religion, determined to avoid harming any life form, to the extent that his followers wore gauze over their mouths to avoid breathing in gnats, and swept the path ahead of them to avoid stepping on ants. Mahavira and Buddha were both welcomed at the court of King Bimbisara of Maghadha (r. 540 to 490 BC) at Pataliputra (Patna) on the lower Ganges. Buddha purportedly endorsed investment, and both Buddhism and Jainism were popular religions with Indian merchants.

However, an aristocratic reaction soon after Buddha's death transformed his teachings. Hindu doctrine transformed Buddhism, the *Jataka* stories telling of Buddha's animal transmigrations in earlier lives. Even this Hinduized Buddhism failed to endure in India, although it continued as Hinayana ('Little Wheel') Buddhism in Sri Lanka and Southeast Asia, and as a further transformed Mahayana ('Big Wheel') Buddhism in central and eastern Asia. The Jains survived in India only as a minor sect. While much of the Eurasian world embraced the new ethical fad, India held to its Bronze Age formula with its rigid caste system. This development did not augur well for future Indian initiatives in trade and war, while it encouraged the foreign trading ventures in Indian waters of Persians, Greeks, and Chinese, who had accepted the ethical teachings favored by the rising urban middle class. However, for a few centuries, Buddhism and Jainism helped to propel Indian trade.

In 550 BC, Koresh (Cyrus) the Great drew on Zoroastrian concepts when he usurped the throne of Persia. At his coronation banquet, he ate a peasant's meal as a sign that he would rule humbly, in the interest of his subjects. By the end of the century, bas-reliefs in the royal palace at Parsa (Persepolis) showed the shahs as champions of Ormuz fighting Ahriman's monsters of darkness and death. This approach appealed to oppressed peoples in surrounding states, who welcomed the rapid expansion of Koresh's realm to Media, Armenia, Lydia, and, in 539 BC, Babylonia. Koresh allowed the

Jews to return to Judea in 538, under such leaders as Zerubbabel and Haggai. Jerusalem and its Temple were rebuilt. It was of use to Persia, with its ambitions against Egypt, to implant a grateful people at the entry gates of that rich prize. This permission facilitated the capture of Egypt in 525 by Koresh's son and heir Kambujiya or Cambyses (r. 530–521 BC). Kambujiya defeated and put to death Pharaoh Psammetichos III. The Persians thereby held both of the western termini of the Indian Ocean trade route, i.e. the Red Sea and the Persian Gulf. Persian trade was aided by the adoption of the Aramaic script, already commonly used by the Jewish merchants in the time of the Babylonian Empire.

By the sixth century BC, coastal trade ran along India's west coast to both Sri Lanka and the Maldives (southwest of India's southern tip). By the fifth century, the supply of pepper from India was large enough in Greece for it to be used as a medicinal ingredient for the treatment of suffocation and (it is said) female disorders. Other spices, too, found use in medicine, as well as in drugs, ointments, cosmetics, perfumes, incense, and food. As this Indian trade beckoned, the Persian Shah Daryavaush or Darius (r. 521–486 BC) rounded out the new Persian Empire by conquering Pakistan, and then, in 512, Bulgaria and Thrace. He sent an expedition under Scylax of Caryanda from the Indus to Egypt. After having the ship canal from the Nile to the Gulf of Suez repaired, he sent a fleet from Egypt to Iran, and rallied his Phoenician and Jewish merchants to conduct the trade. However, Daryavaush soon found himself in the midst of a gigantic struggle with the Greeks for control of Egypt and of its trade in Indian Ocean goods, a conflict that would last for almost two centuries until the final winner was decided. The great difficulty encountered by the Greeks in challenging the Persians in Egypt, compared to the relative ease with which the Greeks had warded off Assyrian and Babylonian threats to Egypt (as described in the previous chapter), is a measure of the success of the Persian Empire in satisfying its subject peoples.

The Greek challenge to the Persians

The long subsequent period of warfare between Greeks and Persians has been traditionally viewed as a clash between civilizations. However, an argument can be made that the Greeks and Persians were more importantly concerned with control of the trade moving through Egypt between the Indian Ocean and the Mediterranean. The Greeks in no way accepted the loss of control of the Indian Ocean trade flowing through Egypt. Instead, they took a defiant stand, pushing for showdowns with Persia. Athens, which had participated in Egyptian trade before the Persian conquest, encouraged Miletos and other Ionian towns under Persian rule to revolt in 499 BC. A major constant goal was control of Egypt's Indian Ocean trade, as will be traced in this chapter. Athens was not the defensive victim merely concerned with independence and democracy that Herodotus presents in his *History of the Persian War*. It is true that Athens and its Greek allies had but a tiny population compared to the huge Persian Empire, yet small but rich societies (including Portugal, England, and Japan) have often been victorious over much larger regions.

In response to the Athenian-spurred revolt of Miletos, Daryavaush in 490 BC had his Phoenician fleet transport a Persian army across to Athens' city-state of Attica. The Persian troops landed at Marathon on the east coast of Attica. Miltiades' Athenian army, although outnumbered two to one, won the ensuing battle thanks to his use of armor and of close-order drill in the phalanx. Athens then lost no time in stirring revolt in Egypt, obliging Daryavaush and, after his death, his son Khshayarsha or Xerxes (r. 486–465 BC), to concentrate on the crisis there. Once Khshayarsha had pacified Egypt, the Persians turned their attention back to bringing Athens to heel. In 480 BC, Khshayarsha led a larger force back to Athens, only to meet with defeat at the naval battle of Salamis and (the next year) the land battle of Plataea. On the same day as the battle of Plataea, the Greeks chased Persian ships to shore at Mycale, opposite Samos, and then defeated the Persians on land, gaining control of the Aegean.

Athens fought for control of Egypt and its trade over the next twenty-five years, led mainly by Miltiades' son Kimon (Cimon). To increase its strength, Athens formed the Delian League, joining Aegean island city-states to fight against Persia. In 465 BC, an Egyptian named Inaros declared himself pharaoh, and defeated the Persians at the Battle of Papremis. A Delian League fleet under Perikles then sailed up the Nile, and helped Inaros take Memphis. When in 454 BC, the Persians defeated the Athenians at Memphis, and crucified Inaros, the revolt continued under Amyrtaeus as pharaoh. Kimon was leading a new Athenian force to Amyrtaeus' aid when he died in Cyprus in 449 BC. Perikles, the new Athenian leader, signed a truce in 446 BC in order to give Athens time to gather strength. He used the peace to strengthen Athen's wealth, prestige, and education, developing Athens' creativity to a feverish height. In the meantime, in 444 BC, Shah ArtaKhshayarsha (Artaxerxes) I reassumed control of Egypt for the time being, and secured his hold by allowing Nehemiah to rebuild the walls of resettled Jerusalem as a military bastion in the Persian province of Israel next door to Egypt. Jews, already important merchants in Persian trade, now also became so in Egypt.

After a twenty-three year truce, the Peloponnesian War broke out between Athens and Sparta (431–404 BC). Sparta eventually prevailed by allying with Persia and its Phoenician fleet. In the very year of 404 BC in which Athens surrendered, Sparta turned on its Persian ally when it helped a rebel Pharaoh Amyrtaeus II to free Egypt from Persia. Sparta prevented Shah ArtaKhshayarsha II from leading an army to reconquer Egypt by supporting an ill-fated revolt of the Shah's brother, Koresh the Younger. A new upstart pharaoh, Nepherites, deposed Amyrtaeus II in 398 BC, but Sparta allied with him in turn. However, various Greek city-states ganged up on Sparta from 395 to 387 BC to take this prize from it. While the war raged, the Athenian leader Konon in 393 BC allied with a new pharaoh, Achoris (r. 393–380 BC), sending the Athenian general Chabrias to serve Achoris in Egypt. In reaction, Sparta in 386 BC concluded peace with ArtaKhshayarsha II of Persia. In 373 BC, Athens helped the latest pharaoh, Nectanebos, to repulse an invasion of Egypt by another Persian army. Athens, Sparta, Corinth, Thebes, and their allies then fell into war among themselves, allowing Shah ArtaKhshayarsha (Artaxerxes) III in 343 BC to reconquer Egypt. Nectanebos fled to Ethiopia. Once again, Greek disunity had endangered the Greek hold on Egypt and the Indian Ocean trade.

Renewed Greek success in the Indian Ocean trade

Frustrated in the hope of dominating Egypt's Indian Ocean trade, and ready for the Asian ideal of a just monarch ruling by divine right, Isocrates of Athens called on King Philippos (Philip) of Macedonia to unite the Greeks. Philippos accordingly defeated the southern Greeks at the Battle of Chaeronea in 338 BC. He then formed the Hellenic League under his leadership. Philippos prepared his army to attack Persia in 336 BC. However, before he could march, he was assassinated, leaving the task to his son Alexandros (Alexander the Great). Alexandros moved his army on a beeline path for Egypt. His 180-ship fleet was not sufficiently strong to challenge the new Persian fleet of about 400, and so he had to rely on success by land. His advance was distinguished by one military victory after another, from Granicus through Issus and Tyre to possession of Egypt. Only after this goal had been attained did Alexander in 331 BC turn his troops to take Mesopotamia, the Iranian Plateau, and the Indus Valley. Alexandros wanted to move on into India, which would have allowed him to control the great source of trading wealth at its heart. However, his soldiers refused to continue, believing that Alexandros was overextending his strength. In 329 BC, Alexandros thus led most of his troops back west.

Alexandros ruled his new empire from Babylon, and turned his attention to encouraging Indian Ocean commerce. He made plans to send ships to sail between the Persian Gulf and the Red Sea, as a preparation for improving contact between Mesopotamia and Egypt. Ordering ships built both in Phoenicia and Babylon, he hired Phoenician sailors, and sent three ships in a preliminary expedition from the Persian Gulf to the Red Sea. He sent an expedition to sail in the opposite direction from Egypt to Babylon, although it turned back part way. He also increased the navigability of the Euphrates River, and made improvements in Babylon's river port. However, in 323 BC, at the age of 32, Alexandros died of malaria. His empire was divided up by some of his generals, remembered as his *diadochi* ('successors'). Of the three main states resulting, the Greek kingdom centered in the new Greek city of Alexandria on the Mediterranean coast of Egypt became the main power, thanks to its dominance of trade in the western Indian Ocean.

Maurya India, the first three Ptolemies, and the India trade

Alexandros' illegitimate half-brother Ptolemeos (Ptolemy) I Soter or 'Awesome Savior' (r. 323–290) founded a line of Greek kings ruling from Greek-populated Alexandria. He constructed a large fleet (using the trireme triple-tier of rowers), and sent it to India, Somalia, and Zanzibar. He fostered trade in the Red Sea by rebuilding ports on its Egyptian coast at Cosseir, Berenike, and Myos Hormos. Southern Chinese and Southeast Asian cinnamon (via Madagascar), Malabar pepper, ivory, and other luxury goods from India and points farther east, as well as ivory and gold from Africa, and the local frankincense were obtained from the south Arabian merchants, especially those of the port cities of Aden, Mocha, Qana, and Dhufar. South Arabian merchants (sailing the monsoon winds southwest between November and April and northeast between May and October) settled in India, in Ethiopia, and at Adulis (Zula) on the Red Sea and other points along the East African coast. Attempts by the Nabataean Arabs of Petra to prevent the Greek takeover of the trade were squelched. Alexandria became the center of the far-ranging Ptolemaic commerce, facilitated by Greek leadership in portrait coinage (Greek coins finding their way to India).

The India that was the object of trade with the Ptolemaic Greeks was divided between a newly formed Indian Empire in the north and various states in the south. Chandragupta Maurya, illegitimate son of the king of Magadha (on the middle Ganges), tried to usurp the throne in 325 BC. When his coup failed, he fled to the Punjab, where he may have urged Alexandros to invade Magadha, which the Greek conqueror might have done had his soldiers been willing to continue to the east of the Indus Valley. In 323 BC, after Alexandros's death at Babylon, Chandragupta organized a popular revolt that ended the rule of the Greek governor in the Punjab. Having acquired a base of power, Chandragupta hired Greek mercenaries, and made himself king of Magadha in 322 BC. Establishing his capital at Pataliputra, he ruled from 322 to 298 BC, and enlarged his kingdom to stretch from Afghanistan to the lower Ganges. He involved the state in business ventures, setting up state slaughterhouses, gambling casinos, houses of prostitution, and metal and wine sales outlets. Indian influences began to find their way across the Bay of Bengal; third century BC inscriptions in the Brahmi alphabet are known from Indonesia.

The Indians seem to have been as active as the Greeks in establishing the new spurt of trade between India and the Mediterranean. Buddhism and Jainism, then flourishing in India, encouraged this involvement, being religions favored by the merchants. A royal highway was laid out between the Mauryan capital of Pataliputra and Taxila. Water routes around the Indian coast and from there to both the Persian Gulf (linking up via the Fertile Crescent with the eastern Mediterranean) and across the Arabian Sea to Aden and Egyptian Red Sea ports were employed by Indian merchants. Indians also acted as middlemen along the route between China and the Mediterranean across Central Asia, and Chinese goods appeared in India around this time. One of the clearest examples of Indian influence on the Middle East at this time was the popularization of the Indian board game *chaturanga*, which would evolve into chess. Indian merchants also moved eastward across the Bay of Bengal, as recounted in Indian adventure tales, inspired by the growing trade to seek new trading items from the 'Golden Isles' of Sumatra, Java, and Bali.

A Graeco-Indian cultural exchange accompanied the Graeco-Indian trade exchange. Indian philosophers debated Socrates' teachings, and Indian astronomers used Greek names for planets, while popularizing the Greek fad of horoscopes. The theatrical use of the clown, the figure of the para- site, and the use of a screen made its way into Indian theater, and the Greek employment of the double die to stamp pictures on both sides of a coin appeared in India. Megasthenes and Deimachos, ambassadors from Antiochos I Soter (the first to Chandragupta Maurya and the second to King Bimbisara of Maghadha), both wrote accounts of India. Perhaps Greek developments in history writing and theater helped to spur prime minister Kautilya to write *Arthasastra*, a history of Chandragupta Maurya's reign, and Visakhadatta to write his play *Mudrarakshas* telling of Chandragupta Maurya's usurpation. Having laid a firm foundation for his dynasty, Chandragupta Maurya abdicated in favor of his son, and (according to Jain tradition) entered a Jain monastery for the rest of his days.

Chandragupta Maurya's grandson Asoka completed the building of the first Indian Empire (r. 272–232 BC). In a series of military campaigns, he conquered all of India except the southern Tamil tip and Sri Lanka. Guilt- ridden after having caused the death and enslavement of thousands of people in his conquest of Kalinga on the Bay of Bengal, Asoka converted to Buddhism. Under Buddhist influence, he suppressed Hindu festivals and rituals, forbade sacrifices, and adopted a vegetarian diet. He issued gentler laws, which he carved into rocks and sandstone pillars for everyone to read. He built hospitals. Buddhist monks were sent as missionaries to the Tamil area, Sri Lanka, Kashmir, Burma, and to the Hellenistic states. Asoka's son Mahinda helped to convert Sri Lanka. Asoka also patronized great Buddhist architecture and art. Stupa reliquary shrines were erected, great sandstone- domed mounds symbolizing Mount Meru, center of the world. His encouragement of Buddhism, along with the development of a Sanskrit script, gave a boost to the Buddhist merchant class. The literary epic, the

Panchatantra ('The Five Senses'), of the fourth or third century BC, reflects a renewed criticism of traditional Hinduism by the reinvigorated middle class. Gods and humans are described as animals in this work, as in Aesop's *Fables.* A jackal (god) named Calila argues for a code of morality against a jackal (god) named Dimna, whom Calila condemns as a devil from Hell. Dimna laughs at the notions of sin and morality, and speaks of karma and reincarnation. Dimna induces the lion king of the jungle kingdom to establish a tyrannical rule from which his animal subjects shrink in fear.

The second Ptolemeos in Egypt, further enhancing the Graeco-Indian trade, restored the old trading canal connecting the Red Sea with the Nile at Anu (Heliopolis) near Memphis, from where commerce flowed on downstream to the delta and the Mediterranean. Greek colonies were established on the island of Socotra off the Horn of Africa and on the Ethiopian coast, the latter to handle the trade in North African elephants used to oppose the Indian elephants used by the Seleucids. The African trade allowed Ptolemeos II to flood the Aegean world with African ivory, breaking the hold of Indian ivory on the Greek market. Ptolemeos II and emperors Chandragupta and Asoka of Maurya India exchanged ambassadors (one of whom, Dionysos, wrote an account of his experiences in India), and colonies of Indian merchants appeared in Alexandria and on the upper Euphrates. The Indian trade of the Seleucid rivals, ruling from Babylon, was restricted mainly to the land route across Iran. Ptolemeos II celebrated his commercial success by staging processions featuring Indian spices, hunting dogs, cows, and women.

Some navigationally linked scientific advances were made at the 'Museon' University and Library of Alexandria in the third century BC. Eratosthenes, following up on Pythagoras' earlier observation that the earth is a sphere, calculated its dimensions fairly accurately. He noticed that at Aswan, in midsummer, the sun shone directly to the bottom of a dry well. So he erected a pole at Alexandria and measured its shadow at the same time of year, from which he determined the angle change between the two cities, which turned out to be one-fiftieth of a circle. Applying the distance between the two cities to that difference allowed him to figure out the whole circle of the earth. Aristarchos concluded from observing an eclipse of the sun that the earth rotates on its axis once a day and revolves around the sun. Euklides (Euclid) wrote the standard textbook for common-sense geometry down to modern times. Archimedes worked out the laws governing the sphere and the cylinder. In architecture, the invention of the crane allowed the construction of the Colossos (statue of Apollo) of Rhodes and the Pharos lighthouse at Alexandria, both designed to guide ships into port. Yet, the continuing division of Alexandros the Great's empire among rival rulers weakened the Greeks. Antiochos III the Great, king of Syria (r. 223–187 BC), planned to invade Egypt and unite the Greek East. However, in 192 BC, time ran out for the Greeks.

The Han Chinese and the Romans

At this point appeared the first significant involvement in Indian Ocean trade of two regions located at a great remove from the Indian Ocean: China and Italy (the states of Han China and Rome). The Chinese established a stable trade coming to India via the Strait of Malacca. For some time to come, Asians would control the eastern Indian Ocean, meeting Greek merchants from the Roman world for a pacific commercial exchange in India. There the Chinese encountered merchants from the Roman Empire.

Indian merchants themselves might have been more aggressive in developing trade expansion had not three developments weakened India in this period. First, a temporary trade disruption weakened Maurya India at this juncture. In 204 BC, Antiochos III the Great briefly expelled the Mauryans from the Indus Valley. In 187 BC, the Mauryan state collapsed altogether in the midst of a Hindu revolt against the Maurya patronage of the Jains and the Buddhists. A rebel general became the first ruler of the Sunga state, which lasted for over a century in the Ganges Valley. Buddhists fled to Sanchi, Bharhut, Mathura, and other refuges. The second problem, leading to a collapse of the Mauryan–Ptolemaic trading dominance, was the failure of either Mauryan Indians or Ptolemaic Greeks to master the Bay of Bengal and to cultivate fully the rich commercial prospects that beckoned from across the eastern Indian Ocean. A third problem was that India was weakened by an invasion of Scythians ('Sakas') out of Central Asia in 165 BC. Despite the emergence of the Kushan state in the region of modern Afghanistan, Pakistan, and Kashmir in the first and second centuries AD, down to AD 319 most of northern India proper remained divided into many small Scythian-ruled states.

The coming of the Han Chinese

Both China and Rome broke into this broadening world trade by forming huge empires. Emperor Shih Huang-ti ('First Emperor') unified China. Inheriting the state of Ch'in as a boy in 246 BC, he conquered all the other Chinese states by his death in 210 BC, ruling from Xianyang (near present-day Xian). His dynastic name of Ch'in (Qin) was the source of the English name for China. He exhibited immense energy in his constant work and travels, giving China a uniform law code, as well as a standardized currency, weights, and measures. He built a vast network of canals and roads radiating out from his capital, and introduced irrigation throughout the country. Shih Huang-ti created China's first standing army, and built various walls, some connected, along the northern frontier to hold out the Xiongnu (Mongols) of the steppe grasslands. This structure was at first built mainly of earthwork, but through the centuries was gradually changed to brick and came to measure fifty feet high and twenty-five feet thick, and to run

1,500 miles. New contacts were made with the outside world, and the Ch'in prime minister Lü Pu-wei expounded on Greece's Pythagorean theorem and musical scale. Shih Huang-ti was buried beneath an artificial mound near Xianyang, in a tomb guarded magically by thousands of six-foot-tall terracotta statues of warriors.

Shih Huang-ti's Chin dynasty did not long survive him. In 207 BC, a peasant-born general, Liu Pang, led his land-owning peasant soldiers in a rebellion against the Ch'in Dynasty, promising milder punishments and a lower tax burden, and became emperor as Kao Tsu ('High Progenitor'), ruling from 202 to 195 BC. His Han dynasty made such an impact on history that the Chinese still call themselves the people of Han. Subsequently, the Han Emperor Wudi ('Martial Emperor,' ruling 142 to 87 BC) set up a meritocracy in which promotions were based on education and achievement on civil service exams. Wudi was an expansionist, who conquered the southern Chinese regions of Chekiang and Fukien. To control the lucrative trade sending Chinese silk and lacquer wares to the new Roman world, between 129 and 119 BC he defeated the Xiongnu in the north and in the west conquered Sinkiang from its Iranian Scythian natives. He then populated Sinkiang with 700,000 forced Chinese colonists. In 139 BC, he sent an embassy to Ferghana, Bukhara, and Bactria, and subsequently conquered as far west as Ferghana. Horses were traded from Ferghana to China, and the vine, introduced to Central Asia by the Greeks, was also brought into China. Silk was traded to the West, where the use of silk caught on in the Roman Empire in the first century BC.

Wudi then sent a Chinese presence to the eastern gateway to the Indian Ocean, using the maritime skills of the southeast coast of China (where the rudder had recently been invented). The fishing fleets and trading junks of Canton (Guangzhou) and surrounding port towns formed the basis for the first significant expansion of Chinese sea power. In 111 BC, Wudi conquered Kwangsi province and north Vietnam, and asserted Chinese naval control of the Strait of Malacca, the eastern doorway into the Indian Ocean. Chinese silks were exchanged for various items, probably including Alexandrian glass.

The coming of the Romans

At the time when China had been moving toward unification and expansion, Rome had begun its own long chain of conquests. The prospering Greek end of the Indian Ocean trade had created and fed Rome, as the child which would eventually displace and then support it. Rome's traditional founding date, in 753 BC, places the start of Rome at the time Greek colonies were being planted throughout the western European Mediterranean, stirring the growth of towns along the commercial routes. Rome's turn to republican government in 508 may have been inspired by the start of Athenian democracy the previous year; Brutus, the father of the Roman republic, had traveled to Greece. Rome's steady military growth reached first for control of the western Mediterranean end of the Greek trade routes, and then took over the Greek eastern Mediterranean itself. After the defeat of the Carthaginian General Hannibal in the Second Punic War, a Roman army crossed to Macedonia, defeated Hannibal's ally Philippos V of Macedon in 198 BC, and occupied Greece. Hannibal fled on to Antioch, and convinced Antiochos III the Great of the Seleucid Empire to lead an army to Greece. Antiochos did so, only to be defeated in his turn. The Roman army followed Antiochos across the Aegean Sea, and defeated him again in 190 BC, obliging him to surrender both his possessions in Asia Minor and his navy. Cornered by the Romans, Hannibal took poison.

Rome's protectorate of Egypt allows it to benefit from the Indian Ocean trade

Antiochos III's son Antiochos IV Epiphanes (r. 175–163 BC) tried to unite what was left of the Hellenistic east against Rome, pursuing a policy of Hellenization to unify the eastern Mediterranean around a Greek identity. In 168 BC, he invaded Egypt, but retreated when he ran up against a Roman army sent in to protect the Ptolemies. Rome's presence in Egypt allowed the Macabbee family in 161 BC to establish an independent Israel freed from Greek rule nestling at the edge of Roman power. Patronage of Ptolemaic Egypt started a Roman interest in Indian Ocean trade, even though the carrying trade remained mainly in the hands of Greeks (along with Jews, Syrians, and Arabs). Cato the Censor led a hard-line faction in the Roman senate that insisted that the only secure way to maintain the Roman Empire was to keep the non-Latin peoples in their place by a harsh rule that would continually remind them who was boss. Despite some minor victories of this line of thought, including the destruction of Corinth and Carthage in 146 BC, the conciliatory faction led by Scipio Aemilianus prevailed. The Roman elite embraced Greek culture, forming the combined Graeco-Roman society that allowed the Greeks high esteem and a continuing importance in the Roman world and the Indian Ocean trade.

Trade sprang up between China and Rome via both the Indian Ocean and the Central Asian silk route. Chinese merchants dominated the eastern part of the sea trade; Indian, Parthian, and Arab intermediaries the central portion; and merchants from the Roman Empire the western extension. Silk goods were given their final form in Alexandria or Antioch for sale in Roman markets. Most of the ships on the Bay of Bengal in this period remained Indian, and the bulk of Chinese trade with India crossed by portage over the Isthmus of Kra where modern Thailand and Burma meet. To reach the shore for this transit required battling strong tides to avoid the shoals created by the deposit of rivers, which could cause a ship to hit bottom as far as 40 miles from the coast, totally out of sight of any land.

'Romans' (actually mainly Egyptian Greeks, Syrians, and Jews) established trading posts that dotted both coasts of India, leaving behind hoards of Roman coins and pottery. The Tamils of south India especially made use of Roman coinage, as Roman trade was particularly strong in the Tamil area. The western merchants picked up pepper and other spices, cottons, gold, pearls, precious stones, palm oil, parrots, eunuchs, and elephant trainers, and brought gold or sold manufactured luxury goods. At first, so few ships were making this hazardous voyage that pepper was selling in Rome for astronomical prices. The Tamil kings were said to have employed Roman bodyguards. The Andhra Empire of south India was also notably influenced by the Roman presence.

The Greeks of Egypt in the early first century BC learned how to build ships sufficiently large to sail directly across the open sea from Yemen to India's Malabar coast. They most likely learned how to utilize the monsoon wind patterns from the Arabs. The pathfinder here was the Greek Hippalus, who may have been a pilot on a voyage from Egypt to India in the 110s BC led by Eudoxus of Cyzicus (sent out by Ptolemeos VIII). The strong wind and rough seas of the summer monsoon (known to the earlier sailors of the Indian Ocean) made the passage to India challenging, but speedy. This route was employed for the rest of the Roman cycle. From this point on, 'Romans' sailed to India in the summer, pushed by the southwest monsoon winds, and returned with the northeast monsoon of winter, bypassing the South Arab middlemen. The South Arabs in protest took to pirate attacks on the Roman ships in the Gulf of Aden. In response, the 'Romans' destroyed Aden, and favored the western Abyssinian coast of the Red Sea. Overall the result was a rapid increase in trade in the Indian Ocean. Ports and other cities sprang up along India's west coast and in Sri Lanka. The 'Roman' ships also made it as far down the East African coast as Zanzibar.

The initial impact of the trading wealth on Rome

A long civil/class war over how to divide the newfound wealth followed Rome's success in dominating the Mediterranean and tapping into the Indian Ocean trade through Egypt. The importance brought to Egypt by its Indian Ocean trade inevitably made Egypt central to resolving the factional struggle in Rome. After Julius Caesar temporarily rose to power in Rome by his victory at Pharsalia in 48 BC, he helped the 21-year-old, intelligent, and alluring Queen Cleopatra VII to prevail in her fight for the Egyptian throne against her brother Ptolemeos XIII. When Cleopatra bore him a son, Caesarion ('Little Caesar'), uniting the blood of Caesar and Alexander the Great, Caesar dreamed of founding an Egypto-Roman dynasty. Returned to Rome, Caesar prepared to have the senate make him dictator for life, on the 15th (Ides) of March 44 BC. However, a group of senators reopened the civil war by assassinating Caesar.

Caesar's great-nephew Octavianus (Octavian) and Caesar's lieutenant Marcus Antonius (Mark Antony) defeated Caesar's assassins in 42 BC. Marcus Antonius, left in charge of the eastern Mediterranean, picked up Caesar's old dream of founding an Egypto-Roman dynasty together with Cleopatra, who gave Marcus three children. However, Octavian, determined to hold on to Egypt, attacked and defeated Marcus Antonius at the naval battle of Actium at the western end of the Gulf of Corinth, in 31 BC Cleopatra hurriedly built a fleet in the Red Sea in order to escape with her family to India. However, at the last minute, local Arabs raided and burned all the ships, foiling this scheme. When Octavian led his army on into Egypt in 30 BC, Marcus Antonius and Cleopatra (after an unsuccessful effort to charm Octavian) committed suicide. Octavian become Rome's first emperor, remembered as Caesar Augustus, and Egypt was converted into a direct province of Rome.

The height of Roman and Chinese trade in the Indian Ocean

The Mediterranean and Red seas were now under Roman supremacy, although the trade was still handled by Greeks, Syrians, Jews, and Arabs. In 20 BC, it is said, Augustus encouraged trade in the Indian Ocean by concluding an alliance with King Poros of India. That year Poros sent a Brahman named Zarmaros as an ambassador to Augustus. The emperor initiated Zarmaros into the Eleusinian mysteries outside Athens and, while Eleusis' fire mystery was being presented, Zarmaros surprised Augustus by walking into the fire. Soon (according to Strabo, the Greek geographer who settled in Augustus' Rome) 120 ships, with archers to protect against pirates, were sailing every year from Egypt's Red Sea port of Myos Hormos to India. In 25–24 BC, Augustus sent an unsuccessful military expedition under Aelius Gallus to subordinate Yemen's Sabaean Arabs, who nonetheless became trading allies of Rome (traveling both by land to Gaza and by the Red Sea).

The Romans traded wine, bronze, tin, gold, and manufactures for frankincense from Yemen, ivory, hides, cinnamon, and slaves from East Africa (obtained from the Arabs of Oman), silk and cotton cloths from northwestern India, and pepper, other spices, gems, and elephants from southwestern India. A temple of Augustus was built at Muziris on India's southwestern Malabar coast by the *Yavanas* ('foreigners,' referring to the many Graeco-Roman merchants in residence there). Somewhere in the period between the 50s AD and AD 110, an anonymous Greek merchant of Egypt wrote the *Periplus of the Erythraean Sea*, a handbook for sailing and trading along the western coasts of the Indian Ocean. *Periplus of the Erythraean Sea* translates into plain modern English as *Circumnavigation of the Indian Ocean*. (As explained above, the Hebrew word for the Indian Ocean, or at least the western part of the Indian Ocean, known to them, was the *Yam Suf*

('Sea of Reeds'), while the equivalent Greek word was the *Erythraean* or 'Red' Sea, the name still used for the Indian Ocean's sea extension from Yemen to Egypt.) This work tells of large Greek ships from Egypt crossing to the Malabar ports for pepper, betel, and silk.

Roman world merchant ventures reached as far as the Ganges delta. Augustus and various later Roman emperors received ambassadors from different Indian states. Rome contributed to a rising demand for spices; Indian merchants sought additional spices in Southeast Asia. Beside the pepper and ginger from India's (southwest) Malabar coast, and the cinnamon by now coming from Sri Lanka, cardamoms were brought from northwest Malaya, camphor from Borneo, from Java and Sumatra, and cinnamon, mace, nutmeg, and cloves from the Moluccas. From East Africa came ivory and tortoiseshell, exported from Somali and Kenyan trading posts in exchange for iron wares (as reported in Ptolemy's *Geographia* in the second century AD). Somalia still provided myrrh, frankincense, and slaves. East Africa's coastline south of Somalia, with its many offshore islands and many coral reefs offering protection from the open ocean waters, and its deep estuaries, provided convenient harbors for visiting ships. The rapid rise in altitude from the coast to the African plateau, hampering communications between the interior and the coast, meant that there were no large political states with which to contend. Products brought from ports farther south on the East African coast included ebony and ivory, shipped to the Mediterranean and India. Gold was not yet a part of this East African trade.

The Chinese merchants may even have braved the considerable dangers of the Bay of Bengal to appear in India; Emperor Wang Mang (r. AD 9–23) sent agents to Bengal to purchase a rhinoceros. The Chinese junks were heavily planked and multi-decked, with several masts, bamboo mat sails, and bows painted with eyes. According to the third-century book *Nan-chou I-wu chih* (*Strange Things of the South*), they carried up to 700 people and 260 tons of cargo. A report from AD 260 by K'ang T'ai, Chinese ambassador to Cambodia, tells about an expedition of Indonesian or Malayan merchant ships sailing to the Roman Empire. The second or third century work *Milindapanha* by Nagasena likewise describes an earlier shipowner of India who traded to Alexandria in the west, and to Bengal, Malaya, and China in the east. However, transhipment from port to port along the long route between China and Egypt would have been the norm. The Malay Peninsula was the terminus for most merchants coming from either west or east, with the Indians dominating the middle segment of the route between China and Egypt.

Oriental luxuries came into great demand in the Mediterranean cities, reaching a height in the second century AD. Pliny warned against the resulting currency drain from the Roman Empire, and many Roman gold coins from this period have been found in India. The extensive use of gold and silver for adornments by the Indians, and their tendency to hoard these metals, meant that they were more highly priced in India than farther west. Rome finally banned Indian muslins on the reasoning that their thinness was undermining the morality of Roman womankind. Emperor Traianus (Trajan) (r. 98–117) dredged out the old Nile–Red Sea canal, which he extended to the western arm of the Nile and hence to Alexandria. He kept a Roman fleet in the Red Sea to patrol against pirates. In AD 106, he turned what was called Nabataea into a Roman province called Arabia, and constructed a road from the Gulf of Aqaba to Damascus. The rock-carved city of Petra in the Wadi el Araba flourished on the resulting trade. In the second half of the second century AD, Ptolemeos the Astronomer wrote that Rome's Greek sailors were trading with Sri Lanka, the mouth of the Ganges, the Malay Peninsula, Vietnam, and China. Some authors read a brief Chinese record to indicate that in AD 166, Emperor Marcus Aurelius sent an embassy to China, encouraging trade between the two empires. However, this is not certain.

Contacts between Rome and India at this time included Christian missionary work. Early Christian tradition insists that St. Thomas was the first to spread Christianity to southern India, where his 'tomb' is displayed. Some have seen a Christian impact on Ashvagosha's transformation in the first or second century AD of Theraveda or Hinayana Buddhism into Mahayana Buddhism, with its emphasis on God's grace (rather than good deeds) and on the writing of lives of the saints (beginning with the *Avadana*). A Christian impact was also exerted over a group of Central Asian nomads called the Kushans, who invaded northern India out of Central Asia in 10 BC, and reached their golden age at the end of the first century AD under a ruler named Kanishka (r. *c.* AD 78–96). Ruling over Afghanistan, the Punjab, Sind, and Kashmir, he patronized a mixture of Nestorian Christian and Manichaean elements into a new blend with Buddhism. Statues of Buddha and bodhisattva saints were carved in a Graeco-Roman influenced 'Gandhara' art style. Kanishka built monasteries and stupas, called a Buddhist council in Kashmir, and sent missionaries to Central Asia, Tibet, and China. The ruins of Idiqut in Turkestan disclose Buddhist and Christian buildings and art side by side. Possible Asian influences coming back into the West with the trade contact include such purported Buddhist contributions to Christianity as the mitre, the crozier, the five-chained censer, the hand blessing, monasticism, the worship of saints, processions, fasting, and holy water.

The height of the trade between Rome and China came in the second century AD. It is said that some sailors from the Roman Empire arrived in Hanoi, which was then part of China, via the Strait of Malacca, having been blown north into the South China Sea by the southwest monsoon. The mastery of the South China Sea, whose reefs and typhoons made it particularly dangerous, was a significant step. China even made an attempt to establish diplomatic relations with Rome. In AD 25, Kuang Wudi

('Shining Martial Emperor') had moved the capital to Loyang (Honan) as a more secure location from increasing Hun raids. Despite the many palace intrigues of the late Han period, and the rise of over-mighty families in the provinces, a golden age of creative energy emerged under three empresses who dominated the government in turn from 88 to AD 150. The prosperity spurred the appearance of new important inventions. Paper was introduced by AD 100, made of rag. Three laborsaving devices also appeared in China: the water mill with its cogwheel, the wheelbarrow, and the horse collar. The open-ended horse collar, attached over the horses' shoulder bones in contrast to the round ox collar, prevented the horse from being choked, and so allowed the harnessing of heavy loads to the horse for the first time.

Why the Han Chinese and Roman dominance of trade ended

In Rome, emperors like Caligula (r. AD 37–41) and Nero (r. AD 54–68) led in the corruption caused by power and the wealth coming in from the extensive trade routes. In AD 67, an army revolt left Nero with no choice but suicide. The emperors of the following century tried to pattern their rule on a more responsible government. The experiment worked fairly well from 98 to AD 180. However, Marcus Aurelius shook the system by leaving the throne to his own son, Commodus (r. AD 180–192), who was the opposite of the meaning of his name ('suitable').

At this point, the Middle Eastern peoples through whose lands the wealth of the East ran, but who had been very marginalized, moved to reassert their importance. These people spoke mainly Semitic and Hamitic languages, like Aramaic and ancient Egyptian. Rome had reconciled its Greek subjects to its rule by the formation of a merged Graeco-Roman culture. However, writers from Cicero to Zosimus slandered Arabs, and Rome had never won the loyalty of its Semitic- and Hamitic-speaking subjects in the Asian and African provinces. The poet Juvenal complained about the (largely slave) Syrians living in Rome as 'sewerage.' The word 'Syrian' was used as a derogatory term to refer to anybody considered inferior, including slaves. At the same time, Rome carelessly recruited large numbers of Middle Easterners into the army. In AD 193, a North African general named Septimius Severus assumed power in Rome and made himself the first of over half a century of Semitic emperors. Septimius introduced a Semiticizing trend to Roman rule, which gained momentum through the first half of the third century. Ruling more from the Middle East than from Rome, he imposed absolute rule for the first time in Rome, executing the (largely Latin) aristocrats in Rome who stood in his way. Additional Middle Eastern subjects were brought into the empire with Septimius' conquest of Mesopotamia in 195, and citizenship was extended to all freeborn inhabitants of the empire by Septimius' son Caracalla in AD 212. Aramaic speech, dress, and customs were introduced to Rome and its court, and oriental religions, including Judaism and Christianity, were favored. Middle Eastern emperors subsequently ruled down to AD 249.

In 249, the Latin general Decius overthrew the last Semitic emperor, Philip the Arab. From 249 to 282, one general fought another for power. At the same time, the Sassanid Persians of Shapur I, the Arabs of Queen Zenobia of Palmyra, and Goths from the Ukraine raided or occupied the eastern provinces of the empire. The Abyssinian kingdom of Axum conquered Yemen, gaining control of the passage of ships between the Mediterranean and the Indian Ocean, and dividing control of the silk trade with the Persians. The steady devaluation of Roman currency may or may not have been related to a gold drain to pay for eastern goods. The Roman Empire had not yet disappeared, but its position in Indian Ocean trade was passing rapidly into the hands of the Sassanian Persians.

The fall of Han China

Han China's fall, like its rise, was closely synchronized with Rome's. In AD 184, Taoist faith healers in Szechwan and eastern China started a revolt which by AD 220 had so weakened China that it broke into three separate states, one covering the Huang Ho ('Yellow River') Valley, one the Yangtse Valley, and one Szechwan (prefiguring the coming split of the Roman Empire into halves). Just as the Romans recruited Germans to fight in their army, so the Chinese hired semi-Sinicized barbarians. In AD 316 steppe peoples sacked Loyang, slaughtering 30,000 of its inhabitants, in a parallel to the Visigothic sack of Rome in 410. Finally, just as the western Roman Empire was divided into Germanic tribal kingdoms, so China was divided up between rival steppe tribes. The later history of China grew out of the amalgam of Chinese and steppe peoples in northern China, just as the Holy Roman Empire arose from the Latin-Germanic admixture in Europe.

Trading shifts in the western Indian Ocean trade

Developments in Iran at this point brought a Persian resurgence. Ardashir I (r. 227–241), a Persian prince of the Sassanian Dynasty, overthrew the Parthian Dynasty in 227, and established his rule at Fars. He then made a bid for a bigger cut of the Indian Ocean trade by founding various ports on the Tigris and Euphrates Rivers and on the Persian Gulf. A disruption of the Central Asian silk road by barbarian attacks induced the Persians to turn to the Indian Ocean route to obtain Chinese silk. Soon Persian merchants were dominant as far away as India and East Africa. In 232, Ardashir conquered Armenia. His son Shapur I (r. 241–273) conquered Mesopotamia and Syria by 260. Shapur was helped by an updated military, fervent warriors, and good allies. He established a heavily armored cavalry army, with big horses and lances, thanks to a new invention coming out of Central Asia, the stirrup. Shapur I (and his son Ormizd) also benefited from religious ardor by championing the Manichaean followers of Mani (Manes, or Manichaeus) (c. 216–c. 276), an Iranian who claimed to be the Mithra or Messiah once prophesized by the Zoroastrian Magi. The fad was useful, but short-lived. The Zoroastrian leaders rejected Mani's messianic claim and his labeling of everything material as evil and everything spiritual as good, and Mani was crucified after Ormizd's death in 274.

Shapur I allied with the Goths and the Semites. As trade moved from the Indian Ocean via the Persian Gulf and the Tigris and Euphrates Rivers to the Caspian and Black Seas, the Germanic Goths moved down the rivers of eastern Europe from the Baltic in order to carry the trade on through northern Europe. Starting in 226, King Kniva's Ostrogothic warriors pushed out from the Ukraine on to the Black Sea in great fleets, raiding the lands along the Aegean Sea, while the Visigoths took Romania from Rome. In 251, Kniva defeated and killed Emperor Decius at the battle of Philippolis, and disrupted Roman shipping in the eastern Mediterranean. Shapur I followed up in 260 by defeating and capturing the Roman emperor Valerianus during a parley on their mutual border. From 266 to 272, Queen Zenobia of Palmyra, Syria, murdered her royal husband, and ruled a buffer state between Persia and Rome that briefly included Syria, Lebanon, Palestine, Egypt, and Anatolia. By the time the Romans defeated Zenobia in 272, Shapur I and the Goths were in control of their respective seas. Alexandria's Greek and Jewish merchants were placed in a difficult position, weakening Rome's hold on the Indian Ocean trade, and Roman coins almost completely disappeared from India.

Under Shah Narseh (r. 293–302), Persia established relations with Somalia and Zanzibar, where South Arabians had established their rule. To gain a counterweight, the Greeks cooperated with the Ethiopian kingdom of Axum, which straddled the southern end of the Red Sea from Ethiopia to Yemen. At the end of the third century, Axum subdued the Hijaz (centered on Mecca) and briefly conquered Yemen. In the mid-fourth century, Greek-born St. Frumentius Christianized Axum, linking it more closely to the Byzantine world, and the Bible was translated into the national language (although in 451 the Ethiopians joined the Egyptian Monophysite Coptic church in insisting that Jesus was purely divine). Byzantine merchants now began a regular trade with Ethiopia with the help of the merchants of Axum. Indian spices again flowed through Alexandria, and Constantinople (Byzantium) grew to 300,000 inhabitants, with three walls. Sea trade connected China, India, East Africa, Egypt, and Syria with Chinese ships meeting Axiomite and Persian ships in the ports of Sri Lanka. Byzantium experienced its golden age in the fifth and sixth centuries, with the erection of the Hagia Sophia church and the introduction of the first extensive manuscript illuminations (on parchment codices).

The Byzantine challenge to Persia

Meanwhile, the Greeks (who had continued to provide much of Rome's mercantile activity) stepped into the vacuum left by a weakened Rome. Emperor Dioclytianos (Diocletian) in 284 relocated his capital from Rome to Greek Nicomedia, on the eastern shore of the Sea of Marmora, between Europe and Asia. This location allowed him to stop the Gothic naval raids and to stabilize the eastern borders. Konstantinos (Constantine) the Great in 330 transferred the capital to nearby Konstantinpolis (Constantinople) on the west side of the Sea of Marmora, at an even more strategic position at the southern end of the Bosporus.

Pulcheria, who dominated the Byzantine government of her retiring brother Theodosios II from 408 to 450 and after his death ruled in her own right for seven more years, gave a further impetus to Byzantine mercantile interests. While Germanic tribes were overrunning the Latin West, the Greeks strengthened their economy in the eastern Mediterranean. In a Byzantine parallel to ancient Egypt's Hatsepshut, Pulcheria gave strong support to the Greek middle class and its industry and trade over the opposition of the Greek nobles. She collected taxes directly instead of going through the town councils, which had overtaxed business, shifting the tax burden to the farming estates of the military aristocracy. She also abolished serfdom, and promoted the middle class in preference to the nobility in the government bureaucracy. When the nobles in opposition used the (originally racing faction) Blue Party to support their goals, Pulcheria supported the opposition Green Party with its middle-class members.

The assertion of Gupta Indian trade in the eastern Indian Ocean

Meanwhile, with both China and Rome having fallen into crisis, India had been left to enjoy the greatest period of importance on the Indian Ocean that it would ever know. This was the period of the Gupta Dynasty. Not that it created a monopoly, for trade remained open to traders from many lands, including the Persians and the Greeks. Chandragupta I (r. 320–330), founder of the Gupta Dynasty, ruled like the Mauryan emperors before him, from Pataliputra (Patna). He triggered a commercial boom by moving away from the Mauryan model of state control of the economy into a free private-enterprise system. Silver coins and cowrie shells (the latter from the Seychelles Islands) were both accepted as currency. Indian navigational understanding was improved with the astronomer Aryabhatta's conclusion that the earth revolves around its axis. The main Indian manufacture sold abroad was textiles. Beside the traditional muslins (plain woven cloth, sold especially to the Mediterranean), they sold brocades (with a raised design as part of the weave, sometimes using gold and silver threads), embroidery (with needlework ornament), and calico (cotton with figures in one color on a background of another). Trade to the Byzantines moved west through the Red Sea. Sailing directly across the bay of Bengal, Indian merchants helped to stimulate trading colonies in Cambodia, Thailand, Burma, Indonesia, and China.

This trading development had started in the pre-Gupta period, when Indian merchants had crossed to Southeast Asia to obtain its gold. New cultural blends resulted from the mixture of Indian with indigenous influences. In the first century AD, Kaundinya planted a Hindu settlement in Cambodia. His descendants were the kings of the Khmer kingdom. Hindu civilization spread to Thailand in the second century AD, where it was reinforced via India and Burma when in the fourteenth century the Thai came to rule Thailand and Laos (from their capital of Ayutthia, named after Rama's capital, Ayodhya). A Shiva- and Buddha-worshiping Hindu dynasty was implanted in Champa (south Vietnam) in the late second century AD. The Hindus colonized Borneo about AD 400, and dominated its society for some time. Buddhist-influenced Hindu kingdoms were launched in Java and in Sumatra in AD 684 In the eighth century, the Hindu Sailendra Empire extended over Java, Sumatra, most of the other Indonesian islands, and the Malay Peninsula (which provided gold to India). This empire's greatest architectural accomplishment was the Borobudur temple, built in Java in the mid-eighth century. As late as the ninth century, East Indian merchant dynasties were still ruling Java, Sumatra, Malaya, and Cambodia. They spread Indian culture with them, inspiring a flowering of culture in these regions, with especially impressive results in Java and Cambodia. The cultural developments based on Gupta influence in Cambodia reached their height long after the Gupta Empire had ended. The island of Bali (named for the king of the *ashura* demons) is still Hindu, a continuing tribute to the strength of Indian commerce and cultural influence in this period.

Chinese merchants for the time being offered no rivalry to the Indians in the Bay of Bengal, due to the weakening of China as a result of its conquest by and wars against the Xiongnu or Mongols. Chinese merchants brought silk and ceramics only to the northern end of the Malay Peninsula, where they were reshipped from the west Malayan coast by Indian merchants via the Andaman Islands to the east coast of India. The last of the nomad dynasties in China was the Wei. By 439, the Wei had conquered all of northern China, and established their capital at Loyang. As Chinese society restrengthened at the time Attila was drawing off Xiongnu (Mongols) to fight in his wars in Europe, the Wei began a conscious policy of embracing Chinese culture. In 494, they made Chinese their official court language, and ordered the nobles to adopt Chinese dress, customs, and surnames, as well as to take Chinese wives. Only then did Chinese merchants begin to expand their trade again along the Asian trade routes. Hoei-Shin, a Buddhist monk during the Wei Dynasty, even wrote of his (imagined?) voyages to a great new land across the Pacific. In the late fourth century, a Chinese Buddhist named Fahien entered India via Central Asia, worshipped at such Buddhist shrines as Bodh Gaya, and returned home by way of Sri Lanka and Java. However, by this time the Gupta Indian merchants had established their ascendancy in the eastern Indian Ocean over to and beyond the Strait of Malacca. Chandragupta II (r. 375–414) extended his realm over India's west coast, and India prospered from the Alexandrian merchant-carried trade with the Byzantine Empire.

The trading wealth helped India to reach a new height of creativity. Mandapas (pillared halls) and shikharas (towers housing a deity) came into fashion at the expense of the free-standing chaitya hall. Indian literary efforts reached new heights with Kalidasa's plays; the *Puranas* collections of Hindu lore; and the *Kama Sutra* manual of how to seduce women and to increase sexual pleasure. A new literary work, the *Dasha Avatar* (*Ten Incarnations*), telling of ten times when Vishnu took on human form to come to earth, heralded the incorporation by Gupta Hinduism of Buddha as the ninth incarnation of Vishnu. Jain influences were also assimilated into Hinduism, including the substitution of animal images in the temples for the sacrifice of living animals, and an emphasis on a vegetarian diet. Chinese creativity under the Wei Dynasty also blossomed from the returning trade, with the invention of block printing, gunpowder, and the kite, and the founding of Chinese landscape painting by Ku K'ai-chih. Japan, with its new extension of the Chinese trade, joined in the creativity with ikebana floral and rock arrangements and the world's first oil painting. With Buddha fully assimilated into Hinduism, and Jainism reconciled with it, the old rural-based priestly religion triumphed over the urban mercantile-linked challenges left from the sixth century BC. At the end of the sixth century, White Hun invaders from Central Asia brought the final blow to the Gupta Empire and the Gupta trading system.

The end of the first period of European Mediterranean trade participation

The collapse of the Gupta Empire and trade invited upheavals in India's western trading partners as well. In the Byzantine Empire, the Semitic- and Hamitic-speaking Middle East remained unhappy with Greek rule, as it had been with the Roman. Its rebelliousness was manifested by Christian heresies, most notably by Monophisitism (asserting that Jesus was only divine, not human), still today the doctrine of Egypt's Coptic church. In the sixth century, the Semites got a chance to break away from Greek rule when Emperor Iustianianos I (Justinian, r. 527–565) overextended Byzantine power. From peasant stock, married to Theodora, the daughter of a bear-trainer at Constantinople's circus, Iustianianos was eager to prove that he could be an outstanding ruler. He built the impressive Hagia Sophia in Constantinople, declaring, 'I have vanquished you, Solomon!' He bolstered the emperor's powers by the new Justinian codification of the Roman law, and he reconquered much of the western Mediterranean from the Germanic tribes.

While thus straining Byzantine resources, Iustinianos failed to dislodge Persian trade in the Indian Ocean. In 531, he asked the king of Axum to challenge the Persian monopoly of the silk trade from China. Silk costs had risen steeply in Byzantium in the early sixth century, after Persia established a monopoly of the silk trade by a trade agreement with the Ethiopian kingdom of Axum. However, the merchants of Axum proved unable to elbow the Persians aside from their position in Sri Lanka. The problem of silk prices was resolved in 552, when silk moth eggs hidden in a bamboo cane were smuggled to Constantinople by Byzantine monks. Soon, silk moths were being farmed in Syria and southern Greece, and silk cloth was being woven in Constantinople, ending the Chinese monopoly of silk production, although China continued significant silk exports. However, because of its higher-quality production Persia was gaining an increasingly strong position *vis-à-vis* Byzantium's Axumite trading partners. Byzantine interests were adversely affected when the governor of Axum's Arabian colony, Abrahah, rebelled in about 540, and held his own against two punitive expeditions from Ethiopia. Abrahah's autonomy was consequently accepted, contingent on the payment of a tribute to the king of Axum. Byzantine access to the Indian Ocean was thus threatened.

Alternate Persian and Greek victories

Iustinianos left his successor a Middle East seething with disaffection. The latest Sassanid shah of Persia, Khusru I Anushirwan (Chosroes), took advantage of this unrest to sack Antioch in 570. In the same year, he took control of Yemen from Axum, cutting off Byzantine access to the Indian Ocean. Persian merchants settled in the ports of Bahrain and Oman, which became dependent on the Sassanid Empire. Many of the Arabs of Oman became worshippers of the Persian creator god Ahura Mazda (Hormuz). The trade in myrrh and frankincense fell off with the ending of the trading prominence of Yemen. Unable to handle the crisis, Iustinos II went insane in 574. After his death, masses of Slavs took advantage of Byzantine troubles to settle permanently in the Balkans. The Persians moved to consolidate their victory under Shah Khusru II Parviz 'the Victorious' (r. 589–628). Khusru ravaged Syria and Asia Minor all the way to the Bosporus between 603 and 610. Encouraged by the Middle Eastern subjects of Byzantium, the Persians sacked Antioch in 611, captured Damascus in 614, took Jerusalem in 615, and conquered Egypt in 616. The patriarch of Alexandria betrayed that city to the Persians.

One short-lived final revival of Indian and Byzantine strength at the start of the seventh century contained this surge of Persian power. In the year

606, Harsha became king of the kingdom of Kanauj near Delhi at age 16, ruling for the next forty-one years. An energetic workaholic and conqueror, he built a realm that ran from the Punjab to Orissa. He was a humanitarian, who prevented his sister from committing the *sutee* immolation suicide upon her husband's death. A patron of learning, he wrote plays and poems, and attracted students from Tibet, Indonesia, China, Korea, and Japan to his Nalanda Buddhist university. The *Jataka*, a collection of five hundred verse tales telling of Buddha's various avatars or incarnations, was written for and presented to Harsha. One story, for example, tells of Buddha's life as a patient ox, emphasizing acceptance of one's lot as the formula for achieving an upward progression in the chain of transmigrations and reincarnations.

Byzantium experienced a last surge of success at the same time. Heraklios I (r. 610–641), an Armenian general who usurped the throne, repulsed two Persian sieges of Constantinople in 615 and 626. In 622, Heraklios went on the offensive, adopting the stirruped, armored cavalry for the Greek army (the so-called cataphracts), as well. He made use of the continuing Greek naval superiority to land troops in Cilicia (at the northeastern corner of the Mediterranean), forcing the Persians out of Anatolia. In 627, Heraklios intercepted a message from Khusru II to his troops, ordering the execution of one of the Persian generals, Shahr-Baraz. Heraklios added the names of four hundred other Persian officers to the list, and then diverted the order to Shahr-Baraz. In reaction, Shahr-Baraz and the other named officers rebelled, and overthrew Khusru II. Heraklios took advantage of the uproar to lead an army into northern Iraq, and in that same year of 627 won a military victory at Nineveh. This success allowed him to occupy the Sassanian capital of Ctesiphon, north of Babylon, at the beginning of the next year. Khusru II died soon after, and Heraklios resumed control of the Levant.

During the millennium considered in this chapter (from the sixth century BC to the seventh century AD), the Greeks barged in to take the leadership and western Indian Ocean trade away from Persia. By conquering the Greeks, the Romans long enjoyed the fruits of their success (in conjunction with a Chinese appearance in the eastern Indian Ocean). After Roman rule faded, the Persians again made a bid for leadership, only to have the Greeks challenge them again, culminating in Heraklios' campaign. However, Heraklios' victory was short-lived. The Semites and Hamites in his restored realm were in no way reconciled to Greek rule, and both Greeks and Persians had exhausted themselves by their continued struggle for control, leaving them vulnerable to outside attack. This attack was about to hit, a mere seven years after Heraklios' great success, and it would end the first period of strong Mediterranean European impact on the Indian Ocean trade. People usually expect that the world that they and their families have always known will not change overnight. History teaches otherwise.

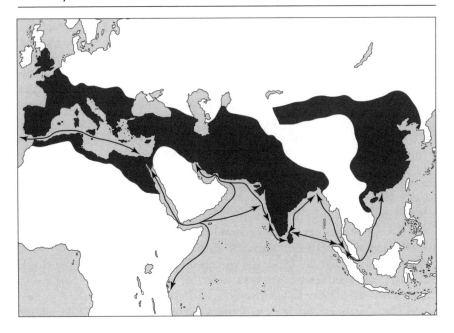

Figure 3.1 Principal lands and sea routes discussed in Chapter 3

Further reading

On India and Southeast Asia: Edward Conze, *A Short History of Buddhism* (London: Allen and Unwin, 1980); W.W. Tarn, *The Greeks in Bactria and India* (Cambridge: Cambridge University Press, 1951); Chai-Shin Yu, *Early Buddhism and Christianity: A Comparative Study of the Founders' Authority, the Community, and the Discipline* (Delhi: Motilal Banarsidass, 1981); Kenneth R. Hall, *Maritime Trade and State Development in Early Southeast Asia* (Honolulu: University of Hawaii Press, 1985); A. Reid, *Southeast Asia in the Era of Commerce, 1450–1680: The Lands below the Winds* (New Haven, Connecticut: Yale University Press, 1989); and D.R. Sardesai, *Southeast Asia: Past and Present* (Boulder, Colorado: Westview Press, 1997).

On China: S.A.M. Adshead, *China in World History* (New York: St. Martin's Press, 2000); Zhongshu Wang, *Han Civilization* (New Haven, Connecticut: Yale University Press, 1982); Xinru Liu, *Ancient India and Ancient China: Trade and Religious Changes AD 1–600* (Delhi: Oxford University Press, 1988); and Yu Yingshi, *Trade and Expansion in Han China: A Study in the Structure of Sino-barbarian Relations* (Berkeley: University of California Press, 1967).

On Achaemenid Persia: Pierre Briant, *From Cyrus to Alexander: A History of the Persian Empire*, trans. Peter T. Daniels (Winona Lake, Indiana:

Eisenbrauns, 2002); Andrew Robert Burn, *Persia and the Greeks: The Defense of the West* (Stanford, California: Stanford University Press, 1984); and John Curtis, *Ancient Persia* (London: British Museum Publications, 1989).

On the Greeks: Sarah B. Pomeroy, Stanley M. Burstein, Walter Donlan, and Jennifer Tolbert Roberts, *Ancient Greece: A Political, Social, and Cultural History* (New York: Oxford University Press, 1999); Charles W. Fornara and Loren J. Samons II, *Athens from Cleisthenes to Pericles* (Berkeley: University of California Press, 1991); Peter Green, *Alexander of Macedon* (Berkeley: University of California Press, 1991); Michael Grant, *From Alexander to Cleopatra: The Hellenistic World* (New York: Charles Scribner's Sons, 1982); Naphtali Lewis, *Greeks in Ptolemaic Egypt* (Oxford: Clarendon Press, 1986); Malcolm Francis McGregor, *The Athenians and their Empire* (Vancouver: University of British Columbia Press, 1987); and Frank William Walbank, *The Hellenistic World* (Cambridge, Massachusetts: Harvard University Press, 1982).

On Rome: Anthony Birley, *Septimius Severus: The African Emperor* (New York: Doubleday, 1972); Ernle Bradford, *Cleopatra* (San Diego, California: Harcourt Brace Jovanovich, 1972); John Buchan, *Augustus* (London: Hodder and Stoughton, 1937); A. Cameron, *The Later Roman Empire* (Cambridge, Massachusetts: Harvard University Press, 1993); Robert B. Kebric, *Roman People* (London: Mayfield, 1997); Yann Le Bohec, *A History of Rome*, trans. A. Nevill (Oxford: Blackwell, 1996); H.H. Scullard, *Scipio Africanus: A Soldier and Politician* (Ithaca, New York: Cornell University, 1970); and C.W. Bowersock, *Roman Arabia* (Cambridge, Massachusetts: Harvard University Press, 1983).

On Byzantium: Michael Grant, *Constantine the Great: The Man and his Times* (New York: History Book Club, 2000); John Moorhead, *Justinian* (London: Longman, 1994); and Warren T. Treadgold, *A History of the Byzantine State and Society* (Stanford, California: Stanford University Press, 1997).

Chapter 4

The Arab golden age

With the fall of the Han Dynasty and the decline of Byzantium, Chinese and European involvement in the Indian Ocean trading scene receded for a time. The difficulties of China and Mediterranean Europe offered an opportunity for the original trading societies of the Indian Ocean periphery to reassert their independence. Most notably, the lands at the western edge of the Indian Ocean that had first led in civilization – the Fertile Crescent and Egypt – now reclaimed their prominence. The rise of Islam gave them a new unity and a rallying ideology, and Muslim networks displaced previous trading patterns. This chapter will look in turn at the four main sub-periods of this Arab-led period:

1   the rise of the newly-Islamic Arabs of Mecca and Medina in the early seventh century;
2   the Ummayad Caliphate of Damascus from the mid-seventh to the mid-eighth century;
3   the Abbasid Caliphate of Baghdad from the mid-eighth to the early tenth century; and
4   the Fatimid Caliphate of Cairo from the tenth through the eleventh century.

The Arab Golden Age witnessed continuing prosperity for the peoples of the Indian Ocean. Arabs vied with Indians and Indonesians for trade in the Bay of Bengal, a competition that reached its height in the eleventh century. Diplomatic relations were established between Arab rulers and their Indian counterparts, and trade increased in the eastern half of the Indian Ocean as well.

This development was spurred by improved shipbuilding (with transverse watertight bulkheads to keep ships from being so likely to sink). The development of larger and more seaworthy compass-guided Arab dhows (and also Chinese junks) allowed an increased transport of bulk cargoes such as manufactures, timber, wheat, barley, rice, salt, and sugar. Both sails and oars were used, along with a stern rudder for greater control. The Arab dhow, whose two masts each carried a lateen sail, could be fast when the huge sails were spread out wide, and maneuverable when they were raised into a high triangle, sailing in zigzag tacks into the wind. Its timbers were fastened with coconut fiber ropes, and pounded tightly together. Holes were stuffed with a paste made of coconut fiber, tree gum, and lime. The biggest weakness of the dhow was that iron nails were long avoided out of fear that underwater magnetic forces would pull them out – a superstition that made dhows very short lived. Wicker rails prevented waves from breaking over the ship's bulwark. Both the ancient Greek astrolabe and the Chinese compass (now improved into a free-swinging needle) were used to navigate. As the astrolabe is not easy to use on the tossing sea (needing to hang freely to find the horizon), a quadrant was also used. Latitudes were estimated from measuring the elevation of the Pole Star, employing a board held at arm's length. Taking aim with the board at the Pole Star, the angle at which a weighted string dangled was then read.

The collapse of Harsha's northern Indian Empire after his death in 647 facilitated a new shift of trading powers. An anti-Buddhist and anti-Chinese reaction brought a Hindu named Arjuna to the throne. The Chinese at his court were massacred, but Emperor Taizong's envoy Wang-Hiuen-tse escaped to Nepal, from where he returned at the head of a Tibetan army. He defeated Arjuna, beheaded a thousand Indians, and took Arjuna as a prisoner back to China.

However, the southeast Indian kingdom of Pallava, centered at Kanchipuram with its main port of Mamallapuram, flourished in the seventh and eighth centuries by selling cinnamon, ginger, pepper, curry powder (a mixture of pepper with pungent spices, originally ginger, and today turmeric and fenugreek), paprika (ground sweet pepper), and cloves to the Arabs, while obtaining cream of tartar (grapes mixed with tamarinds) brought from East Africa.

The great prosperity in the Indian Ocean at this time encouraged the appearance of the world's most sensual major religion, Tantric Hinduism. However, where prosperity leads to sensuality, sensuality does not reciprocate, but rather works to undermine the work ethic and the very prosperity that gave rise to it. Tantric sensuality added an element that would gradually sap India's ability to ward off foreign exploiters. Tantrism deifies *shakti*, the female force believed to be dominant in the universe, venerating the destroyer god Shiva and his consort Kali. India was divided into various small kingdoms that devoted part of their wealth to the construction of monuments. In the late eighth century, the Tamil king Narasimha Varam I of the Pallava kingdom built a shrine to Vishnu at Mamallapuram ('Place of the Wrestler'), including a bas-relief depiction of the descent of the Ganges River goddess from the world of the gods via the Himalayas to the world of humans. At the same time, the Rashtrakuta king Krishna I (r. 760–800) in the area of the later Mumbai (Bombay) contributed two great rock-cut shrines dedicated to Shiva: in the rock quarry of Ellora east of Bombay and on Elephanta Island in Bombay harbor. Holy prostitution was practiced, and even monks lived a life of license. An obsession with lust penetrated the educational institutions, renowned scholars writing obscene books like the *Kuttini Matam* (*Opinions of a Pimp*) by a Kashmir minister, and *Samaya Matraka* (*Biography of a Prostitute*) by the Sanskrit scholar Kshemendra.

T'ang Dynasty Chinese in the eastern Indian Ocean

China at this time was recovering from the invasions by central Asian nomads and the collapse of the Han Dynasty. While a strong Chinese resurgence in the Indian Ocean trade would not come until the late Sung Dynasty, trade between India and China was again important. The T'ang Dynasty was founded in 617 by a usurping general, Taizong (T'ai-Tsung or 'Grand Ancestor'). From his capital of Xianyang (Sian), he conquered the strategic lands along the trade routes out of China. He brought Korea to accept his suzereignty by helping the north Korean king to subdue south Korea, with its Japanese links. He resubjugated Vietnam, giving it the name of Annan ('Pacified South'). In 671, a Chinese Buddhist monk and mariner named I-Ching sailed from Canton via Sumatra to India, and in 717–720, an Indian sailed from Sri Lanka to Canton, leading the way for a two-way trade. Emissaries from the T'ang emperors were sent in the seventh century to Vietnam and India. T'ang China imported a wide range of goods from the Indian Ocean, including cloves and sandalwood from Indonesia, pepper from Burma, dates and pistachios from Persia, and myrrh and frankincense from Somalia.

T'ang goods spread as far west as Constantinople. Post-stations with inns were maintained along the main roads and waterways. A Chinese policy of toleration encouraged contact between various types of people, from the now official state Confucianism through Buddhists, Taoists, Zoroastrians, Manichaeans, Jews, Christians, and Moslems. When, in 713, ambassadors from the Ummayad caliph Walid I refused out of religious scruples to kow-tow (prostrate themselves) before the T'ang emperor Ming Huang, they were released from the requirement. The Chinese economy flourished more than ever. By 748, Persians and Arabs owned vessels sailing to Canton, and lived in a large settlement on the Chinese island of Hainan. They spread Chinese porcelain, silk cloth, and copper coins to Iraq, Egypt, and Zanzibar.

In this period, tea was introduced to China from Southeast Asia. Used at first as a medicine, it soon became a popular drink. To hold the liquid, the Chinese developed the world's first true nonporous porcelain, fused at high temperatures from Kaolin feldspar clay. It would ring when struck, and was falsely believed to show the presence of poisons in food. The resulting Yüeh stoneware was made of white clay under a transparent glaze. As mentioned earlier, China's silk-making monopoly (but not its silk exports) ended when, in the sixth century, Byzantine monks from Syria smuggled silk cocoons into their own land. Porcelain, as well as being useful for ballast, became the main export to the Arabs in the Abbasid period (see page 65ff).

The rise of the Arabs

The towns of the Red Sea coast, with their Jewish merchant communities, had long benefited from the trade up and down the Red Sea. Mecca may have been the main mid-way stopping point for Red Sea traders, distributing goods on through Arabia and up to the Fertile Crescent by camel caravans, although this view is disputed. The pilgrims who visited Mecca, coming to venerate and circle a bowling ball-sized black meteorite kept in the Ka'aba ('Cube') shrine to the moon god al-Lah, further enhanced Mecca's role as a trading emporium. There, Arab traders were free from the blood feud mentality that frequently disrupted trade elsewhere in the Arabian Peninsula. The Umayyad family of the Quiraysh ('Shark') clan especially benefited from Mecca's newfound wealth. However, Arab traders in the Indian Ocean had been losing out in the fifth and sixth centuries in favor of Persian rivals. After Yemen was conquered by a Persian naval expedition sent by the Persian Shah Khusro I in 570, the Red Sea trade was also jeopardized. The rapid changes in control of the Red Sea to Indian Ocean trade route as Persians and Greeks clashed both stimulated and worried the Arab merchants of Mecca. Islam might be seen from one perspective as a creative response in the realm of religion.

Mohammed

In the same year that Khusro I took Yemen, Mohammed was born in Mecca into the Hashimite family of the Quiraysh clan. Grown to manhood, Mohammed found employment leading camel trains between Mecca and Damascus for a rich widow named Kadija. When he was 20, Kadija, then 40, married him. They had four daughters, the eldest of whom was Fatima. When Mohammed was in his early thirties, at a time when some of his acquaintances were calling for a higher spiritual revelation to the Arabs, he had the first of a series of visions. At first, he feared the spiritual forces that had contacted him were jinns. Soon convinced that God was speaking to him through the angel Gabriel, Mohammed committed the messages to writing as the Koran ('Recitation').

Since Mohammed was a merchant, it is not surprising that the religion he announced was friendly to traders. Thus the Koran speaks of honest merchants as equal to prophets and martyrs. Its requirement of the *hajj* or pilgrimage to Mecca at least once by all the faithful if feasible brought a boost to shipping from the many Moslems who sailed to Mecca's port of Jiddah. However, the Koran also incorporated important elements hostile to extremes of materialism. To an extent, it called on Arabs to turn back to the concern for the poor and to community solidarity that were being challenged by Mecca's emergence as a trade center. The charging of interest was forbidden, so that merchants and moneylenders had to resort to third persons or to disguise interest as profit. When Mohammed was in his forties, Persian power, grown still stronger by control of the Indian Ocean trade, swept over the entire Middle East. Shah Khusro II the Victorious declared war on Byzantium, and in 610 conquered Anatolia all the way to the Bosporus. In 611, he took Antioch, in 614 Jerusalem, and in 617 Egypt. These latter conquests fell to him relatively easily, because many of the local Semitic- and Hamitic-speakers were alienated from Byzantine rule.

By the early 620s, Mohammed's adherents began to grow to significant numbers, giving the Umayyad family cause for anxiety. In 622, Mohammed was forced to flee with some of his disciples to Medina ('City') on the Damascus caravan route 200 miles to the north of Mecca. From Medina, Mohammed carried on a war against Mecca, giving a religious militancy that would aid his coming success. His followers were promised that death in such a *jihad* ('holy war') brought guaranteed access to Paradise. The fighting was fierce, and Mohammed sent out assassins to take his opponents off guard. When Medina's Jews refused to accept Islam, the Jewish men were executed, and the women and children were sold as slaves. In 630, the Byzantine emperor Heraklios I defeated the Persians at Nineveh, restoring Greek control of the Middle East. In the same year, Mohammed besieged Mecca. The most astute of the Umayyad leaders, young Muawiya, negotiated its surrender. Muawiya was accepted as Mohammed's private secretary and convert. Mohammed then went on to conquer Yemen, a strategic key to the Indian Ocean, from the Persians. In subsequent campaigns, Mohammed came to control not only the Red Sea coast from Eilat (on the Gulf of Aqaba) to Yemen, but all of the western Arabian Peninsula. The Arabs converted to Islam en masse.

The early caliphs

When Mohammed died, his Hashimite family expected that he would leave the succession to his young cousin Ali, widower of Mohammed's eldest daughter, Fatima. Instead, the position of first *califa* ('successor') or caliph was assumed by Mohammed's best friend and father of his last wife Aisha, Abu Bakr, of the Taym clan. At Abu Bakr's death in 634, power was passed on to Umar (r. 634–644), another of Muhammed's sons-in-law, also from the Taym clan. Since Islam discourages the depiction of human features, leaving faces blanked out, Umar (known for his fiery temper) is identified in Islamic art by the whip in his hand. Indeed, he used his whip to deadly effect, flogging one man for a minor offense and whipping his own son to death for getting drunk. This violence was now instrumental in bringing the Arabs to the forefront of world power.

Unhappy with the collapse of the Persian patronage, the Semites of the Fertile Crescent were in no way inclined to help Byzantine rule. Umar responded to the opportunity in a whirlwind military campaign that swept out of Arabia over the Middle East with the full fervor of newborn faith, and with the promise of control over the crucial commercial routes in the targeted lands. In 635, Damascus was the first city to fall. The rest of Syria followed so rapidly that Heraklios was not even given time to arrive with a relief army. Before the year was out, Umar had taken Iraq as well. Two years later, in 637, Jerusalem surrendered. The Palestinian Jews, who had been faced with forcible conversions to Christianity, worked actively to help the Arab conquest of their region. Another three years brought Umar's conquest of Egypt, in 640. The Monophysite Copts welcomed the Arabs as an escape from Byzantine taxes and Greek Orthodox religious persecution. Umar tolerated both Jews and Copts as Peoples of the Book, merely subjecting them to a mild tax. These groups, along with Syrian Christians and Iraqi Zoroastrians, were allowed to continue holding posts in the administration. The day would come when both Jews and Copts would find themselves persecuted minorities under the Arab rulers of their lands, but for the time being they were satisfied with having exchanged Byzantine Greek rule for that of their Semitic cousins, the Arabs. The last of Umar's conquests finished off the Persian Empire, already driven out of Yemen, Bahrain, and Iraq. In 642, the Arabs decisively defeated Shah Yezdegerd at the battle of Hamadan (Ecbatana). Wherever they conquered, they founded garrison towns (*amsar*) that sometimes grew into bustling cities. Basra in Iraq and Fustat in Egypt each started as a *misr* (the singular of *amsar*).

Umar moves into the Indian Ocean

Attention was immediately given to bringing the Indian Ocean trade under Arab control. In 636, the governor of newly Muslim Bahrain raided the Indian coast near Bombay, while his brother seized ships in the Indus delta. In 638, the next governor of Bahrain raided across the Persian Gulf into Persia. In 641, Umar sent a naval raid across the Red Sea to Abyssinia in reprisal for Ethiopian attacks on the coasts of Arabia. In 642, the new Arab governor of Egypt reopened the old canal between the Nile and the Red Sea. However, Arab control of the commerce from the Indian Ocean to the Mediterranean favored the camel caravans from Mecca to Damascus, causing the Red Sea trade route to Egypt to wither for the following three centuries. Monophysite Ethiopian Axum, still allied with the Byzantines, likewise found itself shut off from the trade routes.

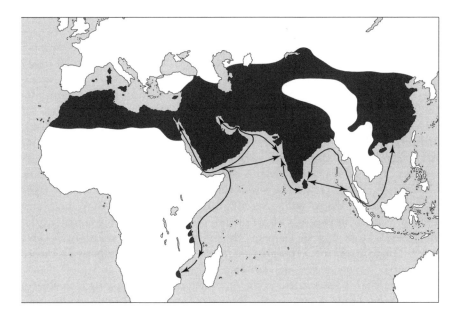

Figure 4.1 Principal lands and sea routes discussed in Chapter 4

The Arab and Muslim presence also spread along to Indian Ocean trading routes eastward and southward. In 710, the Arabs conquered Sind (southern Pakistan today), from which they pushed down the Malabar coast, planting commercial communities in port towns all the way to Sri Lanka. The Persians brought from India sugar cane, rice grains, and saffron that were soon also cultivated in the Muslim regions, becoming staples of the Iranian and Arabic diets. Arabs and Persians also developed Muslim trade centers in East Africa, from where they obtained ivory, gold, iron, and slaves. In return, they sold rugs, iron tools, pots and pans from the Middle East, cloth, beads, and metal implements from India, cowrie shells (for ornaments and currency) from the Maldive Islands, stone pots and jars from Thailand and Burma, spices from the Moluccas, and silks and porcelain wares from China. Less exotic goods such as wheat, rice, oil, butter, and dyes were also traded. From 671 to 748, Persians, Indians, and Malaysians are all listed in Chinese documents as owners of ships at Canton. Gold from the kingdom of Zimbabwe was obtained on the East African coast either at Kilwa (in modern Tanzania) or Sofala (in modern Mozambique). The prosperity that the gold trade brought to Zimbabwe found architectural expression in the high stone enclosures known as 'kraals.' While both Europe and China bought the ivory, the biggest customer was India, as African ivory was superior to Indian ivory for carving into jewelry and ornaments. Slaves, common in

Africa and sold mainly in the Somali port towns, were shipped to China, India (where the practice was acceptable to Hinduism), Persia (where thousands were put to work in the saltpeter mines), and the Middle East.

The Arabs of Oman had long handled the slave and crops trade from East Africa, but only in the thirteenth century did Arab settlements along the African coast become large enough to justify setting up local administrations of independent Arab sheiks there. Beginning with a colony of 'Shirazi' (from Shiraz on the Persian Gulf) around Mogadishu (in Kenya), Muslims spread on to other East African coastal ports. The intermixture of Arab, Persian, and Bantu (and later Portuguese) gave rise to a new lingua franca in East Africa called Swahili (from *sawahil* [Arabic: shores]). Swahili (along with Hausa) grew to be one of the two most widely spoken languages in sub-Saharan Africa, with over 20 million speakers. The Arabian and Persian element in this mix of merchants was strongest in the Somali ports, while the native African element predominated farther south. Arabs also ruled Zanzibar (off the Tanzanian coast). Arab merchants imported Chinese porcelains, carpets, silks and damasks, perfumes, pearls, and glass beads. Indian merchants also settled on the East African coast, bringing iron objects and carnelian beads. However, the Iranians continued to dominate the trade with the regions from the Persian Gulf to China for a while. The Swahili city states used their wealth to construct pillar tombs and mosques with Indonesian motifs.

The spread of Muslim merchants through the Indian Ocean ports was facilitated by the frequent conversions to Islam in the port towns, where native merchants often found the egalitarianism and universality of the new religion appealing. Muslim merchants employed early forms of bills of exchange and formed partnerships, both ideas picked up from earlier times. Muslims charged pagans 10 percent of value on goods, and dhimmis (Jews and Christians) 5 percent, but Muslims only 2.5 percent. The *Dar al-Islam* (House of Islam) was spreading rapidly under Umar, but before he could chalk up his next conquest, he was struck down. Muslim assassinations are often carried out in mosques, while the victim is vulnerable, bent to the floor praying. While Umar was leading the early morning prayers in the mosque at Medina, a Persian slave stabbed him.

The shift of Arab trading control to Damascus

Umar's murder still did not bring Ali and the Hashimites to power. The Umayyad Muawiya (Mohammed's former secretary) had been appointed governor of Syria in Damascus. He had proven himself a good statesman, tempering justice with mercy. Saying, 'I never use my sword when my tongue will do,' he had won the enthusiasm of his subjects. Muawiya was thus in a position at Umar's death to put in as caliph a member of his own Umayyad family, Uthman (r. 644–656), who had married two of

Mohammed's daughters in turn. In 645, Muawiya developed a navy, based in Alexandria and employing the trained Greek sailors of that port city. Damascus emerged as the control point of the Umayyad rule.

Ali challenged Uthman's religious leadership, rallying his *Shi'i* ('Partisan') faction in an attempt to defeat the *Sunni* ('Traditionalist') followers of Muawiya. The issue was finally decided when Ali was murdered in 661 as he prayed in the mosque of Kufa in Iraq. Muawiya then consolidated the rule of the Umayyads of Damascus, and Umayyad authority by 715 had swept across North Africa and Spain. The success was celebrated by the construction of artistically impressive shrines and mosques like Jerusalem's Dome of the Rock and the Great Mosque of Damascus.

The shift of Arab trading control from Damascus to Baghdad

Since the chances of any particular world region rising to primary leader-ship in the Indian Ocean have been greatly influenced by location, some regions have had more than one period of success. This would be true of Egypt and Italy. The first land to return to a second age of such promi-nence was Mesopotamia, or Iraq, in the eighth century. For most of the thirteen centuries since the sixth century BC, Mesopotamia had been ruled from Iran. By 750 the unpopularity and dissipation of the Umayyad caliphs of Damascus gave Iraq a good opportunity for assuming control. Members of Mohammed's Hashimite family led Iraqi claims to political leadership. Abu al-Abbas, of the Abbasid family descended from Mohammed's uncle Abbas, called for an end to the special Umayyad tax status for people of Arab blood. His thirst for revenge against the usurper Umayyad family won him the nickname *al-Saffah* ('the Blood-thirsty'). Replacing the white banner of the Umayyads and the green banner of the Shi'ites with the black flag of the Abbasids, al-Saffah captured Damascus in 750, and put to death the last caliph of Damascus, Marwan II 'the Ass.'

Abbasid trading activity in the Indian Ocean

The Abbasids brought new momentum to trade based on the Persian Gulf. Byzantium had boycotted the Indian Ocean trade route through Egypt and Syria by weakening sales in those regions, and this policy helped to give a new impetus to the alternative Persian Gulf route. Although Egypt was a province of the Abbasid caliphate, the Red Sea route was discouraged in favor of that of the Persian Gulf. Egypt's Red Sea canal was abandoned, Alexandria's population dropped from 600,000 to only 100,000 by 860, and the Pharos lighthouse fell into ruins. Basra (founded as Iraq's main port in 638), Bahrain, and Ormuz returned to their role as prosperous ports on the route to India and (via Muscat in Oman) East Africa. The movement of goods was facilitated by the digging of a canal connecting the Tigris at Baghdad to the Euphrates. The Arabs learned navigational tips from the Iranians, so that via the Arabs various Persian nautical terms eventually passed into English, including 'barge,' 'helm,' 'lateen,' and 'anchor.' Arabic became the lingua franca of trade throughout the Indian Ocean. Pirates based at Bahrain, Qatar, and Iranian harbors were a problem; soldiers armed with 'Greek fire' (naphtha) guarded merchant ships. A large Abbasid fleet was sent in 825 to crush pirates operating out of Bahrain.

Using a Moslem trading colony present in Sri Lanka since the beginning of the eighth century as a midway stopping point, Abbasid Arab merchants pushed into the eastern Indian Ocean with their own ships, sailing through the Strait of Malacca to China. Arab merchants became as important as carriers of Indian Ocean and China Sea trade as the Persians had previously been, although they ran into competition from Chinese merchants in the Bay of Bengal and the South China Sea. The growth of trade spurred the Indonesian islands into their own golden age. In south Sumatra, the Hinayana Buddhist Srivijaya empire based on the city of Palembang arose and became powerful from the late seventh century to the thirteenth century handling maritime trade. In the late eighth and early ninth century, this empire was joined by the Buddhist Shailendra kingdom in Java, noted for building the world's largest stupa, at Borobodur. In Cambodia, the Khmer kingdom was launched at Angkor, famous for its own impressive temples (reaching a height in the twelfth century).

Commerce blossomed between Baghdad, India, Indonesia, Indochina, China, Korea, Egypt, and East Africa. Arabs and Persians made a joint raid on Canton in 758. The Chinese reacted by closing Canton to foreign trade, but in 792 it was reopened and regularly visited by Muslim traders. A large colony of Arabs settled at Canton, and received from the Emperor of China the right to their own *qadi* ('judge'). Jewish merchants moved back and forth between China in far East Asia and France in far western Europe. Both Arab and Jewish merchants constantly came and went from Baghdad, trading in Indian pepper, cinnamon, ginger, and coconuts, Chinese rhubarb, Moluccan nutmeg, cloves and mace, Borneo camphor, Timor sandalwood, Sri Lankan rubies, East African slaves, and many other items. Some of the slaves were put to work in a vain attempt to convert the southern Iraqi marshlands into wheat fields. Others worked on date palm plantations and in pearl fisheries. Caliph al-Mansur (754–775) boasted that there was no obstacle to trade between Iraq and China, and that all ships could come to Baghdad. About 850, Ibn-Khurdadhbih wrote a book describing the routes from the Persian Gulf to China. Bit by bit, the Arabs took over the trade of the East Asian seas from the Indians and Chinese, so that they eventually dominated the entire trading scene. Even Chinese goods were now sent to India in Arab vessels. As a result of the Arab presence in East Asian waters, much of Indonesia was converted to Islam by the end of the fifteenth century.

The Persian Gulf trade route emphasized by the Abbasids brought trade on up the Tigris and Euphrates Rivers, which were navigable as far as the rocky river bars of Hit and Beled. Sailing above these points was difficult, especially on the Tigris, given the strong currents and the unsuitability of the banks for towage. However, at some point the trade continued by portage to the Caspian and Black Seas, and from there up the Volga, Don, Dnieper, and Dniester Rivers of Russia, and on to the Baltic Sea. This commerce stimulated developments in Russia, at first in the form of the Khazar trading kingdom, and later in Kievan Russia.

Harun al-Rashid (Aaron the Just) (r. 786–809) and his sons brought Baghdad to the height of its wealth, power, and creativity. Harun's court reveled in opulence, with women displaying gems hanging over their foreheads, and feasts featuring such delicacies as fish tongues. The court composer Ziryab developed Arabic music with its twenty-one note scale and its intricate meters. The most famous gems of Arabic literature were produced in Abbasid Baghdad, encouraged by the aristocracy's fad for holding literary evenings, with poetry contests. The *Sunna* (a book about Mohammed's habits) and the *Hadith* (a book listing his sayings) were produced. The *Thousand and One Nights* pays homage to the wealth and color of this age, and its tales of Sinbad the Sailor take the reader on trade voyages gathering goods from various parts of the Indian Ocean. The tale of the giant *roc* bird is set in Madagascar, and may represent a fantastic elaboration of such large south Indian Ocean birds as Africa's ostrich and Australia's emu. Sinbad's close escape from cannibals evokes New Guinea; his collecting of coconuts by throwing rocks at monkeys (who threw coconuts in return) suggests the Maldive Islands; his purchase of rubies and slave girls seems to be set in Sri Lanka; and his acquisition of ivory tusks from an elephant graveyard might have taken place in East Africa. The later *Tales of Abu Zayd* (the *Collection of al-Hariri*) is a picaresque novel about a scoundrel whose adventures also follow the Indian Ocean trade routes.

The Chinese invention of paper was adopted with government support. The first Arab paper manufacture was set up in Baghdad in 794, producing paper from linen or hemp rags. Harun al-Rashid founded Islam's first hospital in Baghdad; it was a model which spread throughout the caliphate. In the late ninth century, the Persian doctor al-Rhazi (Rhazes) headed the Baghdad hospital, and wrote both a medical encyclopedia and the first clinical account of smallpox. In al-Kufah, downriver, Jabir carried out chemical experiments. In the reign of al-Mamun (r. 813–833), al-Kwarizmi introduced Arabic numerals, the concept of zero (813), and the decimal system. He also wrote out logarithm tables, thereby giving his name to the logorithm (the exponent indicating the power to which a number is raised to produce a given number). The close trade contacts with Tantric India, with its fakir magicians, levitation, and mid-air rope-climbing tricks, inspired the popularity of Sufi mystics and legends of magic flying carpets in Baghdad by the early tenth century. The Sufis, too, made a religious contribution to the trading impetus by introducing the *baraka* ('blessing') system, whereby merchants bought the protective blessing of Abu Ishaq Ibrahim ibn Shahriyar al-Kazaruniyya, a dead Iranian Sufi saint who had lived in the eleventh century. The *baraka* system would reach its height in the thirteenth century, with adherents located from the Middle East through India to China.

Why Baghdad weakened

As in the fall of the Roman trading and power cycle, the failure to harmonize the needs of ethnic groups within society undermined the Baghdad cycle. Harun's second son al-Mamun overthrew his older half-brother Al-Amin (r. 809–813). Al-Mamun's mother was Persian, and he rallied the Iranian Shiites by promising to make Ali Amida, a Shiite descendent of Ali, his heir, and to transfer his capital to Iran. Al-Mamun sent presents of quality slaves (who were actually trained assassins) to al-Amin and his main supporters, and when al-Mamun gave the signal, al-Amin and his friends were struck down. Al-Mamun (r. 813–833) rewarded his Iranian supporters with important positions, but he never moved from Baghdad, and his promised heir Ali Amida died in mysterious circumstances.

Al-Mu'tasim (r. 833–842), the third son of Harun al-Rashid to reign, was fully Arab, and he purged the government of the Iranian elements brought in by al-Mamun. As a counter-weight, he built up an army and a bodyguard of Turkish slaves (*Mamluks*) from Central Asia, and moved with them to a new palace city, Samarra, outside of Baghdad. However, the Turks in 861 murdered al-Mu'tasim's son and successor al-Mutawakkil, and began making and unmaking caliphs at will. With such chaos at home, the Baghdad merchants were not able to recover from the sacking of Canton by rebel Chinese troops in 878, and regular direct Moslem trade to China ceased. Only in 892 did Caliph al-Muqtadir (r. 908–932) challenge the Turks by building up a new force made up of Berbers from the Maghreb. However, these soldiers, too, became arrogant and, in 932, murdered al-Muqtadir, parading his head as a trophy.

In the confusion following al-Muqtadir's death, the Iranian Buwayid Dynasty (945–1055) asserted power from Shiraz in Persia. As in the sixth century BC (under Darius III), the third century AD (under Shapur I), and the sixth century AD (under Khusro I), Iran was again ready to consolidate its success in controlling world wealth and power. However, in the competition for this position, Iran was destined to be always a bridesmaid and never a bride. The constant ethnic fighting had weakened Iraq and Iran alike. Iran, tantalizingly close to the Persian Gulf world trade route, nonetheless lacked both the populous coast and the navigable rivers to bring that commerce into it. The main water route follows the Tigris and Euphrates

Rivers west of Iran. With Mesopotamia exhausted by Iran's effort to dominate it, Arabized Egypt was about to step to the front stage of world history
for the second time.

The rise of the Egyptian Arabs to prominence in the Indian Ocean trade

The religious and ethnic disunity weakening Baghdad encouraged the rise
of a new power in Tunisia. The Berbers of the Maghreb had never felt
much loyalty to the eastern caliphate. Already in the late eighth century,
Morocco under the Shiite Idrisid Dynasty had followed Muslim Spain in
declaring political independence from Baghdad. The Sunni Aghlabid
Dynasty that ruled the rest of the Maghreb from Tunisia was able to assert
autonomy from Baghdad thanks to its naval strength in the west. Tunisia
had used this naval power to conquer Sicily (by 902), parts of southern Italy,
Sardinia, Corsica, the town of St. Tropez in Provence, and some islands in
the Aegean Sea. Religious fervor was added to Berber ethnic disaffection when
in 893 an Ishmaeli (Sevener) Shiite imam named Abu Abdullah ash-Shii
arrived from the Fertile Crescent. Preaching the imminent coming of the
Mahdi ('Messiah'), Abu Abdullah developed a mass following, with which in
908 he overthrew the Aghlabid Dynasty. He then proclaimed as *Mahdi* and
caliph Obeydallah, a direct descendent of Mohammed through Fatima
and Ali. As the first caliph of the Fatimid Dynasty, Obeydallah embarked on
an expansionist program that swept the remaining Aghlabids out of Sicily
and Algeria, and brought Libya under his rule.

This power base in the Maghreb and the strong navy was used by the
Fatimid caliph al-Mo'izz (r. 953–975) to conquer his way east. Highly
educated, a speaker of Arabic, Berber, Sudanese, Greek, and Slavonic, and
a poet, al-Mo'izz also possessed military abilities. In 958 he subdued Morocco
and then in 696 conquered Egypt from the Abbasid caliphs' semi-
autonomous Turkish Ikhshid Dynasty of governors. Al-Mo'izz arrived in
972 to take up his new residence in the newly founded city of Cairo (al-
Cahira, 'Mars' or 'the Victorious'). The Egyptians, as Sunnis, were not
enthusiastic for Shiite rule, but they were soon pacified by the prosperity
and power brought by the Fatimids.

The Fatimid move into the Indian Ocean

Sending his forces on to conquer Palestine and Syria, al-Mo'izz built
an Egyptian Red Sea fleet that suppressed piracy, and reasserted a dominant Egyptian presence in the Indian Ocean. His fleets sailed regularly from
Egypt via Aden to India, China, and East Africa. The Fatimids wrested the
commercial initiative away from the trade route from the Persian Gulf to
the Baltic Sea, bringing the Viking Age to an end. The Mediterranean was

again revitalized, bringing new vigor to Italy, France, and Spain. As in Phoenician times, Jewish merchants played a role in Fatimid trade, reinforcing their ongoing presence in Cochin, India. Working together with the Egyptian Arab merchants, they kept records in Arabic written with Hebrew letters. A widespread network of (Arab and non-Arab) Ismaili (or Sevener) Shiite merchants was planted around the Indian Ocean. Merchants sailed the Nile to Aswan, then traveled by caravans to board ships on the Red Sea. Aden benefited as a port-of-call on the way to India's Malabar coast. Al-Mo'izz encouraged the glass and lusterware industries in Alexandria to increase exports. Gold, silver, copper, textiles, paper and books, and brass wares were also carried to India in exchange for spices, drugs, and dyes, along with some Chinese silk and porcelain. Egypt used its wealth to cultivate higher learning, founding al-Azhar ('Brilliant') Mosque, which developed into a famous educational centre, and the core of the present University of Cairo.

Egyptian traders were active along the East African coast, adding to the vigor of its increasingly Swahili-speaking society. The Somalis accepted Islam, and intermarried heavily with Arabs. The island of Zanzibar off modern Tanzania sprouted Muslim settlements, and Arabs from Bahrain founded Mogadishu in Somalia in the eleventh century. The two main trading items, gold and ivory, made their way from Zimbabwe, where the wealth allowed the local kings to build high stone *kralls* or simple castles to guard themselves. Several East African coastal city-states were ruled in Arab fashion by sheiks and sultans. Mombasa was founded at the start of the eleventh century, and Swahili-speakers took up residence at Mogadishu and other port cities by the end of that century. They also linked up with trade to Madagascar, to where in the tenth century many Sumatrans had migrated, adding to the Sumatran settlement begun there in the early years of the first millennium AD.

The Indian and Chinese trading partners of the early Fatimids

The Indian merchants of the tenth, eleventh, and twelfth centuries also became more active, Chola Tamil merchants trading from the Coromandel coast and Ceylon eastward to the kingdom of Srivijaya on the Strait of Malacca. The Tamil's Chola realm in southern India and the Chandella realm in north-central India became more important. The Chola kingdom reached its zenith under Rajaraja the Great (r. 985–1018). Ruling from Tanjore, south of Madras, Rajaraja conquered southeastern India, northern Sri Lanka, and the Maldive Islands southwest of India. His son Rajendra went on to conquer Kerala and Orissa, and led campaigns as far as West Bengal, Sumatra, and the Malay Peninsula. He sent ambassadors to China in 1016 and 1033. The Chola government backed an organization of Tamil merchants who traded in every corner of the Bay of Bengal. The Cholas possessed a strong navy, which controlled the Coromandel coast of south-eastern India and the Malabar coast of southwestern India. As opposed to the Malabar coast's emphasis on pepper, the Tamils of southeastern India traded mainly in cotton cloth. However, the Strait of Malacca continued to be controlled by the kingdom of Srivijaya from its capital of Palembang in Sumatra, even though the Cholas sent at least one naval raid to try to win control of this strategic site.

The resulting prosperity brought still more luxuriousness and decadence to Indian culture. Rajaraja built the Rajarajesvara temple in Tanjore with abundant statuary of supernatural beings bedecking the steep temple roofs. This style spread along the trade routes eastward to influence the Khmer style at Angkor in Cambodia. A thirteenth-century temple at Zayton (Quanzhou), China, opposite Taiwan, is in the same style. Chola bronze statues depicted Shiva's cosmic dance of destruction and Kali's fertility mating with and cannibalistic murder of a chosen victim. North-central India's Chandela Dynasty used wealth from local diamond mines (which drew in Egyptian merchants) to build India's largest shrine to Shiva and Kali at Khajuraho ('Place of the Serpent'). Khajuraho still houses a spring mating and fertility festival in which pilgrims annoint Shiva's lingam with water, oil, milk, yogurt, ashes from cremated humans, and perfume, and decorate it with flower garlands. Its sculptures depict the lovemaking techniques described in the *Kama Sutra*. *Kumari* worship grew up in Nepal at the same time. Katmandu and other Nepalese cities each choose a *kumari* ('Princess') from girls of 2 to 4 years of age to represent Kali until she reaches puberty. She validates her selection by walking serenely in a dark room among the twitching and groaning heads of sacrificed buffaloes, billy goats, rams, roosters, and drakes, while devotees dressed as demons dart about.

The weakening of Fatimid Egypt

After a strong start, Cairo's position was shaken by the inadequacy of its later leaders, aggravated by religious developments connected to the millennial expectations around the year one thousand. A chiliastic move-ment, looking to the coming of a divine Savior in the year 1000, shook Christendom. Speculation ran wild based on the statements in Psalm 90:4 and II Peter 3:8 that to God one thousand years are as a day. The growth of Christian fervor spurred by millennial expectation produced a spate of more or less convincingly Christian rulers in Europe, including Romanos Lecapenos of Byzantium, Grand Prince Vladimir of Kievan Russia, Otto I of Germany, St. Stephen of Hungary, Pope Leo IX, Robert II the Pious in France, and King Olaf I Trygvesson of Norway. After it had become clear that their generation was not going to experience the second coming of

Christ, the eleventh-century European monarchs were often markedly anti-Christian in their private behavior, as can be seen in the Greek *bassilisa* Zoe, the German kaiser Heinrich IV, the French king Philippe I le Gros, and William the Conqueror of England.

The shock waves from Europe's millennial expectations spread out over surprising distances. In China and Japan, Jodo (Ching t'u or 'Pure Land') Buddhism had become the most popular form of Buddhism. An admixture of Christian and Buddhist influences (as a result of trading contacts), emphasizing purity and eternal life for the faithful, it was arguably more Christian than Buddhist. It revered the boundless light Amida Buddha of the West, warned of the danger of Hell, and awaited the coming of the divine Savior Miroku and his judgement at the end of 'the millennium.' Buddhist influence had declined somewhat in China due to a persecution in the ninth century, but it continued to be very central in Japan at this time. The Chinese Buddhists now buried *sutra* ('liturgical') scrolls in mounds in preparation for Miroku's imminent return. In Japan, a priest named Genshin in the late tenth century wrote *Essentials of Salvation* as a guidebook. Concern for ethics inspired Lady Murasaki Shikibu's novel in 900, *Genji Monogatari* (*The Tale of Genji*), the world's first great novel, about a self-sacrificing prince. In the eleventh century, these countries experienced a falling away from Jodo Buddhism into a celebration of self-indulgence in the late Sung dynasty of China and the late Fujiwara period of Japan. In twelfth-century Japan, Tobo Sojo wrote an illustrated book of animal parables depicting Buddha as a bloated frog worshipped by timid rabbits. Sung China moved on to an emphasis on enjoyment of its commercial prosperity, due in part to its participation in trade with the Indian Ocean.

This trend made a major impact on Egypt. Shiite doctrine now became soterial, and there was a strong Christian influence over the Fatimid government in Cairo at the very time Christian chiliast expectations were reaching a fever pitch. The mother of Caliph al-Aziz (r. 975–996) was a Slavic slave girl, and the tall, red-haired and blue-eyed ruler raised Christians to high office in his government. His own wife was a Russian Christian, whose two brothers he elevated to the Christian patriarchates of Alexandria and Jerusalem. Al-Aziz prevented Muslims who converted to Christianity from being put to death as was demanded by *Shariah* law. Close contact was maintained with Greek and Italian merchants.

Al-Aziz was succeeded by his equally blue-eyed son al-Hakim (r. 996–1021). With a Christian mother and grandmother, two patriarch uncles, a Slavic regent, and many other Christian officials, al-Hakim was surrounded by Christian fervor. He himself was very puritanical, forbidding the consumption of alcohol, public amusements and games, including chess. However, after the Christian chiliastic expectation was clearly discredited, in 1003 al-Hakim turned vehemently against the Christians. Angry with his Christian mother, al-Hakim forbade respectable women to leave their homes, or even to appear on the roofs or to be seen behind the lattice-work windows. Shoemakers could no longer make ladies' outdoor shoes. Christians were obliged to carry large crosses around their necks, and Jews had to wear bells. In 1009, al-Hakim ordered all churches and synagogues demolished, including Jerusalem's Church of the Holy Sepulchre in 1009. (Bethlehem's Church of the Nativity was spared due to the Muslim prayer services being held in part of its space.) Many Christians were forcibly converted to Islam. Government officials who objected were executed, and a curfew was imposed throughout Egypt.

The anti-Christian reaction led al-Hakim on into an involvement with witchcraft. He began to hold his council meetings at night, and decreed that everyone was to work at night and sleep during the day. He devised a lottery, in which the winners obtained great wealth, but losers were put to death. Al-Hakim's Sevener or Ismailite Shiite followers were organized into grand lodges, centering on the new Mosque of al-Hakim in Cairo. Ancient Egyptian magic rituals were elaborated, with complex initiations and a hierarchy of degrees of rank. Members were used for support and espionage. The Mosque of al-Hakim is today abandoned as a heretical site. As Sunni opposition grew more vocal, al-Hakim had whole families put to death. Many people emigrated from Egypt. Algeria and Tunisia broke away. One night, while inspecting Cairo's merchant 'city' of Fustat on his donkey, al-Hakim came across a manikin of a woman holding a lampoon of him. He flew into a rage, attacking the dummy, and had Fustat sacked and burned, and its population massacred. He then resettled it with people brought in from Egyptian villages.

In 1016, Al-Hakim announced that he was God incarnate. The believers who accepted this claim are known as Druzes, named after al-Hakim's high priest, al-Daruzi. When a mob of outraged Egyptians attacked the Druzes, al-Daruzi fled with a group of followers to southern Mount Lebanon, where the Druze faith still survives. In revenge, Al-Hakim turned his Sudanese troops loose on the residents of Cairo in a new orgy of killing. However, this attack was not carried to the end, for Turkish and Berber soldiers joined the victims in fighting the Sudanese troops. Soon after, on the 13th February 1021, al-Hakim went for a solitary ride on his donkey in the night desert. The next day his donkey was found mutilated, with al-Hakim's coat slashed and blood stained. Al-Hakim's body was never found, and the Druzes believe he lives on and one day will reappear. Al-Hakim's son ez-Zahir (r. 1021–1036) proved to be as unstable as his father, and brought Egypt into further decline. When he invited debutantes to a reception at his palace in Cairo, 2,660 women eagerly crowded into the great hall. However, ez-Zahir had them all bricked into the room, so that they all died of starvation. Ez-Zahir died of the plague at age thirty-one, but his son and successor, al-Mustansir (r. 1036–1094), another cruel and petulant caliph, was incapable of halting Egypt's fall from power.

The short-lived bid of Baghdad for renewed power

When al-Mustansir was 34 years old, in 1070, his Turkish *Mamluk* ('slave') soldiers drove out the Sudanese guard and took control of the caliph's government. Al-Mustansir's mother and daughters fled to Baghdad, where they placed themselves at the mercy of the Seljuk Turkish sultan Alp-Arslan. In 1055, the Seljuk Turks had been welcomed into Baghdad by the Sunni Abassid caliph, to counter the domination of Baghdad by the Shiite Buwayids. The leader of the Seljuks, Tughril Bey, had been proclaimed as Sultan ('Authority'). Tughril Bey and his nephew and successor Alp Arslan (r. 1063–1072) ruled Baghdad with a firm efficiency that renewed Iraqi strength. As Egypt hurtled from one crisis to the next, Baghdad hoped to take back the leadership it had enjoyed in the eighth and ninth centuries. In 1071, Alp Arslan took Jerusalem from Egypt, and Anatolia from the Greeks, defeating the Byzantine Basileos Romanos Diogenes at the battle of Manzikert (north of Lake Van). Central Asian Turks flooded into the Anatolian peninsula, driving the Greek-speaking inhabitants west. Alp Arsaln's son Malik Shah (r. 1072–1092) drew capable men to his service, including his Persian vizier, Nizam al-Mulk, the author of a treatise on government. In 1073, Malik Shah sent an army to Egypt, ostensibly to free al-Mustansir from his *Mamluk* guards, but actually to humble Egypt. The Turks were toppled from power, which was reassumed by Armenian Christian viziers, who ran the Fatimid government from this point on until far into the twelfth century. Malik Shah then took Damascus from Egypt in 1076.

However, Baghdad's chances for launching a new period of dominance were nipped in the bud. This failure was due to side effects of the above-mentioned cynicism prevailing throughout Eurasia in this period, as seen in the impact of three influential ex-school pals. Vizier Nizam al-Mulk had as a student at a *madrassah* in Nissapur, Khorasan, formed a schoolboy pact, of the sort reputedly perpetuated today by Yale's Skull and Bones Society. It was agreed that if one of the three became a success, he would help the other two. Once Nizam had become vizier, Omar Khayyam requested a pension large enough to free him for life to pursue his love of creative writing. Hasan Ben Sabbah asked for a high post in the central adminis-tration. Both wishes were granted. Omar Khayyam used his pension to write the great Persian-language poem, *The Rubaiyat* ('Quatrain'). This influ-ential work questioned faith, turning people to a love of sensual pleasures. In vivid images, the poet evokes the beauty of nature and sensual plea-sures, while sneering at the idea that there is any possible help coming from the heavens. Nizam al-Mulk himself, with his dying breath, quoted the *Rubaiyat* to the effect that we know nothing of what happens after death. Hasan Ben Sabbah tried to rise in the bureaucracy by use of intrigue, for which Nizam al-Mulk dismissed him. Seeking revenge, Ben Sabbah assumed leadership of the minority Ismaili (Sevener) Shiites. Making his center at Alamut ('Eagle's Nest') Castle in the Alburz Mountains north of Teheran, he organized a terrorist society called the *Hashishim* ('Hashish Eaters,' the origin of the English word 'assassin'). There, as the so-called 'Old Man of the Mountain,' he defied Malik Shah's government. In 1092, Nizam al-Mulk was struck down by one of these Hashishim. Malik Shah sent an army to besiege Alamut Castle, but he died before it could be taken.

Malik Shah's sons at once fell into a fight for the succession. Different branches of the Seljuk family established autonomous rule in various parts of the caliphate as *atabegs* ('regents'), while Ben Sabbah expanded his authority over many castles in northern Iran, Iraq, and Syria. The resulting divisions of the Abbasid caliphate weakened Baghdad at the very moment it might have consolidated its power, giving Egypt a chance to resume its leadership. The Fatimid caliph al-Mustali reclaimed Jerusalem in 1098. It looked as if the Arab golden age was going to continue for the indefinite future. By this point, the Arabs had been in the ascendancy for half a millennium. Their power had centered first in Mecca and Medina, then in Damascus, and then in Baghdad, before settling on Cairo. Wherever the caliphal capital had been located, the Arabs had remained in the forefront. However, at this point the Chinese resurged on the eastern extension of the Indian Ocean trading world, just as the northern Mediterranean peoples were reasserting a renewed trading presence from the west.

Further reading

On the Arabs in general in this period: Karen Armstrong, *A History of God: The 4,000-Year Quest of Judaism, Christianity and Islam* (New York: Ballantine Books, 1993); E.A. Belyaev, *Arabs, Islam, and the Arab Caliphate in the Early Middle Ages* (New York: Praeger, 1969); K.N. Chaudhuri, *Asia Before Europe: Economy and Civilization of the Indian Ocean from the Rise of Islam to 1750* (Cambridge: Cambridge University Press, 1990); G. von Grunebaum, *Medieval Islam* (Chicago, Illinois: University of Chicago, 1946); Albert Hourani, *A History of the Arab Peoples* (London: Faber, 2002); George F. Hourani, *Arab Seafaring* (Princeton, New Jersey: Princeton University, 1995); Charles Philip Issawi, *The Middle East Economy: Decline and Recovery* (Princeton, New Jersey: Princeton University Press, 1995); Maxime Rodinson, *Mohammed* (New York: Vintage, 1974); and W. Montgomery Watt, *Muhammad* (Oxford: Oxford University, 1961).

On the Ummayad caliphate: Maulana Muhammad Ali, *Early Caliphate* (Columbus, Ohio: Ahmadiyya Anjuman Ishabt Islam, 1932); and Abd al-Ameer Abd Dixon, *The Umayyad Caliphate in the Reign of Abdal-Malik ibn Marwan, 684–705* (London: Luzac, 1971).

On the Abbasid caliphate: G. Le Strange, *Baghdad during the Abbasid Caliphate* (New York: Curzon/Barnes and Noble, 1972); H. St. John Philby, *Harun al Rashid* (Englewood Cliffs, New Jersey: Appleton-Century/Prentice-Hall, 1934); Al-Tabari, *The Reign of Al-Mu'tasim* (New Haven, Connecticut: American Oriental Society, 1951); and Gaston Wiet, *Baghdad: Metropolis of the Abbasid Caliphate* (Norman: University of Oklahoma, 1971).

On the Fatimid caliphate: Shaukat Ali, *Millenarian and Messianic Tendencies in Islamic History* (Lahore: Publishers United, 1993); Richard Brace, *Morocco–Algeria–Tunisia* (Englewood Cliffs, New Jersey: Prentice-Hall, 1964); Norman Cohn, *The Pursuit of the Millenium* (New York: Harper Torchbooks, 1961); Natalie Zemon Davis, 'Millenium and historical hope,' *Tikkun*, vol. 14, no. 6 (Nov.–Dec. 1999), pp. 57–9; Richard Erdoes, AD 1000: *Living on the Brink of Apocalypse* (San Francisco, California: Harper and Row, 1988); Richard Erdoes, 'The Year 1000,' *Psychology Today*, vol. 23 (May 1989), pp. 44–5; Stanley Lane-Poole, *A History of Egypt in the Middle Ages* (London: Frank Cass, 1968); Bernard McGinn, *Visions of the End: Apocalyptic Traditions in the Middle Ages* (New York: Columbia University Press, 1979); James Reston, Jr., *The Last Apocalypse: Europe at the Year 1000 AD* (New York: Doubleday, 1998); Paula Sanders, *Ritual, Politics, and the City in Fatimid Cairo* (Albany: State University of New York Press, 1994); and Gaston Wiet, *Cairo: City of Art and Commerce* (Norman: University of Oklahoma, 1964).

On T'ang and Sung China: Kenneth K.S. Ch'en, *Buddhism in China: A Historical Survey* (Princeton, New Jersey: Princeton University Press, 1964); Kenneth K.S. Ch'en, *The Chinese Transformation of Buddhism* (Princeton, New Jersey: Princeton University Press, 1973); Jacques Gernet, *Buddhism in Chinese Society: An Economic History from the Fifth to the Tenth Centuries* (New York: Columbia University Press, 1995); and Arthur F. Wright, *Buddhism in Chinese History* (Stanford, California: Stanford University Press, 1959).

Chapter 5

The Chinese and northern Mediterranean resurgence

From the twelfth through the fifteenth century AD, the Chinese again increased their participation in the western terminus of the Indian Ocean trade, and the peoples of Mediterranean Europe also intensified their involvement. The Chinese involvement was far more significant in the short run, and seems to have helped to spark the rise of Italian trade. However, the Italian development was more important in the long run, since it laid the basis for Europe's leading role in modern times. Technological and business advances in both China and the Mediterranean, backed up by a military superiority that also stemmed from innovations, enabled their emergence. This chapter will trace this period through three different stages:

1   when first the Chinese and then the Italians (with French help) reasserted their involvement in the western and eastern extensions of the Indian Ocean trade (in the twelfth and thirteenth centuries, after starts in the eleventh century);
2   when the Chinese reached the height of their participation in Indian Ocean trade (in the late thirteenth to the early fifteenth centuries); and
3   when the Chinese pulled back out of Indian Ocean trade, while the Italian impact continued to grow (through the fifteenth century).

It might be argued that the Italian and Chinese impact was too minor to warrant distinguishing this period as a separate stage. The peoples living on the periphery of the region (including Indians, Southeast Asians, and especially Egyptian Arabs) still played a prime role in Indian Ocean trade. However, China's commercial impact stimulated Indian Ocean trade to an entirely new level, while the emergence of the Italians at the western end of the trade started a shift that would eventually bring control of the Indian Ocean trade and government into European hands.

The increase of Chinese involvement in Indian Ocean trade

The Chinese had been increasing their involvement in Indian Ocean trade since the founding of the Sung Dynasty in 960 by General T'ai Tsu ('Grand Progenitor'). The eleventh through the early fifteenth century represented the height of China's historical involvement in the Indian Ocean area. China's growing strength was based on a rapid expansion in the amount of iron and steel production in Honan and Hopei provinces, as a result of the eleventh-century discovery of the use of coke to smelt iron in blast furnaces (wood was in short supply in northern China). A program of canal building (with a removal of natural obstacles to inland water transport) allowed iron, steel, grain, and other commodities to be transported for sale along the Grand Canal and other canals to central China. Agricultural production increased with a more systematic use of fertilizers and improved seed, and crops grown became more specialized from region to region. Commercial cities arose along the Grand Canal, from the first Sung capital of K'ai-feng at its northern end to their later capital of Hangchow at its southern terminus.

The seasonal use of the canal system due to periods of low water spurred a major increase in coastal trade between northern and southern China as well. Various innovations supported this maritime expansion. The magnetic compass was invented in the form of a flat, fish-shaped magnetized needle resting on straws floating in a bowl of water, and would be passed on to the Arabs by 1119. It was difficult for navigation on a heaving sea, and was at first used to lay out temples for a correct geomantic (feng shui) orientation, but it offered tremendous potential as a concept. Two earlier Chinese inventions were given new applications: gunpowder was now used for weaponry (as land mines and hand grenades) and printing was applied to movable type (not very practical in the system of so many characters), paper money, and scroll books. Paper money was being used at the capital by 1107, allowing taxes to be raised in money rather than in kind. The success of the middle class was facilitated by the introduction of company (often family) partnerships, bills of exchange, and the legal regularization of disputing contracts. The great wealth enjoyed by China in this period encouraged creativity. The cultivated emperor Hui Tsung (r. 1100–1127), whose ships gathered the flowers and stones he fancied, introduced with his own paintings a new 'palace style' of painting, emphasising subtlety. One court-sponsored contest on the theme of a tavern in a bamboo grove by a bridge was won by a painting that showed nothing more than the start of the bridge, with a few bamboo shoots and a sign pointing to the inn.

In 1127, the Jürchen nomads conquered northern China, dragging Emperor Hui-tsung off to imprisonment and death. The Jürchen cavalry was prevented from pursuing the surviving Sung into the south by the rupture of the dikes of the many rice paddies along the Yangtze, flooding the land. In 1135, Hui Tsung's nephew Kao Tsung (r. 1127–1162) relocated the capital to Hangchow at the mouth of the Yangtze. The new capital's proximity to the China Sea turned the attention of the Sung even more to the importance of maritime trade. The government built a navy to keep the Jürchen from advancing south by way of the canals. Armored and paddle-wheel-driven ships, manned by crossbowmen and projectile-hurling machines, were developed for the job. Subsequently, the navy was used to fight off pirates from merchant ships, and joined private interests in running shipyards. Over 50,000 men manned this navy's hundreds of ships. Hangchow battened on wealth derived largely from overseas trade. By the 1130s, about a fifth of government income was derived from excise taxes on the sea trade. China's most profitable exports were textiles, tea, and porcelain, the latter two being products of Fukien province on the southern coast. It was in the later Sung Dynasty (1127–1179) that the idea of a special amusement quarter of a city was introduced.

A new push was given to carrying trade into Indian Ocean waters, with Canton as the principal port of departure. Chinese craft production picked up, and Chinese merchants became paramount in Southeast Asia (where they formed permanent overseas colonies). In the twelfth century, Cantonese junks, with their tall sails, sailed through the Strait of Malacca and continued as far west as Quilon in southwestern India. There Chinese silk cloth and lacquerware, and some iron and steel, were exchanged for southern spices among other products. India's state of Orissa prospered from its end of the trade under King Narasimha Deva (r. 1238–1264), and a resulting burst of activity resulted in the ornate carving of the sun god Surya's sun chariot at Konaraka. Chinese wares found their way as far as the East African coast.

In the early thirteenth century, boosted by their possession of the best boats in the Indian Ocean, the Chinese took over much of the sea trade from the Arabs. Their huge commercial flat-bottomed junks averaged about one hundred feet long, and could carry 120 tons of cargo and several hundred people. The rectangular sails soared into the air, and floating rudders helped to keep the junks stable. Boiled and cooked tung oil provided waterproofing for the sewn boats native to the Indian Ocean area. The floating mariner's compass (mentioned above) was used together with the measurement of speed by throwing a floating object overboard at the bow, and then listening to how many chanted rhymes it took for the ship to pass it up. Star maps showing the constellations aided navigation by night. Ramming was used in sea battles, giving an advantage over the Malay custom of hostile boarding. The increased size of these ships lessened the cost of commercial runs, and brought more trade in bulk goods. The use of the abacus and the decimal system simplified record keeping.

An Arab merchant quarter sprang up in Canton and other Chinese coastal cities. Sung porcelain became common in Cairo and other Middle Eastern cities. Trade guilds are said to have sprung up, grouped by streets as in contemporary Europe. The population mushroomed to 100 million Chinese in all. The wealth of the rising commercial class eclipsed that of the old land-based nobility, creating a more egalitarian and less military society. To serve those who were growing prosperous from this business, amusement quarters grew up in the Chinese cities. Here, *saki* rice wine and tea shops, and live and puppet theaters proliferated. Now that they could afford their wives not working, wealthier men found a way to guarantee a male wish to have his wife always at home. The custom arose of binding a girl's feet so tightly that, as she grew, the toes were bent toward the heel and the arch was gradually broken. The curved stump of a foot could be wrapped over and tied to a small block shoe so that the exploited ladies could hobble a few steps from one chair to the next, but not much farther.

The return of significant Italian involvement

At the end of the eleventh century, Italy reached out to dominate the growing Mediterranean trade in goods coming from the Indian Ocean (the result in part of the recent Chinese stimulus there) via Egypt. The Byzantine Greeks were no longer in a position to return to the millennia-long Greek position in Mediterranean commerce because, since the eighth century, the Byzantine rulers had forbidden Greek merchants to trade abroad. This policy was designed to keep the hitherto Greek-carried European goods such as timber and arms out of Muslim hands, but it allowed Italians to move in to supply this need.

Italian society now nurtured merchants on a large scale, especially in Venice, Genoa, and Pisa, which came into their own as port cities. Venice had progressed from being a Byzantine possession to becoming a favored Byzantine ally, exempt from Byzantine duties since 1082. The Italian expansion into Mediterranean trade was facilitated in this period by commercial innovations. New concepts in banking and finance were borrowed from the Arabs or developed in Italy. Full-scale double-entry book keeping (in which profit and loss were kept clearly separate by using black and red ink) appeared at the latest by the late fourteenth century. Marine insurance, checks, bills of exchange (an early form of traveler's checks), and debt payment (buying on credit) were all employed. The English word 'check' derives from the Arabic *sakk*, but the Byzantine Greeks had used this financial instrument, too, and it had been known in Roman Palestine. By the end of the thirteenth century, the more convenient Arabic (originally Hindu) numerals were being used to keep financial records. The introduction of more adjustable ships with two types of sails also helped. The triangular Arabic lateen sail (useful for maneuvering) was added to the old square sail (better for speed). By raising one or the other of the two sail types, a ship's movements could be tailored to careful route adjustments or to speed. This combination of sails was added to the shallow-draft galleys, favoured by

Venice as necessary for negotiating the lagoons around its islands. For the Atlantic and other deepwater ports, the sails were combined on the deeper-draft large round ships called *naves*, *nefs*, *Koggen*, or tubs, a ship type preferred by Genoa and Pisa.

Two other developments brought an improvement in navigation. The boxed compass put the compass bowl (as invented in Sung Dynasty China) in a box for better retention of the water on which the needle floated on straws. This modification extended sailing on the Mediterranean in rainy weather, provided the sea was calm enough not to toss the water out altogether. Even with this restriction, the number of Italian voyages doubled, which greatly decreased shipping costs. The boxed compass was used in connection with portolan charts, which mapped sea routes by drawing compass roses (lines of intersection over open water) for charting straight routes across the Mediterranean. Use of the direct routes instead of coast-lines cut sailing time and costs. Speed had to be recorded in order to follow one's location on the map. This was done by counting knots, that is, how many knots made at regular intervals in a rope thrown overboard and floating on a piece of wood would float back in a given time. The interval was measured by an hourglass. Today, one knot is now set at 6,080 feet per hour. Winter as well as summer convoys of ships now began to cross the Mediterranean.

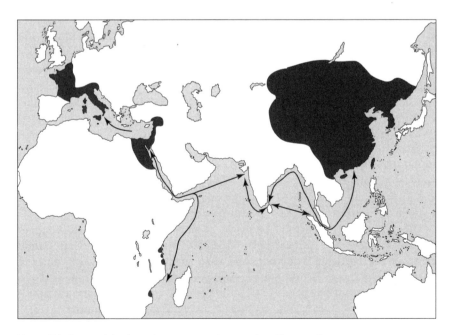

Figure 5.1 Principal lands and sea routes discussed in Chapter 5

In the second half of the eleventh century, Italian city states took control of the western Mediterranean from the Arabs. Pisa and Genoa captured Corsica in 1050 and Sardinia in 1053. In 1063, a Pisan fleet defeated an Arab fleet at Palermo, and in 1087 another Pisan fleet raided the Maghreb. By the 1090s, the Italian city-states were ready to try to dominate the Indian Ocean trade coming through Egypt. The power struggle in the Middle East opened the door to western European conquest. However, such a step needed strong military support, which the Italians sought from the French.

The role of the French

France was in a position to assert itself by the late eleventh century due to many recent technological breakthroughs, including a more efficient harnessing of energy thanks to the adoption of the horse collar and of the crank and cogwheel (both inventions dating back to Han China) as well as of the horseshoe and the tandem harness.

Farm yield had also been increased by use of a heavy plow with a mold-board, and the three-field system. The resulting population explosion encouraged French military adventure abroad in Spain and southern Italy, facilitated by the use of heavy-armored cavalry.

The impact of the *jihad* spirit on the rise of a French crusader mentality

In the late tenth century, the Christian millennialist movement (discussed in the last chapter) had stirred a new militancy on the frontiers of Islam. It might be argued that even developments in India at this time can be tied into this defensive reaction, as Muslims carried out the most massive invasion and conquest that sub-continent had seen since the Aryans. This onslaught left northern India torn and weakened by hatreds, too debilitated to hold her own in the commerce swirling around her. For Muslims, Hindus were not Peoples of the Book, and those Hindus who would not convert, unlike most Jews and Christians hitherto caught in the Islamic expansion, were either massacred or enslaved. The resulting hatred between Hindus and Muslims has been passed down, despite later attempts by various Indian leaders to improve relations between the two religious groups.

The outstanding Muslim conqueror of northern India was Mahmud of Ghazni (a town in Afghanistan). In 1000, Mahmud crushed an Indian army at the battle of Peshawar, and then proceeded to conquer much of northwestern India. While not personally devout, Mahmud plundered the holy Hindu city of Mathura in 1018. In 1019, he conquered Harsha's capital of Kanauj (near Agra), and massacred its inhabitants. Mahmoud's *jihads* against the infidel were even more devastating against Buddhism than against Hinduism. This targeting of Buddhists took place partly because

Buddhism's missionary commitment made it seem the greater threat to Islam. However, there was also a commercial incentive because, while Hindus were mainly farmers, Buddhists were rivals to the Muslims in urban mercantalism. As a result, Buddhists were slaughtered, and Buddhist temples, monasteries, libraries, art, and writings were destroyed, delivering the death-blow to Buddhism in India. By the end of the eleventh century, few traces of Buddhism remained in Central Asia, Afghanistan, and northwestern India. All of northwestern India was reduced to poverty and misery.

Mahmud's Muslim successors ruling northern India in the twelfth and thirteenth centuries continued his brutality. In 1175–1206, Muhammed of Ghur (in Afghanistan close to Ghazni) ravaged northwestern India with repeated massacres. Shifting his capital to Delhi, he launched the Delhi sultanate. While southern India was not immediately affected, this conquest represented the start of a Muslim domination that would in time spread over much of the Indian subcontinent, and impose Muslim control over the ports of Gujarat. A great conversion effort led in the next three centuries to the spread of Islam through India and to Malaysia in the east, and to the East African coast in the west. Kilwa's sultans led conversion *jihads* into the interior, while Mogadishu became the heart of East African Islam. The resulting wide-flung Muslim communities cooperated in trade throughout the Indian Ocean to the benefit of Muslim merchants involved in this networking.

The conquest of India spurred creative results under Mahmud, who wanted to be remembered as an exceptional leader, despite having risen from Turkish Mamluk slave status. He founded a university and a museum at Ghazni, and patronized al-Biruni as his court astronomer, al-Farabi as his court philosopher, and Firdausi as poet – he was author of the Persian epic poem the *Shah Nameh* ('King's Book'). Mahmud also tried in vain to woo the philosopher Ibn Sina (Avicenna) to his court.

At the same time, a strong *jihad* spirit flared up in Spanish al-Andalus at the opposite end of the Islamic world. There an upstart leader named al-Mansur (r. 976–1002) led a reaction against the increasingly Christian-influenced Umayyad caliphs of Córdoba. Caliph Abd al-Rahman III (r. 912–961), who was the nephew of the Christian Queen Toda of Navarre, had placed Christian *mozárabes* (Arabized Christians) in leading positions in the army, and had surrounded himself with a Slavic bodyguard. When al-Mansur took power, he unleashed a persecution of Christians and Jews that foreshadowed al-Hakim's coming attack on those groups in the Middle East (discussed in the previous chapter). He led repeated *jihads* against the Christians of northern Spain, leaving the area devastated. The church of Santiago de Compostela was burned, and Christian prisoners dragged its bells as trophies to Córdoba. Since a Koranic *sura* stated that the dust of a *jihad* is pleasing to God, he collected dust from each of his campaigns to revere in reliquary boxes. Al-Mansur also turned his disapproval against the pro-Christian Fatimid caliph al-Aziz of Cairo, sending him a letter of criticism. Al-Aziz sent a contemptuous letter back to al-Mansur, saying that if he had ever heard of (the upstart) al-Mansur, he would have sent him a reply, but since he had not, he would not.

French princes and knights poured into Spain in the eleventh century to fight in the *Reconquista* to push the Muslims back south. Exposed to the Muslim *jihad* spirit, they imitated its religious fervor to their own advantage. Count Raymond of Toulouse, who had married an illegitimate daughter of King Alfonso VI of Castile and had lost one eye fighting the Moors in Spain, became a principal leader of the First Crusade to Jerusalem. This religious warfare in Spain was encouraged by the papacy, which was then militantly asserting its power in the investiture controversy (the struggle for power between popes and kaisers in the Holy Roman Empire). The conjunction between Italian merchants and French warriors was a natural one, just waiting for coordination. Pope Urbain/Urbano (Urban) II, a French Cluniac monk ruling from Rome, forged that link.

The First Crusade boosts Italian merchants in the eastern Mediterranean

At a church council in 1095 at Clermont, Urbain made a call for his native Frenchmen to join the great military expedition that became the First Crusade. The goal was to free the Bible lands from the Infidel. Genoa, Pisa, and Venice provided naval support, for which they were rewarded with special trading privileges in the Levant. In July 1099, the crusaders conquered Jerusalem. Baudouin I of the new so-called Latin Kingdom of Jerusalem (r. 1100–1118) met defeat at the hands of the Egyptians at the naval battle of Ascalon in 1102, but under Baudouin II (r. 1118 to 1131) Egypt was cowed into cooperation. In 1128, a Venetian naval force annihilated a Fatimid fleet off the coast of Palestine. The Fatimid caliph al-Amir and his Armenian Christian vizier made peace with Baudouin II, and the Italian merchants won an important position in carrying Egypt's Mediterranean trade. King Foulques of Jerusalem (r. 1131–1143) subsequently tightened his links to an Egyptian government dominated by Coptic and Armenian Christian administrators. Caliph al-Hafiz (r. 1131–1149) interested himself in Christianity, and was fond of vacationing at the monastery of St. Catherine in the Sinai. Fear of the Seljuk Turks and the Kurds allowed Foulques to conclude a triple alliance between Jerusalem, Egypt, and Damascus. Al-Hafiz even gave an annual payment to Foulques to help strengthen the Latin Kingdom's army.

The impact of the First Crusade on Indian Ocean trade

Egyptian merchants continued their prominent role in the Indian Ocean trade, bringing rice and cotton from India, silk, porcelain, and steel from

China, and slaves and ivory from East Africa. However, the Egyptian trade was now interlinked with Italian economic cooperation. The 'Franks' (mainly Italians), just like the Greeks, Syrians, Yemenites, and Iraqis, were granted their own assigned *funduq* ('lodging-house', *caravanserai*) in Alexandria. The Italian merchants did not personally penetrate into the Indian Ocean region. The Fatimids periodically filled in Necho's old canal between the Red Sea and the Nile in case the Italians would try to use it to sail their ships into the Indian Ocean. For all that, the Italians exerted a significant indirect impact on the Indian Ocean trade. Flemish textiles were introduced as one exchange item for goods from the east. The Italians also provided Egypt with timber and new slaves for the Mamluk troops upon which Egypt depended. The greatest impact, however, was due to the new European consumer market (influenced by western contact with the Levant during the crusades) for eastern textiles and pepper and other spices. A concurrent development of a luxury consumer market of the same sort occurred in China during the Southern Sung Dynasty. Mogadishu emerged as the main trading center on the East African coast between 1150 and 1250 by controlling the flow of gold north from Sofala (modern Mozambique).

The Italians who carried much of the Mediterranean trade in this cycle celebrated their rising fortunes in the eleventh century by erecting such striking cathedrals as San Marco basilica in Venice and Pisa's classically influenced *duomo* with its (now) famous 'leaning tower of Pisa' *campanile* ('bell tower'). The first medieval universities began to take form in Italy at the end of the eleventh century, with the emergence of Bologna emphasizing the study of law and of Salerno for the study of medicine. Stimulated by the trading wealth and helped by the Middle Eastern contacts, France likewise showed evidence of great new cultural energy. In southern France this new prosperity and stimulus led to the development of troubadour verse and Romanesque architecture and statuary. Paris's emerging reputation as a leading city of Latin Christendom was greatly enhanced by the growth of the University of Paris. Gothic architecture was introduced, beginning with the royal burial church of St. Dénis. Nôtre-Dame de Paris developed harmonic singing, with a four-part score for soprano and alto (sung by boys) and tenor and bass (sung by men).

The French become a liability to Egyptian and Italian trading co-operation

The French had played an essential role in establishing Italian merchants in Egypt. However, they increasingly became a hindrance once their religious militancy proved embarrassing to the new and mutually profitable Italian–Egyptian trading *entente*. The springboard of French power in the Levant, the Latin Kingdom of Jerusalem, collapsed in all but name before the end of the twelfth century. The Second Crusade in 1147–1149 was so mishandled that it only accelerated the decline of French strength in the Levant, and the Christian domination of the Egyptian government was brought to an end in 1164 by the Kurdish Sunni general Salah ed-Din (Saladin, 'Reformer of the Faith').

The Italians continued to benefit from the Egyptian trade, but Salah ed-Din refused to allow the entry of the Italian merchants personally into the Indian Ocean, or even into Cairo. In part to prevent the Europeans from breaking into the Indian Ocean trade, Salah ed-Din conquered the Hijaz (the eastern shore of the Red Sea), Yemen, Aden, Eilat, and Syria, leaving the Latin Kingdom surrounded on the southeast, west, and northwest. Reynauld de Châtillon, the prince of Karach, led the attempt by the French to break into that trade nonetheless. In 1183, he oversaw the construction of a fleet to clear the way for French merchants to trade in the Indian Ocean. The Italian merchants remained loyal to their Egyptian allies, refusing to betray the secrets of navigation in those eastern waters. Built on the Mediterranean coast of the Latin Kingdom and reassembled in Eilat, Reynauld's French fleet asserted a Latin presence on the Red Sea. Salah ed-Din was fast to respond. He sent his brother al-Adil with a fleet, this fleet built on the Mediterranean coast of Suez and reassembled on the Red Sea. When Reynauld's fleet attacked Medina and Mecca for the second time, al-Adil cornered and destroyed it at the port of Jidda, executing all of the men aboard.

This challenge to the Indian Ocean sea routes brought an end to the Latin Kingdom of Jerusalem as a significant state. In 1187, at the Horns of Hittin (on the west side of the Sea of Galilee), Salah ed-Din defeated the crusaders, conquering Jerusalem and most of Palestine. The Latin Kingdom was reduced to a tiny enclave on the Mediterranean coast. The Egyptian government instituted a new concept that was to be imitated by prevailing naval powers in the Indian Ocean for centuries to come, namely a system of safe-conduct passes which merchants had to purchase in exchange for protection and permission to sail. Salah ed-Din's government (in conjunction with that of Yemen) elbowed Jews and Copts out of the Indian Ocean trade, helping a particular group of Egyptian Muslims called the *Karimi* to gain a monopoly. In the thirteenth century, Egyptians launched a triangle trade between Aden, Cambay in Gujarat, and Kilwa in East Africa. Kilwa now passed Mogadishu as the main Zimbabwe gold-trading nexus on the East African coast, an importance reflected in the quantities of Indian glass beads and Chinese porcelain found from this period there.

Subsequent crusades proved incapable of truly restoring the Latin Kingdom of Jerusalem. Nevertheless, Salah ed-Din, his brother and successor al-Adil (r. 1193–1218), and the later heads of the family still continued the Italians' commercial importance in Egypt, allowing them to retain their commercial base in Alexandria, as well as in Akko (Acre to the French), Tyre, and other Lebanese coastal towns. Muslim merchants traveled freely on Italian ships, while the European courts of Palermo and Toledo cultivated

Islamic culture. Muslim merchants traded in southern Italy and in the crusading ports of the Levant.

The arrangement between Egypt and the Italians in the thirteenth century despite the Muslim reconquest of Holy Jerusalem left the French and the papacy at a loss. For the French in general, the crusades were a war for the cause of Christ, while for the Italians, with their commercial concerns, the crusading fervor from which they had originally benefited had become a major inconvenience, threatening to disrupt their lucrative trade with Egypt. These cross-purposes eventually developed into confrontation. The changed situation is evident already in the Fourth Crusade of 1203–1204, in which the Venetian doge Enrico Dandolo managed to divert the French soldiers into the conquest of Christian Constantinople, which both spared Egypt, and expanded the Venetian naval hold on the eastern Mediterranean. French energies were dissipated by the imposition of five Frenchmen in turn as Byzantine emperors from 1204 to 1261. The takeover also allowed Venice to set up a prosperous military-backed trading-post empire with control of the Pera dock and shipbuilding district of Constantinople. Venetian Crete acted as the central control point, with other garrisons at Negroponte in the Peloponnesus and (later) at Akko (Acre). In 1212, merchants similarly betrayed the participants of the Children's Crusade by selling them in Egypt and Tunisia as slaves.

Al-Adil's son al-Kamil (r. 1218–1238) continued the pro-Venetian policy. Tolerant toward Christians, he returned many of the victims of the earlier Children's Crusade to their homes, and in 1219 allowed the Italian friar San Francesco d'Assisi to preach to him. The French continued to oppose this Egyptian–Italian collaboration. Jean de Brienne invaded Egypt in 1221, to no effect. When the thoroughly Italian King Federico II of Sicily was obliged by crusading sentiment to at least seem to invade Palestine in 1228, al-Kamil (preoccupied with his own civil war) agreed to grant him wall-less and defenceless Jerusalem (minus the Dome of the Rock, and without true control) as a friend and ally. The pope denounced this farce, and Palestine soon reverted to Egyptian rule. The future King Edward I of England, who in 1270–1272 fought on crusade, was typical of northern Europeans in criticizing the Venetians for continuing their trade with Egypt.

The French urge Mongol intervention

The repeated French attacks in the name of Christ moved from being a controllable nuisance (from the Egyptian and Italian viewpoint) to becoming a deadly threat when the Mongol explosion out of Central Asia spilled over into the Middle East. The French and some of the popes formed the hope of converting the pagan Mongols to Christianity, thereby creating a formidable ally against the Muslims. In 1245, friars Gian Piano Carpini and Simon de Saint Quentin were sent by Pope Innocenzo IV to try to convert the Mongols. In 1246, Innocenzo sent two more missions of the same sort. All three missions failed to win either converts or allies. Carpini returned with his report in 1247. Nonetheless, a Mongol commander sent his own envoys to Cyprus in 1248, where they proposed joint military action against the Muslims to (St) Louis IX of France, who was preparing to lead the Seventh Crusade to Egypt. In 1249, Louis invaded Egypt, only to be defeated, taken prisoner, and ransomed. In 1250, Louis sent André de Longjumeau to win continued cooperation with the Mongols, who proved unreceptive at this point. Undiscouraged, Louis in 1253–1255 sent William of Rubruck to Mongolia and China to try again, but again without success.

This potential conjunction of French and Mongols was too serious a threat for Egypt to overlook. Turkish Mamluk soldiers took control of the government, and under Sultan Baybars in 1260 stopped the Mongol advance at the battle of Ain Jalut ('Goliath's Spring') in Palestine. Further negotiations between the French and papacy on the one hand and the Mongols on the other hand did nothing to alter this outcome. In 1260, a Dominican friar named David of Ashby went as envoy of the Pope and Louis IX to Genghis Khan's grandson Hülegü. Since this Mongol ruler's wife Doquz Khatun and his commander-in-chief were both Nestorian Christians, since he was already allied with Christian Armenia and Georgia, and since he had spared the Christians and their churches when he took Baghdad in 1258, St. Louis IX looked to Hülegü as a potential convert and ally. Hülegü responded by sending his own envoy to Pope Urbano IV in 1263. However, Hülegü died in 1265, before anything concrete could be accomplished. A final envoy, Raban Sauma, sent to the French king and the pope from the Mongols in 1287, was far too little, too late. By his death in 1277, Egypt's Mamluk sultan Baybars had re-established the (puppet) Abbasid caliphate in Cairo, and had eliminated the Frankish presence in the Levant. The Venetians retained their role in the trade from Egypt through the Mediterranean thanks to their undermining of the zealous French, and thanks to Baybar's halting of the Mongols. All the same, the Mongols delivered a shock that brought a new major shift in Indian Ocean and world trade, power, and civilization.

The rise of the Mongols

In the early thirteenth century, an eventual change in the Indian Ocean trading pattern was put into motion when ferocious and barbaric peoples burst out of Mongolia in a conquest of the greater part of Eurasia. This eruption has been explained as the last major historical clash between herders and farmers. From the first introduction of agriculture, farmlands had reduced the land available for grazing herds. At times, farms blocked crucial passages from one pastureland to the next. A hostility between the two groups developed which had led to repeated wars through the millennia.

Timuchin, better known as Genghis Khan ('Heavenly Lord') gave direction to Mongol pastoralist discontent. When Timuchin was a boy, his father was defeated and killed by a rival tribe. Thirsting for revenge, Genghis later built up a military force of 130,000 men. He employed gunpowder weapons and catapults to overwhelm city walls and gates. His main fighting tactic was the old trick of feigning flight, and then turning his horses back on the pursuing enemy, surrounding and cutting him down. Genghis was also a master of espionage (using merchants as spies) and of psychological warfare (showing great brutality with those who resisted him). He demanded that wholesale destruction follow conquest. He was irritated if he saw so much as one live cat or dog where his army had passed. Prisoners were beheaded, and pyramids were constructed out of their skulls. After uniting Outer Mongolia, in 1205 Genghis Khan destroyed Inner Mongolia. In 1211 to 1215, he conquered the Jürchen state of Chin in Manchuria, and in 1219 to 1221 Turkish Khorezm (Turkestan) in Central Asia. Then he wrapped up his conquests by laying northwestern China waste.

Genghis's son and heir Ögödei carried on the expansion, conquering Korea in 1231. Three grandsons pushed the Mongol campaigns farther afield: Batu into Europe in the 1240s, Hülegü into the Middle East in the 1250s, and Kublai Khan into China, Southeast Asia and the Indian Ocean in the 1260s through the 1290s. Batu conquered the Volga Bulgars in 1237, and Russia in 1240. In 1241, he ravaged southern Poland and Hungary. Vienna beckoned, but at this point, Khan Ögödei died, and Batu was called back to Mongolia for the election of his cousin Möngke. Thanks in part to the woods of Europe, in which Batu's plains-loving men felt claustrophobic, the Mongols never returned. Möngke's brother Hülegü conquered Iran and Iraq. He cleared Lebanon of the *Hashishim* assassins, whose survivors fled to Bombay, where they are still ruled by the Agha Khan (descendents of Ismael, the seventh Imam). The Turkish Mamluk sultans of Egypt came to be virtually Mongol-blooded through intermarriage with Mongol princely families. Aladdin's marriage to a Chinese princess in the 'Tale of Aladdin,' an Egyptian addition to the *Thousand and One Nights* from this period, is a reminder of the Mongol wives of the Egyptian sultans. Hülegü's elder brother Kublai Khan (r. 1260 to 1294) pushed farther south into China, founding the Yüan ('Origin') Dynasty, with his summer capital at Shang-tu or Xanadu in Inner Mongolia, and his winter capital at Beijing. In 1279, his armies and new navy completed the conquest of southern China with the help of large ships equipped with catapults, flame-throwers, rockets, and burning arrows.

China's resurgence in the Indian Ocean trade under Kublai Khan

The Mongols caused one of history's most dramatic changes in the world trade centered on the Indian Ocean. After Hülegü's conquest of Iran and

Iraq, they strangled the Persian Gulf trade route. The Egyptian sultan Baybars' destruction of the crusader ports of the Levant, which had passed the Persian Gulf goods on farther west, magnified the crisis. Masses of Muslims fled from Mongol-devastated Central Asia, Iran, and Iraq to settle in India, Southeast Asia, and East Africa. Just as at the start of the Bronze Age, the main trade routes of the Arabian Sea shifted toward the south. Arab and Persian merchants were weakened to the benefit of Gujarati Hindus from Cambay, who now became prominent from Aden to Malacca.

When merchants later tried to revive the Persian Gulf route, they found themselves up against the rivalry of Mamluk Egypt's Red Sea route. However, even the Red Sea route had been negatively affected by political problems and the immense loss of lives in the recurring waves of the Black Death. At the same time, Kublai Khan's expansion by sea from China into the Indian Ocean directed much of the Indian Ocean trade eastward. Also, the exorbitant taxes required by the Mongols drove many landowners out of business and undermined reinvestment needed for continued productivity. Wars between the Tamils and the Sri Lankans had left much of the Ceylonese rice lands abandoned. Cambodia experienced a similar economic collapse after Thai attacks ended the Khmer kingdom. On the other hand, the Mongol Empire made the land trade between the Black Sea and China across Central Asia more secure, while its move into the Indian Ocean using Chinese merchants gave a new impetus to Indian Ocean trade in general. Yet in the long run the negative impact of the Mongols was not overcome.

Kublai Khan expressed a sustained interest in expanding foreign trade, promoting the sale of Chinese porcelains and silks, and forging new commercial ties with Southeast Asia. As soon as he completed the conquest of southern China in 1279, he sent envoys to Annam (north Vietnam) to promote commercial ties and procure spices, pearls, medicines, and animals. The king of Annam responded by sending trading missions to China in the guise of tribute bearers. Moving a step closer to the Indian Ocean, in 1273 Kublai sent three envoys to the Burmese kingdom of Pagan, requesting tribute. When the envoys were executed, Kublai sent an avenging army to Burma in 1277, which in the course of the next decade obliged the Burmese to cooperate. When Champa (south Vietnam) likewise refused tribute, a Yüan army invaded in 1279, only to find itself bogged down in a losing war against guerilla raids, humid heat, and disease. However, Kublai Khan pushed the trade impetus forward.

In 1289, Kublai Khan tried to elbow his way into Java, sending an envoy to demand its submission. King Kertenegara branded the envoy's face, and so Kublai sent a 20,000-man Chinese army on a thousand ships to conquer the island in 1292. After defeating a Javanese fleet, the Chinese troops landed, and were victorious for a time, but eventually were ambushed, routed, and forced to return to China. Nonetheless, Kublai encouraged a revolt that toppled the Javanese king Kertanegara, and supported the founding by his son-in-law Widjaya of the Hindu kingdom of Madjapahit. The resulting Yüan presence in Vietnam and Burma, and influence in Java gave Kublai Khan key control points along the trade route between China and India. Kublai Khan then used his fleet to assume control in the Indian Ocean proper. He sent envoys to Sri Lanka in 1281, and to Malabar in 1285 and 1290, set up trading posts in Sri Lanka and southern peninsular India, and made ten Indian kingdoms tributary to Mongol China. Chinese merchants settled in Sumatra, Sri Lanka, and Calicut on the west coast of India. The Chinese domination of the eastern Indian Ocean was so complete that the Arab ibn-Battutah, who visited China in the fourteenth century, noted that only Chinese junks plied the waters between China and India.

However, Italian–Chinese trade contacts still followed up on the initial Christian missionary conversion and alliance efforts of the French (and the popes) in the previous generation. In 1287, Kublai Khan sent a Chinese Nestorian monk named Rabban Sauma to Rome and Paris to explore a suggested anti-Islamic pact. Venetians and Genoese from trading posts in the Crimea purchased eastern goods in exchange for silver (obtained by selling Greek wine in western Europe and then buying Flemish and Italian cloth woven from fine English wool to sell in the Levant). Venetian merchants Niccoló and Maffeo Polo claimed to have traded with Beijing. Niccoló's son, Marco Polo, in his book of travels, claimed to have traveled overland to China, and to have served Kublai Khan for seventeen years (1275 to 1292), returning home via the Indian Ocean route. Genoese merchants resided at Zayton, near Amoy, in south China, in the fourteenth century, and Christian missions were founded there and at Beijing. In 1291, the Italian friar Gian di Monte Corvino traveled with a merchant named Piero di Lucalongo to Beijing, where Monte Corvino established a church and translated the New Testament and Psalter into Mongol.

Africa also experienced a shift in trading pattern at the turn of the thirteenth to the fourteenth century, with Kilwa's crushing of its rival Sofala and consequent monopoly of the export of the gold from Zimbabwe. Kilwa also exported ivory, along with the coastal towns north of it as far as Mogadishu. Kilwa's success allowed it to mint coins (as did Mogadishu and Zanzibar), and found architectural expression in Kilwa's great mosque and royal palace.

Devastation of much of the civilized world opens the door to Europeans

Even though the Mongol period brought a further push to China's Indian Ocean trade, as well as new overland Eurasian trading contacts with the Italians, it left the leading countries of Asia as well as Egypt seriously weakened for centuries to come. The two main reasons for this decline were the military devastation wrought in many areas by the Mongol occupations, and the catastrophic drop in population caused by the Black Death picked up by the Mongols during their conquests of Yunnan province and Burma, and spread by them through Eurasia and North Africa.

Russia's relative prosperity in the period of Kievan leadership were shattered by Batu's impact. In the north, the Swedes and the Germans took advantage of the weakening of the Russians to conquer part of their territory. The Mongols laid a heavy tribute on Russia, in money, young men (for soldiers, some of whom had been sent to help to conquer Vietnam for Kublai Khan), and young women. Petitioners to the Khans were required to approach on all fours, beating their foreheads on the floor in the *kow-tow*. Russia was brutalized, impoverished, isolated from trade, and left with a heritage of autocratic government.

Iran, Iraq, Egypt, and India were all similarly hard hit. The Middle East has never recovered its former prosperity. When Hülegü took Baghdad in 1258, Baghdad's precious collection of beautifully illuminated manuscripts was thrown into the Tigris River, where they damned up the water, which turned black with dissolving ink. Almost the entire population of the city was massacred, so that the stench from their rotting corpses obliged a Mongol retreat. Iran and Iraq were hit by depopulation from the Black Death, political instability, farming decline, and a withering of trade. The Mongol Il-Khan ('Vice-ruler') dynasty of Iran and Iraq, founded by Hülegü, had little interest in the sea, and Baghdad, with Basra and the other Persian Gulf ports, lost all international significance for the next half millennium. It is true that Marco Polo's book relates that at least the port of Hormuz at the mouth of the Persian Gulf continued to flourish, but his accuracy has been questioned. Egypt was badly hit by population loss from the Black Death, by the corrupt government of the Mongol-connected Turkish Mamluks, and by a constriction of commerce that ruined Cairo's great Muslim and Jewish merchant families. Nonetheless, the Mamluks maintained Egypt's previous prominent position in Indian Ocean trade. They did not, in fact, create a permanent navy, but they maintained ports on the Red Sea, used by Egypt's so-called Karimi Muslim merchants. The Karimis sailed in convoy to Calicut and Quilon in India, where they picked up pepper and spices for resale in Europe through their Venetian trading partners. India's Hindus, intimidated by the subordination of Indian rulers to the Chinese emperor, stopped trading in large numbers around the Indian Ocean by the fourteenth century (although the Muslimized merchants of Gujarat and south India enjoyed an upsurge in business).

China also suffered. Northern China was devastated, depopulated, and thrown into misery by the Mongol conquest and the internecine wars between the Mongols. Vast sums of tax money were demanded to finance the continuing Mongol expansion. Northern China's canal system of transport, disrupted and damaged by flooding, was never restored, permanently losing its importance. The system of education was disrupted, and the civil service examinations were suspended. Kublai Khan showed a certain appreciation of Chinese culture, but within limits. He had tents pitched in the imperial parks, where his family members lived in preference to buildings. The great inventiveness that had hitherto marked Chinese culture came to an end. Mongols left behind mainly military architecture such as the massive defense towers in Beijing's old city walls. In the area of creativity, Yüan rule brought a shift from the Chinese preference for subtle coloring to the Mongol love of gaudy colors, making lavish use of gold next to reds and purples. The most positive cultural development was the flourishing of vernacular Chinese plays, written by professional native storytellers who kept alive the memory of earlier greatness by presenting heroic deeds, often from T'ang times.

Korea's economy was hard hit by Mongol commandeering of vast quantities of grain and men. The nervousness set off in Japan by the Jürchen Tungus' conquest of northern China in 1127, the Mongol conquest of China starting in 1224, and Kublai Khan's failed attempt to conquer Japan in 1274 and 1281 militarized Japanese society under the Kamakura shoguns, creating the Japanese Feudal Period. Japan was frightened into centuries of defensive isolation, interrupted only temporarily in the sixteenth century. Western Europe's fortunes also went into a downward spiral. The trade disruption caused growing unemployment, malnutrition, and lack of resistance to disease. Soon epidemics were sweeping Europe. The Black Death (bubonic and pneumonic plague) in its first attack in 1347 to 1350 may have taken the lives of a third of the population. As wealth collapsed, the nobility and the middle class disrupted law and order with their struggles for control.

The fall of the Mongols

Built on brutality, Mongol dominance was doomed to a rapid demise, like the Assyrian, Babylonian, and Chin states before it. The Mongol population, overextended by conquests, dropped so drastically that the Mongols could no longer hold back encroachment on its pasturelands by its neighbors, much less dominate them. In the second half of the fourteenth century, nativist reactions sprang up on all sides.

After Il-Khan rule failed in Iran in 1340, anti-Mongol revolt in China brought in the Ming Dynasty (1368–1644). The revolt was launched by Hung-Wu, an orphaned commoner from the area of Nanking. Raised and educated at a Tendai Buddhist monastery, he grew into a physically ugly man, with a face described as pig-like, and with a cruelty and nasty temper to match. At the age of 25, Hung-Wu joined a robber band called the White Lotus Society, and eventually rose to be its leader. From this base, he stirred an expectation that a Buddhist savior god called the Maitreya (the Boddhisatva or manifestation of Buddha of the Future) would appear to save the light trapped in the darkness of material bodies. This sect added religious fervor to the revolt against Mongol rule of China. Taking advantage of a civil war among the Mongols, in 1356 Hung-Wu seized Nanking, and by 1367 controlled all of the Yangtze Valley. In 1368, he captured Beijing, and assumed the throne as the first emperor of the Ming ('Bright') Dynasty.

The effort to drive the Mongols out and to keep them out by military measures on the northern Chinese border brought a high degree of despotic centralization that undermined individual initiative. It also required a financial effort that diverted Chinese funds from more productive investment. The nostalgia to reassert traditional Chinese culture after the Mongol intrusion also played its part by orienting Chinese society to the past, an outlook bolstered by the triumphant Confucian bureaucracy with its contempt for industry and trade.

Dmitri Donskoi, grand prince of Muscovy (r. 1359–1389) won a victory in 1380 at Kulikovo Pole ('Snipes Field'). In Uzbekistan, Timur Lenk (Tamerlane or 'Iron Man the Lame'), a Turk descended on his mother's side from Genghis Khan, assumed control of Central Asia, turned the Mongol terror tactics back against the Mongols. His revolt put a decisive end to the Silk Road across Central Asia, which had already been seriously weakened by Mongol depredations and epidemics. By 1394, he incorporated Iran and Iraq into his realm, and in 1398 he captured Delhi, slaughtering its population or selling them as slaves.

Height of the Chinese push in the Indian Ocean

For a time, however, the Ming Dynasty restored and increased China's primacy in the Indian Ocean. In 1407, a Chinese army occupied Annam (north Vietnam). In 1420, the Chinese navy consisted of 1,350 fighting ships, some of which displaced as much as 1,500 tons (in contrast to the 300 tons displaced by the flagship of Vasco da Gama). A large number of private Chinese merchant ships were trading with Korea, Japan, Southeast Asia, India, and East Africa. Japanese Zen creativity flourished under the Ashikaga shoguns with the tea ceremony, 'No' plays, meditation pavilions, rock gardens, and origami paper arrangements. A superior type of *fuchuan* junk was created for this distance travel with high prow and stern, and pointed hulls to cut through the ocean waves, and four overhanging decks. A keel running the length of the hull stabilized the craft. So-called dragon eyes were painted on the prows. At a length of about 400 feet, this ocean-going *fuchuan* was one of the largest wooden sailing ships ever built. The Chinese admiral Cheng Ho (or Zheng He), a Muslim court eunuch who hailed from Yunnan, led seven great cruises between 1405 and 1433, touching on Borneo, Malacca, Java, Sumatra, Sri Lanka, Calicut, Aden, Ormuz, Yemen, Malindi, Mogadishu, and Zanzibar, among other spots. His ships bristled with naptha-shooting crossbow archers, and one of his main assignments seems to have been to suppress the widespread piracy that was pushing up prices and hampering trade.

The Washanga subclan of Pate Island in the Bajun Islands of the Lamu archipelago off the coast of Kenya believes it descends from Chinese sailors shipwrecked there. They form part of the Swahili-speaking 'Bajuni' fishermen, who have a lighter skin, a slighter build, and finer features than their neighbors. There are various hints of Chinese influence on the Bajuni, including the men's flowing beards; the women's two side braids from hair parted in the middle; the production of rich silk cloths; and Asian-like music with drums played in Asian style with the fingertips (rather than with the palm of the hand as elsewhere in Africa). Chinese Ming ware has been discovered in large quantities on Pate Island. Washanga folklore records a story also told in Chinese records of how the king of Malindi sent giraffes to the Chinese emperor. Zanzibar, a Chinese trade base in this period, retained a tradition of intense commerce and of rice cultivation.

Those princes who resisted the Chinese emperor's authority were punished, and pirates were squelched. The Chinese helped the Thais (from whom they obtained hard mahogany for rudders) to fight the Khmers, and annexed Annam or northern Vietnam (in 1408). The Chinese already controlled Palembang, Sumatra, thanks to the action of Chinese pirates a few years earlier. From Sumatra, the Chinese derived pepper, ginger, medicinal herbs, camphor, frankincense, and sulfur (used for medicines). The trade to China from Indonesia and Malaya represented the main source of income of the Southeast Asian city-states. Malacca, founded on the Malaysian southern coast about 1391 by Iskandar Shah, an exiled prince from Palembang, was made a vassal state of China. Malacca's Chinese merchant community took shape at this time. Iskandar's conversion of the area to Islam smoothed commercial relations between Malacca and the Arabs. Islam now replaced Hinduism and Buddhism in Malaya and most of the islands of Indonesia, with the notable exception of Bali, in the late fourteenth and fifteenth centuries. Being a Muslim was an advantage to Admiral Cheng Ho in his dealings with the Islamic rulers of the Indian Ocean region. Arabs (and to an extent Indians) carried spices and dyes from Indonesia and Malaysia, Indian cotton and silk cloth plus pepper, and Chinese silks and porcelains to Aden and Egypt. China made Malacca its preferred port of call in Southeast Asia, and a Chinese community took root there. Sumatran pepper and Indonesian rice were exported from Malacca in exchange for cotton from Gujarat.

Cheng Ho also visited the Maldive Islands, the source of coconuts and cowrie shells, southwest of the southern tip of India. Chinese envoys helped to bring a friendly candidate to the throne of the newly significant port of Calicut on India's Malabar coast. Calicut provided China with pepper, cinnamon, ginger, cardamom, and turmeric from its Western Ghat mountain hinterland, making Calicut south Asia's most important port. Pearls, coral, and gemstones were also exported from India to China. The Chinese likewise traded with Calicut's neighbor Cochin. Chinese forces occupied Sri Lanka from 1408 to 1438, and Bengal, Ormuz, and East Africa sent various trade missions back to China. Hormuz at the mouth of the Persian Gulf was of interest for obtaining pearls (sent from Bahrain), rubies, sapphires, topaz, coral, amber, gold, silver, iron, copper, cinnabar, carpets, woolens, and salt. Cheng Ho also visited with the sultan of Aden, from whom the Chinese obtained gems, pearls, coral, amber, and rose water in exchange for porcelain, pepper, gold, silver, and sandalwood. From Jidda and Dhufar, the Chinese purchased frankincense, myrrh, aloe, and medicines. Cheng Ho also reached Mogadishu, Somalia, and Malindi, in Kenya, whose dhows carried local agricultural products to Arabia to exchange for silks, damasks, carpets, perfume, pearls, glass beads, and Chinese porcelain.

However, China groaned under the taxes needed to maintain this naval effort. Chinese Confucians, with their lack of sympathy to the crass materialist drive of the merchants, criticized the effort. The strain became all the greater when in 1420 Emperor Zhu Di (r. 1399–1424) built Beijing's grand Forbidden City. The next year, he discovered that two of his concubines were engaging in sexual relations with the eunuchs. Zhu Di held an investigation, and executed many of the concubines, but as they faced death, some of the women placed the blame on the 61-year-old emperor's sexual neglect of them. Immediately after, lightning struck and burned the Forbidden City's three great ceremonial halls. Zhu Di, feeling that the god of heaven was angry with him, entered the Altar of Heaven to pray. When he came out, he announced that he would cut back on public spending so that taxes could be lowered.

This development helped to convince the Ming government that their maritime involvement was a mistake. At any rate, the introduction of deepwater locks on the Grand Canal in 1417 had freed the Chinese of the need to use the sea route for trade between northern and southern China in periods of low water on the canal route. In 1428, after almost a decade of Vietnamese military resistence, China pulled its troops out of Annam. In 1436, the Chinese government ended the construction of seagoing ships, along with the voyages of the navy ships already in existence. All further maritime trading by Chinese subjects was forbidden. Successful private businessmen, frowned on by the Confucianist prejudice against profit-making, were subject to excessive taxation or government take-overs of their businesses.

The fifteenth century resurgence of Italian influence

The Mongol impact left a negative impress on the Middle East, Russia, and China that can be detected to this day. The end result of Mongol ascendancy was that China, Japan, Iran, and Iraq (and to an extent Egypt) were all knocked out of a leading position in world history for centuries to come. The defeat of the Mongols by the end of the fifteenth century was too little, too late to save the health of these once thriving and civilized lands. The only part of the old civilized world not badly hurt by the Mongols was western Europe. Weakened by economic disruption and plagues but still independent, experimental, and enterprising, the Europeans were thus left free to dominate world trade, wealth, power, and creativity with no strong outside competition. Thus the leadership in trade and historical progress in modern times was left to Europeans by sheer default.

After China bowed out of the Indian Ocean in the east, Italian influence in the western end of the Indian Ocean trade (from Egypt west) reached a new height. The credit of the Turkish Mamluk Dynasty of Kalaun in Egypt, long intermarried with the Il-Khans of Iran, was damaged by the declining power of the Mongols. The collapse of Mongol rule, first in China in 1368 and then in Iran in 1380, emboldened the Circassian (mainly Slavic) Mamluks to take power in 1382. Barkuk, the first Circassian sultan (r. 1382–1399), continued Turkish as the government language, while keeping records in Arabic. In contrast to the earlier Turkish Mamluks, the line of Circassian Mamluks was not hereditary, sultans being elected by the Circassian soldiers. This system encouraged factionalism, with constant street fighting.

The decline of Persian Gulf trade in the thirteenth century and the withdrawal of the Chinese in the early fifteenth century left the Egyptians, their South Arab trading partners (especially of Oman), and the Gujaratis of western India (all of these groups Muslim) as the main merchants in the Arabian Sea. As the Chinese pulled out after 1436, these traders moved to dominate the Strait of Malacca, now controlled from the city of Malacca. Egypt's aggressive Sultan Bars-Bey (r. 1422–1438) expanded Egypt's Indian Ocean trade, developing Mecca's port of Jeddah, and granting trade monopolies in the Indian Ocean to rich Egyptian merchants. In the fifteenth century, Arab dhows dominated the trade of both the Red Sea and the Persian Gulf. The center of Egyptian mercantile control in India was established at Calicut, the main pepper port. Pepper bought for 50 dinars in Calicut was resold to the Venetians in Alexandria for 130 dinars. European demand for spices, silk, gold, and ivory was on an upswing, as Italy's trade recovery spread economic revival on to its northern neighbors. Tamerlane sent a request for an alliance to Egypt, but Sultan Barkuk, determined not to share Egypt's re-emerging wealth with the Central Asian bully, replied that Tamerlane's flattering letter read like the scraping of a bad fiddle. Exhibiting his strength in the Levant, in 1424 Bars-Bey wrested Cyprus from its king, Jacques de Lusignan. Egypt's hopeful mood was continued from 1468 to 1495 under Qait Bey, another wealth seeker, who had the eyes and tongue of his alchemist torn out for failing to produce gold chemically.

Barkuk's revitalization of the Red Sea trade route also brought a new flood of business back to Egypt's Italian trading partners, who managed to establish an economic advantage in their dealings with Egypt. The wealth and leisure brought to Italy in the fifteenth century created the Renaissance. The Mamluk Egyptians had inherited a close commercial relationship with the Italians from the period of the crusades, and continued the old partnership. This time, Italy acted without France, which was no longer needed for a military assertion in the Middle East and was still struggling to recover from the disruption begun in the fourteenth century.

Venice's military victory over Genoa in 1380 left it as the dominant maritime power in the eastern Mediterranean. The 3,000-ship Venetian fleet was the largest in the whole Mediterranean. Faster ships were built by placing three masts on each ship. This innovation was expensive, requiring pine masts imported from Prussia and additional expensive sails. The three-sail method was applied to the old flat-hulled galley to make the new galleon and to the round-hulled nave to make the new caravel (becoming 'expensive sails'). The magnetic compass was somewhat improved in the form of the fly compass, with the magnetic needle placed on a paper disk fly wheel marked with degrees. However, even this innovation required a relatively calm sea.

The Venetians passed the test for super-merchants by selling back to Egyptians goods (sweets and linen textiles) produced from crops cultivated in Egypt (sugar cane and flax). The Egyptian middle class (including the Karimi merchants) had been so devastated by the Black Death that the government had felt obliged to take over the production of sweets and textiles that had recently been thriving businesses, as well as establishing a government monopoly over the pepper and spice trade (in 1429). Bureaucracy and over-taxation subsequently inhibited technological development, and encouraged the Yemenites to grab back part of the trade of the western Indian Ocean. The Egyptian sugar industry still depended on water- or oxen-turned wheels, while the Venetians were developing new sugar-refining methods. Slave-worked sugar plantations in Cyprus and Crete provided part of the Venetian sugar, from which sweets were now sold far and wide, in place of the former sweets produced from Fustat in Egypt. The Italian name for Crete, Candia, gave us our very word for candy. Likewise, Egyptian flax was now turned into linen cloth in such Italian textile centers as Florence. The Venetians were granted two large warehouses in Alexandria (along with one small one each for the Genoese, French, and Catalans), and a corrupted form of Italian with an admixture of Arabic and Greek words became the lingua franca of trade in that city.

Florence shared in Venice's trade bonanza as a much needed military ally. Venice was willing to cooperate with Florence due to the need to pull together in face of threats both from the expansionist Duke Gian Galeazzo Visconti of Milan and from the rival port of Genoa. The Venetian–Florentine alliance was secured by an exchange of resident ambassadors, a new development. After having conquered much of the Po Valley, in 1402 Gian Galeazzo marched against Florence. However, before he could take the city he took ill and died. Florence gained new lands from the military campaign, and most importantly conquered the port of Pisa and the mouth of the Arno River in 1405. Venice also benefited, creating the Veneto as an expanded city-state under its sway on the mainland. Mantua and Ferrara survived as buffer states. Later, Venice's old rival Genoa lost power with the fall of Constantinople to the Turks in 1453, while Venice's control of the eastern Mediterranean grew with its domination of Crete and Cyprus.

While Milan, Venice, and Naples all grew to over 100,000 inhabitants, the most notable of the Italian trading cities in many ways was Florence, with its 40,000 inhabitants and its port of Pisa. The success of the Florentine merchant-bankers, and most notably of the leading Medici family, rested on sophisticated banking and trading techniques. The Florentine merchants were freer than the Venetians, who had to rent their ships from the Venetian government. The Medici had learned to give each of its branch banks independent responsibility, so that the collapse of one branch would not spread to them all. Illegal practices such as double bookkeeping (with one set of books to show to the government tax officials and another to record the truth) and pseudonym accounts (to hide questionable profits) also gave the Medici an edge over the competition. The Mamluk economy used Italian (as well as Egyptian) money as a leading reserve currency.

The shady innovation that gave the Italians the cutting edge in commerce in this period, combined with the great profits derived from the trade coming in through Egypt, also allowed them to achieve an impressive accomplishment in (equally competitive and self-serving) creativity. Fifteenth-century Italy's creative gift to history was the Italian Renaissance, centered originally on Florence and then spreading out, most notably to Rome. The Florentine creativity in the early fifteenth century was partly sparked by Florence's defense against Gian Galeazzo Visconti. To show Florentine greatness, a contest was held for the commission to produce two new bas-relief bronze doors for Florence's Baptistery. Lorenzo dei Ghiberti won the contest, and Michelangelo later dubbed one of his doors the Gates of Paradise. Donatello Bardi triumphed in sculpture with his realistic marble statues for the Cathedral's campanile, while Filippo Brunelleschi completed the Cathedral's construction with a 308-foot dome. Artistic realism was also furthered by the paintings of Massaccio, Paolo Uccelo, and Leon Batista Alberti, with their rules of perspective and three-dimensional effect.

The second generation of Renaissance creativity in the mid-fifteenth century was dominated by the emerging wealth of the Medici under Cosimo Pater Patriae, and hence took on a more secular tone as it was centered more on secular wealth than on the Church. Brunelleschi created the grand Palazzo Pitti, and Michelozzo the Palazzo Medici, whose courtyard Donatello decorated with the Renaissance's first nude statue (of David in a foppish hat). Marsilio Ficino, who burnt candles before a statue of Plato, and popularized the *Corpus Hermeticum* book of magic, headed Cosimo's Platonic Academy.

The third generation of the Italian Renaissance between 1469 and 1492 was led by the sybaritic Lorenzo il Magnifico into an outburst of unabashed hedonism. Pollaiuolo and Verrochio created playful statues to decorate Lorenzo's palaces and gardens, and Sandro Botticelli celebrated youth and spring in such paintings as *The Return of Spring*. Pico della Mirandola in his *De Hominis dignitate* (*On the Dignity of Man*) praised man as greater than animals and angels, and studied Hebrew in order to master the Cabbala books of Hebrew magic and mysticism.

The fourth generation of the Renaissance saw Rome join Florence as a major creative center. While Leonardo da Vinci flitted around the map scattering masterpieces from Florence to France, Pope Giulio II (r. 1503–1513) rebuilt the Vatican Palace and St. Peter's Basilica as a memorial in part to his own family's importance. Donato Bramante and Michelangelo acted as architects, with Raffaelo painting the papal reception rooms, and Michelangelo depicting God's judgments on the ceiling and east wall of the Sistine Chapel. The proclamation of Italy's trading-based wealth and power blared at its loudest in this Vatican creative triumph, but it was about to be seriously diminished.

The weakening of Italy

The collapse of the Medici Bank and political leadership in Florence in 1492 and 1494, along with the conquest of Naples by Spain and of Milan by France, left Rome and Venice as the two strongest remaining Italian states. Giulio II (Giulio della Rovere), pope from 1503 to 1513, was led by dreams of grandeur to wage war against Venice's doge Leonardo Loredano, and to conquer Florence in 1512. When Michelangelo was designing a statue of Giulio for Bologna, the pope instructed him to put a sword in his hand, rather than a Bible. It was said that Giulio had kept the sword of St. Paul and thrown away the keys of St. Peter. In 1506, Giulio had conquered Perugia and Bologna. Then, in 1508, he formed the League of Cambrai, bringing France, Germany, and Aragon into the war on his side. When Giulio threatened to turn Venice back into a fishing village, Loredano retorted that he would turn Giulio back into a parish priest. These enemies were so wrapped up in their petty local war that they paid insufficient notice to a new power asserting its position in the Indian Ocean trade.

Down to this point, trade in the Indian Ocean, with its gifts of unprecedented wealth, power, and creativity, had been dominated by nations on the Indian Ocean and its sea extensions, with two periods of intensified Mediterranean European and Chinese activity. The preceding four hundred years had seen the participation of both Italians and Chinese in trade extending from the Indian Ocean. In the late thirteenth through early fifteenth centuries, China had seemed to be laying the foundation for centuries of Chinese influence of that trade. China's retirement from the Indian Ocean in the fifteenth century had left Italy as the main distant beneficiary. However, a brand new region (that of Atlantic Europe) and a brand new entry route (the Cape of Good Hope) were about to make a major alteration for the following half millennium in the old link between an Indian Ocean trading presence and world wealth, power, and creativity.

Further reading

On crusader age Egypt: R. Irwin, *The Middle East in the Middle Ages: The Early Mamluk Sultanate, 1250–1382* (Carbondale, Illinois: Southern Illinois University Press, 1986); and Peter Thorau, *The Lion of Egypt: Sultan Baybars and the Near East in the Thirteenth Century* (London: Longman, 1987).

On the crusades and the Latin kingdom of Jerusalem: Karen Armstrong, *Jerusalem: One City, Three Faiths* (New York: Ballantine Books, 1996); James A. Brundage, *The Crusades: Motives and Achievements* (Boston, Massachusetts: Heath, 1964); Amin Maalouf, *The Crusades Through Arab Eyes*, trans. Jon Rothschild (London: Al Saqi Books, 1984); and Jonathan Riley-Smith, *The Crusades: A Short History* (Athlone: Orca Book Services, 2001).

On the Indian Ocean in this period: Jan Julius Lodewijk Duyvendak, *China's Discovery of Africa* (London: A. Probsthain, 1949); Abu-Lughod, *Before European Hegemony: The World System AD 1250–1350* (Oxford: Oxford University, 1989); David R. Ringrose, *Expansion and Global Interaction: 1200–1700* (New York: Longman, 2001); and Morris Rossabi, *Voyager from Xanadu: Rabban Sauma and the First Journey from China to the West* (Tokyo: Kodansha International, 1992).

On China and the Mongols in this period: William H. McNeill, *The Pursuit of Power: Technology, Armed Force, and Society since AD 1000* (Chicago, Illinois: The University of Chicago Press, 1982); Luan Baoqun, *Tales About Chinese Emperors: Their Wild and Wise Ways* (Hong Kong: Hai Feng, 1997); Wolfram Eberhard, *A History of China* (Berkeley and Los Angeles: University of California Press, 1971); Louise Levathes, *When China Ruled the Seas: The Treasure Fleet of the Dragon Throne, 1405–1433* (Oxford: Oxford University Press, 1994); Mauricio Obregón, *Beyond the Edge of the Sea: Sailing with Jason and the Argonauts, Ulysses, the Vikings, and Other Explorers of the Ancient World* (New York: Random House, 2001); Kevin Reilly, *The West and the World: A History of Civilization* (New York: Harper and Row, 1989); and Morris Rossabi, *Khubilai Khan: His Life and Times* (Berkeley: University of California Press, 1988).

On Europe in this period: Barbara Tuchman, *A Distant Mirror: The Calamitous 14th Century* (New York: Knopf, 1978); D.S. Chambers, *The Imperial Age of Venice, 1380–1580* (San Diego, California: Harcourt Brace, 1970); Hans Baron, *The Crisis of the Early Italian Renaissance: Civic Humanism and Republican Liberty in an Age of Classicism and Tyranny* (Princeton, New Jersey: Princeton University, 1955); Gene A. Brucker, *Renaissance Florence* (New York: Wiley, 1983); John Rigby Hale, *Florence and the Medici: The Pattern of Control* (London: Thames and Hudson, 1977); Garrett Mattingly, *Renaissance Diplomacy* (Boston, Massachusetts: Houghton Mifflin, 1955); and Raymond de Roover, *The Rise and Decline of the Medici Bank, 1397–1494* (New York: Norton, 1966).

Chapter 6

The first assertion of North Atlantic influence

The sixteenth century opens up a period, extending down to the present, in which the lands on the coasts of the North Atlantic have played a pivotal role in the power and trade picture of the Indian Ocean region. The devastating impact of the Mongols on Asia and Egypt, either through war or epidemic, facilitated the emergence of the Atlantic Europeans (whose wars and epidemics at the same time were eclipsed in scale by those in Asia and Egypt). The immediate beneficiary of this situation had been Renaissance Italy, but Italy was now replaced by the Iberian Peninsula thanks to the discovery of the fourth main sea route into the Indian Ocean. Other Atlantic peoples, notably Dutch and English (who played an important role in the Iberian success story from the first), and later Americans (tutored and helped by England), would follow.

The reason the South Atlantic nations failed to profit by the shift is explained by Africa's weather pattern (and the consequent subsistence economy with its restricted population) and river cataract barriers to trade; and by the remote and thus relatively backward nature of South American society. This chapter will investigate the initial period of North Atlantic involvement in the Indian Ocean trade, when the Iberian Peninsula was leading developments with its superior nail-based ship construction, its use of cannons, and its possession of the gimbel compass. It will look first at how the Portuguese launched the move into the Indian Ocean at the start of the sixteenth century; next consider the period of growing Spanish influence in Portugal from 1525 down to the assumption of the throne of Portugal by the kings of Spain in 1580; and then consider the impact of this Spanish connection down to its dissolution by the middle of the seventeenth century.

This chapter will examine the height of Iberian power in the Indian Ocean in the sixteenth century; the period of Dutch initiative in the Indian Ocean through most of the seventeenth century; the emergence of the English presence by the end of the seventeenth century; the wars for trade control between England and France from 1689 to 1815; and the final consolidation of British success in the early nineteenth century. It will see the imposition of British in place of Indian Ocean area manufactures, as a result of the British success by the end of this period.

India in this period was weakened by the hatred between Muslims and Hindus, the slow and incomplete Islamic conquest of the subcontinent, and the lack of maritime involvement of the Moguls. Tamerlane's great-great-grandson Babur or Baybar swept out of Turkestan, reconquering Kabul, Afghanistan in 1504 and Delhi in 1526. This launched the Mughal Empire, so named because Tamerlane had been half Mongol (i.e. Mughal). Baybar, like his gruesome ancestors, employed brutality (erecting the traditional Central Asian towers of human heads after his victories) and advanced weaponry (including matchlock muskets and cannons). By the time of his death in 1530, Baybar controlled much of northern India, which he organized as a military state. Every official held a rank in the army, and all obeyed the emperor as commander-in-chief.

After the reign of the bibliophile son of Baybar, Humayun, Baybar's grandson Akbar (r. 1556–1605) completed the conquest of northern India. His conquests gave him access to both the Arabian Sea (at Gujarat in 1574) and the Bay of Bengal (at Bengal in 1576). As the previous main Gujarati port of Cambay was silting over, Surat took its place as the principal port of the region. Various Bengal ports were used to make trade contacts with the Coromandel coast, Burma, Thailand, and Southeast Asia. Akbar's empire, with his road-building program, facilitated the movement of goods across northern India to and from these ports. However, Portuguese and Asian pirates placed a limit on the Moguls' maritime success. Akbar was also handicapped by resentment between his conquered Hindu subjects and the minority Muslim elite. He tried to reconcile his Hindu subjects, in a new, more positive start, by building a brand-new capital city, Fatepur Sikri. He wed a Rajput Indian princess, placed Hindus in high offices of state, and removed the one-sided poll tax on Hindus. In 1582, he announced a new Din Ilahi ('Divine Faith') mingling elements of Islam and Hinduism. However, his new approach failed to win converts and, at his death, Akbar left an India still divided politically and religiously. Before these problems could be resolved, western European control had been tightly clamped on the Indian Ocean trade.

Henrique the Navigator

In the 1380s, all over Europe, the middle class had been making a bid to become part of the national political process. This bid was expressed through a wave of rebellions, which failed in their goals almost everywhere. Portugal was an exception since the bourgeois revolt coincided with the more generally popular cause of national independence. When King Fernão I of Portugal died in 1385, the Portuguese middle class refused to accept the rule of Fernão's daughter Beatriz and her husband Juan I of Castile. Juan I promised to keep out of Portuguese affairs, but the Portuguese people recognized that little Portugal would probably end up by being absorbed into militaristic Castile. At a parliament held in Coimbra, João (a shy illegitimate son of a former king, Pedro I) was raised to the throne as João I of the new house of Avis. A royal council was formed consisting of lawyers, merchants, clergymen, and representatives from the guilds. When Juan I led an army to take control, and was joined by many of the Portuguese nobles, João turned to Portugal's traditional ally, England. At the battle of Aljubarota on 14 August 1385, the English longbow archers brought victory for Portugal. As a result, the middle class was able to retain a strong position in Portuguese society, infusing it with their energy and commercial orientation.

The new trade impetus coming from Portugal's trade with England and Flanders attracted pirates from the Barbary coasts of Morocco, Algeria, Tunisia, and Libya. To contain these attacks, João I's government sent an expedition with the assigment of capturing and holding the Moroccan port city of Ceuta as a base from which to guard the Strait of Gibraltar. Nineteen-year-old Henrique O Navegador (Henry the Navigator) captured Ceuta in 1415, remaining as its governor. Needing major financing in order to make Ceuta an effective base for defeating the pirates, Henrique made note of the Arabs' flourishing trade in gold from mines near the Gulf of Guinea. He realized that if he could establish sea connections with the Gold Coast, he could bypass the Arab middle-men and put the lucrative gold trade in Portuguese hands.

The Arabs were familiar with the West African coast, and a Catalan map of 1380 shows the Gulf of Guinea, but sea trade had not been established between Europe and the Gold Coast because of the dangers of the seas off Cape Bojador (on the coast of the western Sahara). Known to Catalans for a century, the towering cliffs, desert hinterland, thick fogs, and sometimes 50-foot waves of Cape Bojador formed a hitherto impassable barrier. North of the Equator, the doldrums, a vast area of calm sea lacking wind or current to move ships along, also discouraged travel. What was called for was an exploration of how to swing many miles out into the Atlantic to obviate the Cape. This line of thought brought Henrique to a study of navigation to overcome the difficulties of forging such a new sea route. Henrique therefore founded a school of navigation at the University of Coimbra, as well as a center of navigational studies at his Vila do Infante at the Cape of Sagres, the southeastern point of Portugal. Genoese navigators, shut out of the eastern Mediterranean trade by the Venetians, poured in.

Inventions and adaptations made in these schools helped the breakthrough. Earlier, they had used the quadrant, the sextant, and the astrolabe to determine latitude by the height of Polaris (in the Northern Hemisphere). The portalan chart from thirteenth-century Italy allowed the plotting of a course over open sea. A central rudder, long known to the northern Europeans, was placed on the ships. Now the old box compass was replaced by the new gimbel compass, moving freely on a double pivot, to allow the final element for feasible ocean navigation. These improvements allowed Henrique to send his ships far out into the Atlantic, establishing Portuguese colonies in Madeira in 1419, and in the Azores in 1432. Cape Bojador was obviated in 1434, and by the time Henrique died in 1460, Portuguese colonies had been founded in the Gulf of Guinea, and were dominating the gold trade. The Portuguese crown was able to mint a pure gold coin called the cruzado, modeled on the Italian florin and ducat. Profits went as high as 700 percent for one voyage.

João II and Manoel the Fortunate

For two decades after Henrique's death, Portugal was content to enjoy the fruits of Henrique's labors. Then the energetic João II (r. 1481–1495) continued the maritime exploration program, setting his sights on a trans-African entry into the world's big trade prize, the Indian Ocean. Portuguese probes were sent farther down the west coast of Africa, and in 1486 Bartolomeo Dias reached the Cape of Good Hope (as João diplomatically dubbed it) at the southern rounding of Africa. Dias wanted to push right on to India, but his crew mutinied. Dias's return suited the cautious João II, who wanted to be careful to prepare the way for such a momentous step. He gathered information about the area into which his explorers were moving, in 1487 sending an Arabic-speaking agent named Pero de Cobilha on a secret mission via Cairo to Aden and India. Cobilha returned with detailed information about spices and the military power of the Mamluk Egyptians.

João II in 1495 then arranged for an expedition to India. Vasco da Gama rounded the Cape of Good Hope, and in 1498 found in Melinda, Kenya, an Indian pilot willing and able to conduct him on to the pepper realm of Calicut on the west coast of India. The wealthy Hindu *zamorim* (from *Samudri Raja*, 'King of the Seas') or king of Calicut (Kanara) on the Malabar coast of southeast India, realized that these newcomers had little to trade and could well displease the dominant Mamluk Egyptians. As Vasco da Gama sailed away, Zamorim sent warships after him. The Portuguese were much relieved to escape. By the time Vasco da Gama's expedition arrived back in Lisbon in 1499, João II had died, leaving as king his nephew Manoel O Afortunado, 'the Fortunate' (r. 1495–1521). In 1500, a new expedition was sent to India under Pero Cabral, who claimed Brazil for Portugal on the way. After Cabral bombarded Calicut, the *zamorim* agreed to trade with Portugal, granting the Portuguese a warehouse at the port. The Portuguese bronze cannons were the decisive factor since the Indian ships, with planks held in place by ropes, could not withstand either a Portuguese bombardment or the recoil of large cannons firing from within. The occasional cannon or two found on a native Indian Ocean ship (whose lighter hull did not support many gun ports) was in any case not made of bronze. Cabral sailed for home with a rich load of merchandise.

Hoping to reverse the bad luck he had experienced in his first voyage, Vasco da Gama commanded the next merchant voyage back to the Indian Ocean, in 1502. Returning to the *zamorim*'s court prepared for the co-operation Cabral had received, he found the *zamorim* once again sullen and uncooperative. Cabral had demanded the expulsion from Calicut of all Muslims. Instead, the *zamorim*, along with the sultan of Gujarat and the emir of Yemen, had sent to the Egyptian Mamluk Sultan al-Ghuri pleas for help. A forty-galley Mamluk fleet soon appeared in the port and attacked the Portuguese ships. The main Mamluk tactic was to come gliding in at the side of an enemy ship, shearing off its oars. However, the Portuguese ships had no oars. What they did have were those fearsome cannons, and with these they won the victory. Vasco da Gama then sailed home with a rich cargo at last.

At this point, a flourishing trade commenced between Portugal and India, diverting commerce from the Red Sea route. Portugal sent copper, lead, mercury, and African gold to India and brought back mainly black pepper, cinnamon, ginger, cloves, nutmeg, and mace. Fleets left Lisbon in March to benefit from the summer monsoon in the Indian Ocean, which pushed them north to India. The return fleets left India in January, and were pushed back south to the Cape of Good Hope by the winter monsoon. To consolidate the Portuguese hold on the trading profits, in 1504 Afonso de Albuquerque defeated the *zamorim* in a land battle in which 20,000 Indians died. The *zamorim* retired to a Hindu monastery, while Albuquerque built a Portuguese fort dominating Calicut. The Egyptians tried in vain to shift their spice routes to Indonesia and Sri Lanka, for the Portuguese blocked them there, too. Groups of merchants began to lease the right to import and sell pepper and spices from the king of Portugal. Prices were set, and the merchants bringing pepper and spices from Asia had to sell them in Lisbon, from which other merchants by contract with the king could then resell them elsewhere in Europe.

The Italian response

By 1504, no more spices were coming into the Italian ports. However, Pope Giulio II and Doge Leonardo Loredano were too obsessed with their War of the League of Cambrai against each other to turn their full attention to this external threat. Giulio bent his efforts to the conquest of Perugia and Bologna, which he would accomplish in 1506. The Italian powers thus contented themselves with half-measures to counter the Portuguese in the Indian Ocean. Loredano allied with Egypt against Portugal. Giulio ordered King Manoel to end the Portuguese presence in the Indian Ocean, rationalizing that it exposed the Christian minorities in the Middle East to Muslim reprisals. The Venetians helped Egypt build a new, cannon-armed fleet, but kept their main energies concentrated on fighting the pope. In 1505, Sultan al-Ghuri sent this more modern fleet, manned by 1,500 Mamluks, to reassert his hegemony of the Indian Ocean. Off Sri Lanka, it waylaid a Portuguese fleet under Lourenço de Almeida, son of the first Portuguese viceroy of India, Francisco de Almeida. Lourenço was killed with a shot in his chest, and his fleet was defeated.

The Italian jubilation over this victory was short-lived. Portugal had its attention riveted on this struggle, and Muslim religious truculence was met blow for blow, crescent for cross, with Iberian Christian crusader zeal. In 1506, Afonso de Albuquerque sailed to India with a new fleet and instructions to defeat the Mamluks and to replace Almeida as viceroy. Albuquerque captured Ormuz, controlling entry into the Persian Gulf. In 1507, Sri Lanka (the center of cinnamon production) became a vassal state of Portugal, but a combined Egyptian and Indian fleet defeated the Portuguese in a battle off the port of Chaul near Bombay. Emboldened, the emir of Ormuz helped the Persian shah to conquer the town. In a fury, Albuquerque vowed not to cut his beard until he had recaptured Ormuz.

In February 1509, Albuquerque undid the effects of the battle of Sri Lanka by decisively defeating a combined Egypto-Persian fleet at Diu, across the Gulf of Cambay from Bombay. The Portuguese ships were still vastly superior in cannon power. Indeed, only the stout, round-hulled caravels of the Portuguese could remain stable while firing large numbers of cannons from the decks. Other, slimmer makes of ships were threatened with capsizing under multiple cannon firings. Even at that, the battle was so fiercely fought that when Albuquerque boarded the Mamluk flagship, he found only twenty-two men still alive, and they were all mortally wounded. Returning a hero to Calicut, Albuquerque found himself thrown into a prison by Almeida, who refused to step down as viceroy. Not until a brusque second order arrived from Lisbon three months later was Albuquerque released and placed in command as viceroy.

With the Venetians defeated by Giulio II's coalition that same year of 1509 at the battle of Agnadello, Doge Loredano in 1510 surrendered all of Venice's mainland territories. Too late, the Italians finally pulled together in an effort at Italian solidarity. In 1511, Giulio II joined a humbled Venice, along with Spain, England, and Switzerland, in forming the Holy League, sworn to drive the French back out of Italy. Venice reconquered its territories. However, the benefit went not to Italy but to Spain, as Carlos V extended his power over most of the peninsula after the Spanish conquest of Milan and sack of Rome in 1527.

While the Italians were failing to restore their strength at home, Albuquerque was establishing Portuguese control of all entries to the Indian Ocean. In 1511, he captured Malacca, commanding the Strait of Malacca leading east out of the Indian Ocean. With 800 soldiers, he captured this city of 100,000, put its palace and much of the city to the torch, and built a Portuguese fort there. Local attacks on this Portuguese fortress by the king of Java in 1514 and the sultan of Bintang in 1518, were beaten back. Portuguese merchants moved to take control of the trade in cloves, nutmeg, and mace from the Moluccas, along with the trade with Java. Timor emerged as the Portuguese trading center for southeastern Indonesia. The Islamic missionary expansion, which had been proceeding apace down to this point, now came to an abrupt halt, contained by the Portuguese Christian missionary and 'civilizing' mission and inherited crusading spirit against the Muslim trading rivals. A trading presence in China was launched in 1514.

In 1513, Albuquerque bombarded Aden, but failed to take it. Instead, he began a yearly naval blockade of the Bab al-Mandeb ('Gate of Lamentation') Strait into the Red Sea during the trading season. He left a garrison to control the island of Socotra, to keep Arabs from leaving the Red Sea. Trading ships in the Indian Ocean had not traveled previously in military convoys, but now the Portuguese forcibly channeled most trade to their two main ports, Goa and Cochin. They established a variation of the Egyptian Mamluk system whereby ships were not supposed to sail without a permit, called a *cartaz* by the Portuguese.

It has been argued that the Portuguese takeover was eased by the landward orientation of most of the large Asian states involved in the Indian Ocean region, including Mogul India, Safavid Persia, and Ottoman Turkey. However, these states were not insensitive to maritime interests in the Indian Ocean. While the Italians waged war in Italy, the Egyptian Mamluk sultan al-Ghuri turned to the Turkish Ottoman sultan Selim the Grim (r. 1512–1520) for help against the Portuguese. Selim sent al-Ghuri firearms and cannons to equip a new Mamluk fleet, again with some financing from Venice. In 1515, this Mamluk fleet set out down the Red Sea under an Ottoman admiral, and managed to conquer Yemen. However, Albuquerque bottled up the Mamluk fleet inside the Red Sea, repulsing all of its attempts to break out. Selim decided that he needed to take over control of Egypt to give it leadership strong enough to stand up to the Portuguese. Al-Ghuri allied with Shah Ismail of Iran, in vain. In 1516, Selim's forces took Aleppo from al-Ghuri, who died on the battlefield. The Egyptians chose Tuman Bey to be their next Mamluk sultan, but in 1517, Selim the Grim took Cairo and hanged Tuman Bey from the Zawila Gate. The puppet Abbasid caliph in Cairo was acknowledged in return for passing on his caliphal title to the Ottoman sultans at his death in 1528. However, the Straits of Aden remained closed for three decades more before a trickle of trade reopened to Egypt and Italy.

With the Turkish and Egyptian challenge checked for the time being, in 1515 Albuquerque retook Ormuz, bottling up the Mesopotamian and Persian entry into the Indian Ocean. The emir of Ormuz, in his fury at losing the city, burned down his own palace, the so-called 'Pearl of the Orient.' Colombo, Sri Lanka was occupied in 1517. Albuquerque then chose Goa on the southwest coast of India to be the seat of power for Portuguese rule of the region, taking up residence in the palace of its emir. He arranged alliances with various rulers of important coastal areas around the Indian Ocean. He also encouraged his men to marry native women, to provide soldiers and sailors locally without having to depend on reinforcements from Portugal. Jews, before their expulsion from Portugal, moved as merchants to Cochin, India, where a sixteenth-century synagogue, rebuilt after being burned in the 1660s, has survived. Soon Portuguese would become a new lingua franca in the Indian Ocean, alongside Malay in the islands of Southeast Asia, and Persian at the Indian courts. Portuguese garrisons were planted in such strategic trading ports as Sofala (to control the gold export from Zimbabwe), Diu (by the Gujarat textile industry), Cochin (for the pepper of Malabar), and Colombo (dominating cinnamon exports). The Portuguese attempt to profit from the East African gold trade was frustrated by the smuggling of gold by African and Arab merchants to ports farther north on the coast. The Portuguese responded by raiding the coastal cities, and by stopping virtually all Arab and Persian trade in East Africa. Kilwa went into an irreversible decline, as did Gedi and other ports, while the Portuguese merchant ships sailed straight from the Mozambique coast to India.

So complete was the Portuguese triumph that in 1515 Venice had to buy spices in Lisbon. At the end of that same year, Albuquerque was recalled to Portugal just when all his hard work had been completed. Disappointed, he exclaimed that he had lived too long and that it was time to go to his tomb. Ten days later, he died, and his remains were subsequently buried in a church he had built in Goa. The Portuguese presence in the Indian Ocean thus began a new era in which militarism, colonialization, and trade exclusivism replaced a period of relatively greater multinational cooperation.

Spain's merger with Portugal

Portugal was too vulnerable to hold on single-handedly to the lucrative position it had achieved, and soon passed into the Spanish sphere of influence after all. After the 1474 union between Isabel la Católica of Castile and Fernando el Católico of Aragon had created a united Spain, the new country used its geographic proximity to Portugal and its superior military power to elbow its way in on the Portuguese bonanza. The Spanish Inquisition, founded in 1484, had burned two thousand Christian or pseudo-Christian victims, while Isabel had expelled the Jews in 1492, and the Muslims in 1504. The newly won power and confiscated wealth had allowed the crown to drive the last Muslim rule from Iberia, with the conquest of Granada in 1492. However, these victories had been won at the cost of seriously weakening the Spanish middle class for centuries to come.

Isabel had moved into making her own overseas conquests by winning the services of a renegade navigator, Cristóbal Colón (Christopher Columbus). Perhaps a Genoese of Catalan extraction (he wrote letters in Catalan), Colón had picked up some of the secrets of the Portuguese navigators by marrying the daughter of one of them. He had tried in vain to persuade João II that he could reach India by sailing west, believing that the earth is half the size it really is. Adelard of Bath in the twelfth century had re-measured the earth's circumference with reasonable accuracy (as had Eratosthenes in Ptolemaic Alexandria), and João's navigators had warned him not to buy Colón's argument.

At first skeptical, Isabel had finally granted Colón minimal backing in 1492. Never admitting that he had not made it to Asia, Colón had been lucky enough to discover gold in Hispaniola. Isabel and Fernando had induced the Spanish Pope Alessandro VI in 1493 to mediate a division of the globe into two spheres of colonization rights between Spain and Portugal, everything east of a north–south line 370 leagues west of the Azores to be reserved to Portuguese exploration, and everything west to Spanish. The Portuguese in 1494 negotiated the treaty of Tordesillas, shifting the dividing line 270 leagues farther west (to about 46°W) (which would later allow them to claim Brazil).

Portugal had also been detached from its traditional English support. England's shaky Tudor dynasty had needed Spanish recognition and support, and in 1501 Isabel's youngest daughter Catherine of Aragon was

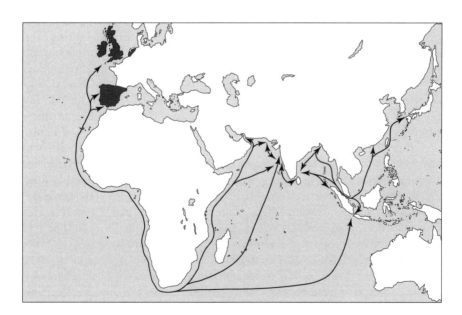

Figure 6.1 Principal lands and sea routes discussed in Chapter 6

married to Henry VII's son Arthur, prince of Wales. Arthur died soon after, but in 1509 his brother Henry VIII picked up the bride and the alliance. However, after Isabel la Católica had died in 1504, the new queen of Castile, Juana, had fallen victim to insanity, postponing further pressure on Portugal.

Isabel's policy of imposing Spain's influence on Portugal bore fruit under her grandson Emperor Carlos V, numbered Carlos I as king of Spain (r. 1516–1556). Carlos ruled over a powerful set of lands that the new king of Portugal, Manoel's son João III (r. 1521–1557), felt unable to resist: Spain, southern Italy, the Lowlands, Burgundy, the nominal kingdom of Germany with the Holy Roman Empire, Austria, Bohemia, and the new colonies of Spanish America. The double wedding in 1521 of João III's sister Isabel to Carlos V and of Carlos's sister Catalina to João sealed the new dominance of Spain in world wealth. Portugal henceforth followed Spain's lead, introducing the Inquisition (in 1536), inviting in the Jesuits, closing schools, banishing foreign influences, and introducing censorship of books. By the time Henry VIII sought a divorce from Carlos V's aunt Catherine of Aragon in 1527 (opening again the possibility of an English interest in an Anglo-Portuguese alliance against Spain), Portugal was firmly in the Spanish sphere of influence.

The trading partners

However, Spain, with a weakened middle class, was no more equipped than Portugal to keep the wealth of its world trade in its own hands. The profits slipped to the northern European centers of manufacturing and banking, in the Netherlands, Germany, and England. This money drain made it vital for Spain to maintain control over the northern centers under its control to prevent the tail from wagging the dog. Resisting this attempt at Spanish imperial domination, the Germanic North found its rallying point of rebellion in the Protestant Reformation. Carlos's ability to discipline the Lutherans was undermined by threats from François I of France and the Ottoman sultan Suleiman the Magnificent. After the Turks had swarmed over the walls of Constantinople in 1453, ending the Byzantine Empire, Greek sailors had been used to create an aggressive Turkish fleet. As the mastery of the western Mediterranean passed from Italy to Spain, so mastery of the eastern Mediterranean passed to the Greek-manned Ottoman fleet. Pressure was now applied against Carlos V in Europe and the Mediterranean with the Ottoman siege of Vienna in 1529, and the Ottoman admiral Kheir ed-Din Barbarossa's conquest of Algeria in 1530 and Tunisia in 1534. A Habsburg–Persian alliance against the Ottomans finally brought a respite from the Turkish threat in the 1540s. This entanglement kept Suleiman tied down on his eastern border, relieving the pressure on Carlos V.

The impact of Carlos V on the Indian Ocean

The Spanish–Portuguese rapprochement worked well for the interests of both countries in the Indian Ocean under Carlos V. The Portuguese continued to block the Red Sea route, and large amounts of spices and pepper were shipped around the Cape of Good Hope to Lisbon, to be marketed mainly through Carlos V's Flemish port of Antwerp. Asian exports were paid for with Mexican and Peruvian silver. By the 1529 treaty of Saragossa, the Moluccas spice islands were conceded by Carlos V to belong to the Portuguese crown. Everything west of a north–south line 297.5 leagues east of the Moluccans was reserved to Spain, and everything east to Portugal (with the exception of the Philippine Islands, which were reserved to Spain). In 1535, Sultan Bahadur of Gujarat (hard pressed by the Moghul emperor Humayun's attempt to conquer his kingdom) allowed the Portuguese to build a fort at the port of Diu in return for their promise of military assistance.

The Portuguese made commercial contact with Japan in 1542, and began to export Japanese silver in exchange for Chinese silk. Huge cannon-guarded wooden castles were built by flourishing Japanese trading cities like Osaka to protect them from raids on their wealth from envious *daimyo* lords. The Chinese port of Macao, at the mouth of the Pearl River by Canton, was 'given' to Portugal by a Ming emperor in 1557 in return for Portuguese aid against pirates in the China Sea and the payment of an annual tribute. By the mid-sixteenth century, in Africa the Portuguese also settled Mozambique, exporting its placer gold. Spanish Jesuit missionaries moved freely through these Portuguese colonies and trading posts. The most famous of these Spanish Jesuits was Francisco Xavier, who in the 1540s missionized in Goa, Malacca, China, and Japan.

The Ottomans also demanded access to the Indian Ocean trade. Piri Reis, the Ottoman cartographer and admiral, had written a book in 1521 about the world's seas, in which he underlined the importance of expelling the Portuguese from the Indian Ocean. Sultan Suleiman the Magnificent was persuaded to give the major effort needed to take Yemen, with the passage from the Red Sea to the Indian Ocean, away from the Portuguese. The Ottomans established mercantile relations with western India and East Africa, supported by a fleet in the Indian Ocean. The Ottomans also conquered Iraq in the 1530s, taking control of the port towns of Basra and Kuwait. Mombasa and other towns of the East African coast looked to the growing Ottoman Empire for help, although Mombasa's weaker rival Malindi saw its opportunity to lie in cooperation with the Portuguese. While Ottoman ships raided as far south as Malindi in 1542, the hope placed in the Ottomans proved to be misled. Carlos's alliance with the shah of Persia launched a long Turko-Iranian war, and partly checked the Ottoman challenge in the Indian Ocean, as in the Mediterranean and Europe. Admiral Piri Reis conquered the Arab coasts of the Red Sea for the Ottoman Empire, grabbed control of Aden in 1547, and attacked the Portuguese garrison at

Ormuz in 1552, but was forced to retreat back to the Red Sea. Nonetheless, by the end of Carlos V's reign, the trade route from the Indian Ocean to the Mediterranean via the Red Sea and Venice was back in operation. In 1558, the Augsburg banking firm of the Fuggers transferred their Lisbon branch to Alexandria, which was soon handling as much pepper and spices again as was Lisbon.

Felipe II's struggle with the northern Europeans

In 1552, the German Protestant princes formed an alliance with the French king Henri II, sealed by their transfer of French-speaking territory in Lorraine from the kingdom of Germany over to France (in defiance of Carlos V). The French involvement meant that the religious war could not be decided in Germany until it was decided in France. Carlos abdicated between 1556 and 1558, leaving his son Felipe II to deal with the challenge from France. The French Protestants drew strength in turn from the Dutch, shifting the center of focus in the religious wars to the Lowlands. Felipe II's inheritance of the throne of Portugal in 1580 strengthened his hand. However, England's Elizabeth I sent an army to help the Dutch rebels, so that the focus of the religious wars moved to her country.

In 1585, English ships and merchandise were banned from Spain, and in 1588 Felipe II sent the formidable Spanish Armada to topple Elizabeth. The fleet set sail in May 1588 with 130 ships and 22,000 men. When its crescent formation entered the English Channel on 29 July, 150 English ships attacked. The English cannon were better made, with a longer range, and their ships had a more shallow draft, going into waters where the Spaniards ran aground. The smaller English ships could go under the high-decked Spanish cannon fire, while firing holes point blank into the sides of the Spanish ships. Under this attack, the Spanish admiral headed, not into the port where the Duke of Parma's troops were waiting to be transported to England, but rather into French Calais. This harbor was too small for all of his ships, which had to squeeze close together to dock. That night, the English sent fire ships into Calais, so that fire spread to many of the Spanish vessels, causing the rest to scatter in the dark. The next morning, the Armada was spread out on the Channel. Seeking to flee the renewed English attack, the Spanish fleet headed north, past Parma's waiting army, in order to circle around the British Isles and return to Spain. On the way the Armada was caught in stormy weather, so that less than half of the ships and a third of the men ever made it home. In the wake of England's victory over the Spanish Armada, the Dutch resistance was consolidated, the 1598 edict of Nantes ended the religious war in France on the basis of toleration, and the focus of the religious wars shifted back to Germany. Meanwhile, Spain and Portugal worked to reinforce the Iberian position in the Indian Ocean.

The impact of Felipe II on the Indian Ocean

The Portuguese–Spanish cooperation still worked to some extent to their mutual advantage in the Indian Ocean in this period. After Spain's colonization of the Philippines in 1564 (Manila emerging as the provincial capital in 1572) and the Spanish takeover of the Moluccan spice trade, Portuguese Goa organized an oriental branch of its commerce based on Manila, Macao, and Nagasaki. A Chinese merchant community grew up in Manila, to the irritation of the local Philippinos who carried out massacres of the local Chinese in 1603 and 1639–40. In Japan's Momoyama period (1568–1598), two powerful generals in turn protected the towns trading with the Portuguese. Oda Nobunaga (r. 1568–1582) seized Kyoto, ending the Ashikaga shogunate, and allying with the mercantile interests. After a treacherous vassal murdered Nobunaga, he was succeeded by one of his generals, Toyotomi Hideyoshi (r. 1582–1598), who built his main castle on Momoyama ('Peach Hill') in Kyoto, and conquered Korea in 1592. Furthermore, in 1578, the sultan of Gujarat, after his subordination to the Moghul Empire in 1573, signed the Praças do Norte, granting the site of the future city of Bombay to the Portuguese. These developments tied Indian Ocean trade into a new global economy encompassing the Atlantic, Pacific, and American colonial worlds. American and Japanese silver were used to pay for the Indian Ocean products. Felipe II's confrontations with the Ottoman Empire extended into the Indian Ocean, where between 1585 and 1589, the Turkish sea captain Amir Ali Bey rallied the Muslim city-states of East Africa to join him in a common cause against the Iberians. However, in 1589, a large Portuguese fleet sailing from Goa attacked Amir Ali Bey, then entrenched in Mombasa. As it happened, the Zimba tribe, feared for their cannibalism, attacked Mombasa from the land side at the same time. The Zimba briefly took the city, and the Portuguese captured Amir Ali Bey, putting an end to the Turkish bid for power on the coast. In 1593, the Portuguese built Fort Jesus to control the harbor of Mombasa, and placed the ruler of allied Malindi in charge of that city.

However, Portugal also suffered from attacks by Felipe II's foes. After about 1560, the half-century-long Portuguese blockade of the Strait of Aden collapsed, and pepper, spices, cotton and silk textiles, and dyes began to flow to Europe again via the Red Sea route. In return for an Ottoman promise of support against the Portuguese in 1563, the sultan of Aceh at the western tip of Sumatra converted his land to Islam (a gesture of defiance to the Christian Iberians). Although the Ottomans never managed to send more than two supply ships, the Aceh navy successfully drove off the Portuguese. Soon huge ships from Aceh were carrying Sumatran pepper in large quantities through the Red Sea to the Mediterranean. The defeat of an Ottoman fleet at Lepanto off the west coast of Greece in 1571 took pressure off the Iberians in the Mediterranean, but did not stop the trade flow past Aden. On the contrary, the Ottomans provided the Aceh sultanate with bronze guns that allowed it to defy the Portuguese. After the defeat of the Spanish Armada in 1588, both English and Dutch ships dared to push their way into the Indian Ocean. Captain James Lancaster headed the first English probe from 1591 to 1594; and Cornelis de Houtman directed the first Dutch appearance between 1595 and 1597.

The Iberian contribution to civilization

Down to this point, Iberian energies were focused on Spain's religious and political wars. England's defeat of the Spanish Armada in 1588 brought a pause during which an outburst of creative reflection erupted in both Spain's *Siglo de Oro* ('Golden Age') and England's Shakespearian Age. However, the results in Spain and England provide a study in contrasts. Looking at their government, the Spaniards called for better rule. Lope de Vega's play *Fuenteovejuna* criticizes government oppression, and the paintings by Estéban Murillo and José Ribera of poor and ragged street children highlighted the government's neglect of social needs. The English for their part praised their government in such works as Edmund Spenser's *The Fairy Queen*, and Shakespeare's *Henry VIII*. In foreign affairs, the beleaguered Spaniards argued for an ending of the war policy. Miguel de Cervantes in his picaresque novel *Don Quijote* warned against Spanish idealist heroes fighting windmills. Tirso de Molina's play *El Burlador de Sevilla* (*The Jokester of Seville*) poked fun at the idea of fighting to the end merely for the sake of honor. The English, enjoying their rise in power, called instead for continuing warfare in works like Shakespeare's *Henry V*. The most predictive difference between the two societies was Spain's lack of emphasis on science, and England's involvement in scientific endeavors, shown by such Englishmen as Francis Bacon and William Harvey.

The decline of Iberian power

The decline of Iberian power was linked to the steady decline in American silver yields through the seventeenth century. Felipe III (r. 1598–1621) followed a retrenchment policy, concluding peace with England in 1604 and with the Dutch in 1609. His milder attitude emboldened the English and Dutch to greater efforts. Their use of the joint stock company allowed them to accumulate capital far beyond the ability of single merchants so that they could build and man factories and forts, and plan a unified marketing strategy. In 1600, the English East India Company received its royal charter, and in 1602 the Vereenigde Oost-Indische Compagnie (the Dutch East India Company) appeared. In 1605, the Dutch, forging a new trade route east from the Cape of Good Hope to the western coast of Australia and then north to Java (see page 118), took Amboina, Indonesia. In 1620–1621, the Dutch conquered Banda in the Moluccas with its nutmeg trees, and handed out nutmeg plantations to Dutch settlers. They drove out the natives by cutting off their supply of rice, and imported slave labor to replace them. In 1641, the Dutch wrenched Malacca from the Portuguese. The Dutch then forged a new route by sailing directly from their new port of call at Cape Town, South Africa, to western Australia (utilizing the 'Roaring Forties') and then on to Java. For years, the Iberians and the Dutch competed for control of the spice trade. The Muslim merchants, who remained involved in the carrying trade down to the nineteenth century, benefited from that struggle to regain strength. The policy of forcible conversion to Islam continued in Southeast Asia, where *jihads* at the turn of the sixteenth to the seventeenth century forced several ports (including Makassar on the island of Celebes in 1605) to accept Islam.

Spain was pulled into a disastrous struggle for primacy by the final return of the religious wars to Germany with the Thirty Years War. The government of Felipe IV (r. 1621–1665) threw Spanish troops into the war in support of the Austrian cousin house of the Habsburgs against German (and Dutch) Protestants. Simultaneously, the Dutch (and, to a lesser extent, the English) elbowed their way deeper into the Indian Ocean trade. Under Dutch direction, Java and Sumatra replaced Malabar as the main supplier of pepper to the world market. The Dutch occupied Mauritius (near Madagascar), exterminating its dodo bird in order to export its salted meat to the Cape of Good Hope. They also erected Fort Zeelandia in Formosa (Taiwan) in 1624. As in Manila earlier, now a Chinese merchant community grew up in the Dutch colony of Batavia, Java, with the same negative reaction of the natives, who massacred local Chinese in 1740. The Spaniards likewise were pushed out of the Japanese trade. In 1598 the *daimyo* lords, led by Tokugawa Ieyasu, took back control of the government. In 1600, Ieyasu crushed his opponents at the battle of Sekigahara, east of Kyoto. Then in 1603, he assumed the title of *shogun*, launching the Tokugawa period. The middle class was resubordinated to the nobility. Great honor had to be shown to the poorest *samurai*, who was legally entitled to kill a disrespectful commoner on the spot. Ieyasu isolated Japan from the outside world step by step, and the Spaniards were expelled in 1624. In 1626, a combined Dutch and English fleet was sent to combat the Portuguese in the Persian Gulf. The Iberian troubles prompted the Moguls to expel the Portuguese from Bengal in 1632.

In 1635, France's Cardinal Richelieu intervened to fight Spain directly in the Thirty Years War in Germany. The strains in Europe encouraged accelerated attacks on the Portuguese position in the Indian Ocean. The Portuguese were expelled from Japan in 1638. By 1640, only the Dutch (along with the Chinese) were still allowed to trade in Japan (at Nagasaki). Tokugawa also crushed Christianity, martyring thousands of Japanese Christians. This reactionary Japanese policy would prove to be a boon to England, leaving the world seas free from a potentially vigorous Japanese competitor. The Dutch began a yearly blockade of Goa in 1636 (that would continue to 1645). Spain's provinces of Cataluña and Naples rebelled, and Portugal in 1640 declared independence under a new king, João IV. The 1648 treaty of Westphalia allowed peaceful coexistence in Germany on the old basis of a largely Protestant north and a largely Catholic south. However, the war between France and Spain continued until Spain's defeat was acknowledged by the 1659 the peace of the Pyrenees. Spain fell to the status of a second-rate power.

It is moot whether Portugal's detachment from a declining Spain saved more for it in the Indian Ocean than would have been held under the Spanish crown. The Dutch finally captured Malacca from the Portuguese in 1641. In 1650, the Portuguese lost Muscat in Oman to the Omani. In 1652, the queen of Zanzibar launched a revolt against the Portuguese as well. That same year, the Dutchman Jan van Riebeeck founded Cape Colony, dominating the main entrance into the Indian Ocean from Europe. Arabs once again took control of East Africa's coastal trade. In 1656, the Dutch captured Colombo, Sri Lanka, taking over its cinnamon exports. In 1662, the shah of Persia with English East India Company help from Surat recaptured Ormuz from the Portuguese. In 1663, the Dutch East India Company took Cochin on India's Malabar coast from Portugal. Spain's Indian Ocean interests were also hurt. In 1662, the Spanish troops were evacuated from the Moluccas in order to help defend the Philippines from a threatened attack from China. By 1668, the Dutch took over Makassar in the Celebes Islands, and established a monopoly over the Indonesian trade in cloves, nutmeg, mace, and cinnamon. Indian textiles and raw silks, and Japanese silver also became central elements in their trade. The Dutch, like the British, adopted the maritime pass system from the Portuguese. Thus the period of Iberian prominence in the Indian Ocean trade had started with Portuguese enterprise, had slipped into domination by Spain, and had finally returned to (a now debilitated) Portuguese control. The only question at this point was which of the northern European powers would rise to the top in the vacuum left by an exhausted Iberia. Would the leadership pass next to France (which had defeated Spain); to the Netherlands (already a hub of much of world business); or to mercantile England?

The Dutch and English East India Companies

England's defeat of the Spanish Armada in 1588 had opened up the possibility that England might succeed to Spain's position in the Indian Ocean and world trade. While France had confronted Spain in the early seventeenth century in Europe, the English and the Dutch had been relatively free to establish a position on the world seas. However, the English spent the years between 1588 and 1605 consolidating their position in Ireland. When they moved to establish their own trading presence in the

Indian Ocean, they found that the Dutch had already made a considerable head start there.

After Felipe II of Spain ended the participation of Dutch merchants in the trade with Lisbon, some of the Dutch merchants at the end of the sixteenth century began to look for their own independent commercial contacts in the Indian Ocean. Under the leadership of Grand Pensionary Jan van Oldenbarnevelde (r. 1603–1618), a merchant and cofounder of the Dutch East India Company, the Dutch made rapid moves to implant themselves in the Indian Ocean trade. Dutch prosperity was helped by the welcome Oldenbarnevelde extended to the persecuted Portuguese Jews (and their wealth and trading contacts). Ship size and cargo capacity were increasing in this period, allowing more trade in such cheap bulk commodities as grain and textiles. The guns carried on ships, and their nautical charts, added to their safety. Large square-stern three-masted ships were employed, normally ranging between 130 and 150 feet long. The round-sterned flute or fly-boat, which allowed the Dutch to carry a considerable cargo with a minimum crew, was also often used, even though its stern was prone to split in the tropical sun. On the other hand, such large ships were expensive, often left cargo space underutilized, and required larger crews than the Arab dhows.

Pepper, spices, tea, and silk were paid for with precious metals, since Europe (except for some Haarlem and Leiden textiles) had few goods wanted in Asia at the time. Asian goods were purchased with the silver from Spain's American colonies, which flowed north from Spain to pay for manufactured goods (despite a Spanish government prohibition of such purchases). The fact that Amsterdam was the world center for this trade in precious metals gave the Dutch a major advantage in Indian Ocean commerce. This trade imbalance unfavorable for Europe continued through the seventeenth and eighteenth centuries. The Dutch sold part of the pepper in England, which had also been barred from trade with Lisbon. It was in reaction against the exorbitant prices demanded for the pepper by the Dutch, that a group of London merchants had grouped together to form the English East India Company, with a charter granted by Elizabeth I. By 1601, it was successfully doing business in the Indian Ocean market. Stirred by this example, the Dutch government (as mentioned) formed their own East India Company (the Vereenigde Oost-Indische Compagnie) in 1602, and the French established theirs in 1604. These companies, thanks to enjoying a monopoly on all Dutch trade with Asia, made better decisions by minimizing price uncertainties at home, enjoyed governmental support, and protected themselves by hiring their own navies and armies. The many shareholders helped to finance the ventures. This step eliminated the open competition that was starting to drive up the purchase prices in Asia, while simultaneously lowering the sales price in Europe. The mere safety of their sea passages helped to draw the silk and spice trade to them.

The Dutch, as so many powers before them, applied religion to the service of trade and power. Oldenbarnevelde's business partner Hugo de Groot (Grotius) popularized Deism, arguing that God had at creation withdrawn from the world, leaving it to be run by laws, including moral laws, conveniently for Dutch propaganda. De Groot founded international law as a way of using a supposedly moral imperative to take trade control from an Iberia which had forfeited its right to it by its use of cruelty. While the Dutch were equally ruthless with the people they conquered, de Groot found it convenient to twist Padre Bartolomé de las Casas's attacks on some of the *conquistadores*' abuse of the Amerindians into the notorious 'black legend,' tarring all Spaniards with the charge made by the good friar (ignoring the fact that Carlos V had as a result moved to protect natives).

While the French at this point sailed no farther than to Madagascar, the Dutch established their presence in various parts of the eastern Indian Ocean, setting up 'factories' (commercial establishments). The Dutch were especially attracted to Indonesia, despite the relative unimportance of Indonesian spice profits compared to the trade in pepper, as it was politically and militarily the weakest region of the important mercantile points of the Indian Ocean region. In 1605, the Malaccan Banda Islands agreed to sell all of their nutmeg and mace to the Dutch, and the islands of Amboina and Ternate made a similar agreement regarding their cloves by 1609. The Dutch resold the spices with a profit that sometimes ran as high as 1,000 percent.

In India, the Dutch started a 'factory' at Petapuli on the Coromandel coast in 1606, where they could obtain Indian textiles to exchange for the Moluccan spices, as well as slaves to work the spice plantations of Amboina and Banda. In 1618, the Dutch began to purchase Indian textiles from Surat as well. Jan Pietersz Coen established a central Dutch control point at Batavia (modern Jakarta) at the western end of Java in 1619, challenging the Muslim city of Aceh (at the western end of Sumatra) for control of the region's trade. Chinese junks brought porcelain, silk, gold, sugar, and coarse textiles to Batavia to exchange for pepper, spices, sandalwood, and other goods. When smuggling by the English, Portuguese, Spanish, and Asian merchants cut into the Dutch control of Indonesian spices, in 1621 Jan Pietersz Coen executed or deported most of the population of the Banda Islands. Dutch settlers then took over, employing slave labor to work the nutmeg plantations. Dutch trading patterns followed the monsoons from one of their ports to the next. Trips from Batavia to Japan were in May or June; to the Moluccas in November through February; to India in July or August; and those to points farther west in August or September.

Repulsed by the Dutch when they attempted to trade in the eastern Indian Ocean, the English merchants tried to win participation in the trade of Mogul port of Surat on India's Gujarati west coast. In 1608, James I sent William Hawkins, a relative of the pirate hero John Hawkins, to the Mogul emperor Jahangir (r. 1605–1627) to request permission for English trade in Surat. Jahangir (in spite of his name, which means 'world grasper') was mainly a lover of food, alcohol, and opium. Hawkins could speak Turkish, which was then spoken at the Mogul court along with the court language of Persian. This helped Hawkins hit it off with Jahangir, who presented him with a Christian Armenian girl as his concubine (Hawkins married her) and a post at his court in Agra. However, Felipe III of Spain raised such objections that Jahangir felt obliged to turn down the English request for a trading post, and sent Hawkins, bride in tow, back to England.

James I determined to fight Iberia for the right to trade in India, and sent two English ships back to India in defiance of Felipe. In 1613, in the waters off Surat, three Portuguese galleons attacked the intruders, but the lighter and faster English ships, better provided with cannon power, drove the galleons on to a sand bank and destroyed them. Jahangir was impressed. He received the new English ambassador, Sir Thomas Roe (who refused to kow-tow before him), with the comment that one Portuguese will beat three Indians, but one Englishman will beat three Portuguese. He then granted the English East India Company the right to trade in the Mogul trading post of Surat, where it would work in rivalry with the Portuguese, the Dutch, and later the French. The English jumped into the export of pepper and cloth, trading the cloth in China in exchange for tea. In 1619, the English set up trading posts in Burma, including one at Rangoon, exporting ivory, timber, and tung oil for tanning leather. In 1622, they helped the Persians retake Ormuz from the Portuguese in return for a trade agreement that allowed the English to sell Iranian silk and silk cloth and rugs in Europe. Heartened by this example, in 1650 Oman recaptured its own Persian Gulf port of Muscat from the Portuguese, as well.

James I's son Charles I (r. 1625–1649) proved to be an incompetent king under whom the navy was neglected, the finances misused, and the monarchy overthrown after a ruinous civil war. This English mismanagement allowed the Dutch to entrench themselves still further in Indian Ocean trade, despite some setbacks. Under the leadership of Stadtholder Frederik Henrik van Oranjen (r. 1625–1647), Dutch colonies were founded in New Amsterdam (later New York) and Pernambuco, Brazil. With the rise of Dutch and English commerce, the Portuguese hold on the East African trade weakened. Yusuf bin Hasan, son of a ruler of Mombasa put to death by the Portuguese, had been raised as a Catholic in Goa. In 1631, he reverted to Islam, and conquered Mombasa by a surprise attack. The Portuguese later reconquered Mombasa, only to be challenged again after 1650 by the Omanis. In 1698, Oman conquered Fort Jesus, and with it total control of Mombasa. Catholicism was eliminated to the benefit of Islam on the coast north of Mozambique. Oman replaced Portugal as the controlling power over East African coastal trade in the eighteenth century, setting up forts at Mombasa, as well as at Pemba and Kilwa, among other ports. Mombasa was the Omani regional control center, and Oman immigrants poured in. The Arab-controlled trade in the eighteenth century concentrated on slaves (sent mainly to Arabia, Persia, and India) and ivory, but the supply of gold fell off so much as to end once again the importance of this trading item.

However, things went well for the Dutch elsewhere in this period. In 1625, the Dutch East India Company increased its control of the clove trade by allowing the cultivation of cloves only on their island of Ambon. Clove trees on any other island the Dutch could reach were destroyed. In 1635, the Dutch began to trade at Hugli in Bengal, from which the Mogul emperor Shah Jehan had recently expelled the Portuguese. Other Bengal 'factories' were soon added. Bengal became the major supplier of raw silk and fine textiles shipped to Holland and England. In 1638, the Dutch East India Company in an anti-Portuguese treaty with the king of Kandy won a monopoly of the cinnamon and pepper exported from Sri Lanka. The Dutch then expelled the Portuguese from the island by force. In 1639, the Japanese excluded all European traders except for the Dutch, giving them most importantly control of the silver and copper exports from that island nation. The handling of the Japanese silver and copper gave the Dutch a great advantage. They bought silk in China with American silver, and then traded the silk in Japan for silver and copper, which they exchanged in India for Indian textiles, which they then traded in Indonesia for cloves, mace, and nutmeg. In 1642, the Dutch also commenced a lucrative trade in tin from the Malay Peninsula. Commercial success in the Indian Ocean again stimulated cultural creativity, as Peter Paul Rubens painted court portraits, Rembrandt van Rijn depicted Amsterdam's rich burghers (as well as religious scenes), and Franz Hals portrayed jolly commoners.

Breakthrough under Charles II

Oliver Cromwell, who rose to dictatorial power out of the English Civil War, restored the English presence on the high seas, allowing the English government after his death to look back to the Indian Ocean. Meanwhile, the Dutch were proceeding to new triumphs under the leadership of the Grand Pensionary Jan de Witt (r. 1653–1672). When, the year before de Witt's takeover in 1652, Jan van Riebeeck had founded Cape Colony at the southern tip of Africa, he implanted a settlement of Dutch *boers* ('farmers') there to help hold the crucial entryway into the Indian Ocean. In 1663, the Dutch took Cochin, on India's Malabar coast, from the Portuguese, giving them a good source for pepper and central Indian opium (which they sold in Indonesia). By their conquest of Makassar in the Celebes in 1667, the Dutch also obtained a total control of the clove trade, for the time being. The cultural results of the ongoing Dutch success in the Indian Ocean included advances in science: Anton van Leeuwenhoek's breakthrough with the microscope, Christian Huygens' pendulum clock, as well as the paintings of Jan Vermeer, Jakob van Ruysdael, and Jan Steen's paintings, and Baruch Spinoza's religious pan-syncretism.

After so much preparation, the British Empire finally blossomed into a major world power in the reign of Charles II (r. 1660–1685), the son of Charles I. France had just subordinated Spain in the peace of the Pyrenees a year before Charles became king, and a showdown for control of the world's seas between France and England could have rapidly taken shape. Instead, good relations were maintained between Charles and his cousin Louis XIV due to their mutual interest in driving the Dutch out of the running. Charles patronized the new Royal Society, housing it next to his 'Queen's House' palace at Greenwich. This group of scientists led the way in stimulating inventions that gave England an edge in the Indian Ocean, including the Greenwich tables of movements of the moon, better maps showing measurements by degrees, and Halley's table of wind movements (1686). The more widespread use of older inventions like the telescope also helped. In the eighteenth century, accurate shipboard chronometers made precise measurement of longitude at sea possible. The result was that the English were able to follow trade routes that had never before been used.

The 1662 Anglo-Portuguese alliance, sealed by the marriage of Charles II to the Portuguese princess Catherine of Braganza, gave Britain the start of its true empire. The old alliance between England and Portugal that had been disrupted by Isabel la Católica and Carlos V was thereby restored. Since its break from Spain in 1640, Portugal needed help to maintain its independence. It was willing to pay a high price in exchange for help from England, and thus allowed the English to trade in its territories and to take over some of its key colonies in India and Guinea. Portugal's gift of Bombay gave England a major port on the west side of India. In 1668, Charles leased Bombay with its magnificent bay to the English East India Company, which built a strong fort on Elephantine Island in its harbor. However, since it lacked either good local soil or contacts with a productive hinterland, Bombay became a military and banking center rather than a trade emporium. The East India Company navy stationed there was used to protect trading interests at Surat. Also, in 1663 England took Cochin on the Malabar coast from the Dutch. The Dutch tried to counter the English move by buying up all of the Malabar pepper, but the English prevailed by being willing to pay higher prices for the pepper than the Dutch.

The English also emphasized trade at the other two corners of the Indian subcontinental triangle: at Madras (the present-day Chennai) in the south (where they had held a fort ever since 1639) and at the new city of Calcutta (springing up from an older village around the new British Fort William after 1696) in the northeast. By 1735, a trade in selling cloth from Bengal and India's southeastern Coromandel coast would be booming. Bengal also provided opium, silk, and sugar. William Pitt the Elder's grandfather founded the family fortunes by dealing in diamonds at Madras, at the same time that the American Puritan founder of Yale University, Elihu Yale, was wheeling and dealing there. The new English possession of St. Helena helped to protect the English trade route through the South Atlantic.

The enhanced English position in the Indian Ocean after 1662 was tested in the Second Dutch War of 1665 to 1667. The resulting treaty of Breda gave England a theoretical right to form a colony in Australia at the southeastern corner of the Indian Ocean. However, until the invention of 'great circle sailing' English ships could reach Australia only by a thousand-mile passage through the Dutch East Indies, so England's right to settle it lay dormant for the time being. In 1668, the Japanese government dealt the Dutch a major blow by forbidding the export of silver, restricting Dutch exports mainly to copper, lacquer ware, porcelain, and silk. England fought in the first part of the Third Dutch War (1672 to 1674) as an ally of Louis XIV of France. Willem III, the stadtholder, used his position as army head during the emergency to topple de Witt, who was murdered by a mob along with his brother. Willem III then launched a stronger executive control of the government by his family, weakening the power of the merchants who had created the great Dutch success in the Indian Ocean. Subsequently, the Dutch lost Taiwan (on the route of trade between China and Japan) to the Ch'ing Dynasty in 1683. However, they did take Bantam at the western tip of Java into their sphere of influence in 1682, which allowed them to compete with the pepper exports from Aceh. Meanwhile, the English trade exchanging Indian opium, pepper, and cloth for Chinese tea was flourishing. In 1688, Willem III of the Netherlands became King William III of England as a result of the Glorious Revolution. The Dutch were thereby neutralized as a threat to the English in the Indian Ocean, just as the French were moving to take over the role of England's main rival.

Aurengzeb's wars to hold back England

The Mogul emperor Aurengzeb took alarm at the growing British presence as a threat to his control of India. In 1658, he had usurped the throne of India from his father Shah Jehan, whom he had imprisoned in Fort Agra. From there Shah Jehan had constantly gazed at the Taj Mahal he had built as a tomb for his beloved wife Mumtaz Mahal, Aurengzeb's mother. He employed a mirror to view the tomb even as he lay in bed until Aurengzeb in irritation had had his father blinded. Aurengzeb was a devout Muslim who opposed cultural activity, dismissing the court musicians, writers, and authors. He ordered all Hindu temples destroyed, Hindu clerks dismissed from the civil service, and once again all non-Muslims had to pay a special tax. When these measures spurred a revolt of the Hindu princes of Rajputstan, he crushed the insurrection. In the 1660s, the Moguls suppressed the Eurasian pirates hampering trade in the Bay of Bengal. Aurengzeb conquered Golconda on the northern Coromandel coast, and made use of its port of Masulipatnam to exchange Indian cloth for Sumatran pepper. He also employed the services of a mercenary Arab fleet based south of Bombay to combat pirates based on the Malabar coast. Nonetheless, his ban on Hindu worship caused a trade disruption as Hindu merchants in 1669 flooded out of his main port of Surat.

To counteract the British, Aurengzeb encouraged the French. Louis XIV's Compagnie des Indes Orientales set up trade in three main ports: Surat (north of Bombay), Pondicherry (south of Madras), and Chandernagore (16 miles from Calcutta). The English reacted by supporting the Hindus. The impressive Great Temple to Shiva built at Madura in this period, with its florid statuary of Shiva, Kali, and their attendants, proclaimed the prosperity English trade had brought to the Tamil state in southern India. With revolt increasingly disrupting his empire's economy, Aurengzeb at age 88 gave up the struggle and retired. His empire was subsequently divided into many virtually autonomous principalities, some Hindu and some Muslim. Persia's Safavid Empire and Turkey's Ottoman Empire joined the Mogul Empire in a general decline of the large hinterland states of the Indian Ocean area, leaving the Europeans in a much stronger position.

The European pirates that swarmed over the Indian Ocean at this time did their part in driving out Asian merchants from the competition. Through much of the eighteenth century, the English (and Dutch) East India Company exported Indian (and other South Asian) textiles to Europe, America, and the West African slave markets. By the 1720s, textiles from Bengal were in the greatest demand, passing up those of Surat in Gujarat and of India's southeast Coromandel coast. The British also carried Chinese porcelain and silk, Japanese copper, Yemen coffee, South Asian saltpeter, and Maldivian cowry shells (the latter used as money in Africa). Although at this time European demand for pepper fell off with the greater availability of fresh food, reducing the need for pepper to override the taste of rotting foods or to spice up bland meals, by the end of the seventeenth century India was accounting for 10 percent of Britain's public revenue.

England's victory over France

With other competitors removed from the running, England and France turned to fighting out the issue of which country was to control world wealth and power. In a memorial written for Louis XIV, Gottfried Wilhelm Leibnitz recommended that France concentrate its energies on building up a great navy and conquering Egypt, in order to control the trade of the entire Indian Ocean area. Such was the key, according to Leibnitz, to world power and leadership. William III, sovereign in both England and the

Netherlands, rallied both of his nations to fight the French. In this, he enjoyed the full support of the English merchants. The resolution of this contest in favor of Britain would require seventy-four years of conflict and four world wars, not counting the following forty-eight years in which the French tried to reverse the outcome by still more warfare. In the War of the League of Augsburg (1689–1697), the English naval victory of La Hogue in 1692, fought off the northeast corner of Normandy's Cotentin peninsula, obliged Louis XIV to cancel his planned invasion of England, and left Britain with an upper hand on the world seas. The imam of San'a now opened the trade from the Red Sea coffee port of Mocha to the English (as well as to the Dutch) East India Company. A European craze for Arabian coffee (and later Chinese tea) sprang up, stimulating imports of these products. Two new important financial institutions were founded in London: the Bank of England in 1700, and Lloyd's of London Insurance Company for merchants, the latter begun about the same time in a London coffee house. Despite budget strains in both Britain and France, Britain's advances in banking and credit gave it an advantage in the coming rounds of conflict.

The War of the Spanish Succession (1701–1713) precipitated the 1707 Act of Union, by which England and Scotland united into Great Britain for their mutual interests. Gibraltar at the southern tip of Spain was occupied by Britain. In 1710, the French East India Company occupied Île de France (now called Mauritius) and Bourbon (now renamed Réunion) in the southwestern Indian Ocean. These two islands provided naval links between the East African coast and India. In the same year, the Dutch acknowledged the right of the English East India Company to join in the China trade in tea, porcelain and silk (to provide Europe's *chinoiserie* fad). The treaty of Utrecht (1713), among other concessions, allowed England to keep Gibraltar. British merchants were eager to jump right back into a new war to finish the contest with France. Yet Britain held the peace from 1713 to 1740, while France recuperated.

The reason for this long lull was a blackmail policy in which France threatened to invade Hanover, beloved homeland of the newly imported English kings George I (r. 1714–1727) and George II (r. 1727–1760), warning that they were willing to help the Stuart Pretenders to the throne return to England. France took advantage of the respite to recuperate, develop French Louisiana, and buy slaves from the imam of Oman's East African ports to sell in India, Java, and the Caribbean. The slaves allowed the Île de France to develop a sugar plantation economy. The French also strengthened their Indian Ocean position by the occupation of the Seychelles and Rodriguez Island. At the end of the 1730s, a group of pro-war English Whigs formed a lobby group called the Boy Patriots. Their spokesman was William Pitt the Elder, the grandson of 'Diamond' Pitt, whose family wealth derived from India. Under their impress, the rationale for the British presence in the Indian Ocean began to shift from commercial benefit to national glory. The War of the Austrian Succession (1740–1748) brought little gain, but the Seven Years War (1756–1763), settled the contest. William Pitt as prime minister concentrated on capturing India. In June 1756, Suraja Dowla, a Moslem prince allied with France, captured Calcutta's Fort William, defended by only 800 men against 50,000 Indian soldiers. Sixty-four British prisoners of war were locked in a room under the fortress. When this tiny cell, only 18 by 14 feet and with only two small holes for air, was reopened the next morning, all but twenty-three men were found to have died of suffocation. The news of this 'Black Hole of Calcutta' helped to stir the British resolve to win.

By this time, British (and other European) armies had gained a major military lead thanks to light and cheap field artillery that could be loaded and fired as fast as a musket. In June 1757, a British army commanded by Robert Clive defeated Suraja Dowla at the battle of Plassy with an artillery bombardment. Clive then turned against the French and their other allies in India, taking one fort after another from the French. In January 1760, the count of Lally was decisively defeated at the battle of Wandiwash. In January 1761, the last French fort in India, Pondicherry, was razed to the ground. The pro-French Mogul emperor of India, Shah Alam (r. 1759–1806) was obliged to place his realm under British protection. At the same time, the British also conquered French Canada.

The treaty of Paris in 1763 left Britain in control of India, Canada, and of the world seas. In 1765, the English East India Company won *diwani* rights of revenue collection in Bengal, giving them control of the local opium traffic (a control extended to Bihar in 1773). The opium, sold exclusively to the English East India Company at a price set by that company, was at first resold to merchants at auctions held in Calcutta. In 1797, the company assumed direct control of the growing of opium, which was sent (along with Indian textiles) to China to pay for Chinese tea, which was in turn sent to Europe. In the meantime, in 1773 the English East India Company was transformed into a government by being given responsibility for the financial affairs of Bengal, Bihar, and Orissa, and by its political functions being transferred from its board of directors to royal officials. Having been almost totally eliminated from the India trade, the French turned their concentration in the Indian Ocean to East Africa. One of the French merchants, named Morice, won a monopoly of the purchase of slaves from Kilwa and Zanzibar, backed up by a treaty between the French government and the sultan of Kilwa. The resulting prosperity of Kilwa induced the imam of Oman to conquer that island port in 1780.

England's Industrial Revolution

The victory over France spurred the English into the creation of their Industrial Revolution. The British East India Company, of which the king was the main shareholder, was given charge of managing India. The company's governor, Robert Clive, guaranteed that the Indians would buy British goods. Indian merchants and industrialists were forced to pay prohibitively high taxes and to sell their goods only to the British East India Company for artificially low prices. The profits long accruing to the shareholders of the Royal African Company, centered in Liverpool, were applied to the use of newly invented machines that allowed England to produce vast quantities of goods for sale in India and elsewhere. Inventions including Abraham Darby's improved iron, smelted with coke (1709), Thomas Newcomen's steam pump (1712), and James Watt's steam engine (1769) allowed the emergence of a major heavy industry center in Birmingham. Simultaneously, John Kay's flying shuttle (1733), James Hargreaves' Spinning Jenny (1764), and Edmund Cartwright's power loom (1785) underlay the creation of a major textile industry in Manchester.

The native Indian middle class rapidly collapsed, and soon British manufacturers were the main providers of the vast Indian market. The Indian merchants were squeezed out of the running, leaving towns like Cochin and Calicut to stagnate. The central items of an emerging triangle trade were manufactured products from Britain traded to India for opium, which was carried on to China to be exchanged for tea for sale in Europe. In this way, the Indian Ocean trade was integrated still more into the new global economy. The Indian market was so vast that immense profits were soon being lost by the inability of the tiny British work force to turn out sufficient quantities of goods. This was the problem solved by the invention of machines to take over the main burden of production, mainly for the textile and the iron manufacturing industries. Key breakthroughs came with James Watt's steam engine to provide the power, and the power loom, to weave cloth by machine. By this means the Industrial Revolution siphoned the wealth out of India and the other colonies into the mother country. India (and neighboring regions) became dependent economically on Europe as a supplier of raw materials in exchange for British (and other European) manufactures. While India sank into poverty, England rose to great prosperity.

A renewed French challenge strengthens Britain in the Indian Ocean

When Louis XVI became king in 1774, the French were seething with resentment that their government had lost control of the world's seas and with it the chance to sponsor their own Industrial Revolution and the wealth and power that would come from both. Help was extended to the American Revolution in 1778 in the expectation that the new United States would then help France to resume its lost position of dominance around the globe. In the same year, the French encouraged an anti-British alliance in India between Haider Ali, the Nizam of Hyderabad, and the

Marathas of the Mahratta state centered in the northwestern Deccan. That same year, a British expedition arrived from Surat, and broke up this coalition, while the British East India Company's Governor, Warren Hastings, occupied French Pondicherry and Mahe, in the Seychelles, in 1778. In an attempt to soothe Indian nerves, Hastings formed personal friendships with leading Indians, had the traditional Indian laws translated into English, and founded the Asiatic Society for the preservation of Indian culture. In 1781, Haider Ali was defeated at Porto Novo in Mysore (although his son Tipu Sahib fought on until the French withdrew their aid in 1784). As the coming victory of the British had become ever more likely, the Yemen coffee port of Mocha gave them preferential treatment, charging them only 3 percent import duties, plus a few low fees. Muslims had to pay 7 percent plus up to 8 percent more in fees, to the anger of the Jiddah and Cairo merchants. Furthermore, involvement in the American Revolution proved to be a major blunder for the French government. It left the French treasury bankrupt, and brought virtually none of the expected benefits.

The strengthening of the Anglo presence around the Indian Ocean

Instead of weakening the British Empire, the American secession propelled Britain into establishing a whole new set of major overseas Anglo settlement colonies, the so-called 'Second British Empire.' The British government tightened its control over India in two steps. In 1774, with trouble brewing, the Regulating Act set up a governor-general and council to govern British India, within certain limitations of company rights by the crown. Then in 1784, the India Act placed the British East India Company under crown control, in a double-government system that involved both the East India Company and the monarch. The governor-general for India was appointed by the British East India Company with crown approval, and functioned as a government minister. He was to hold one vote in a Calcutta-based council to run India, alongside four British East India Company agents. A supreme court for Indian affairs was established, using English common law with English judges. Charles Lord Cornwallis, the general who surrendered to the Americans at Yorktown and the first governor-general of India under the new system (1784–1795), prohibited female infanticide, and the *suti* burning of widows was abolished in 1812 for women who were pregnant, under 17 years of age, or unwilling to die. However, Anglo-Indian relations were marred from the first by racism. Cornwallis would allow only Britons to hold office, declaring that Indians were 'inherently corrupt.' The few remaining Indian-owned factories were fined so stiffly for back taxes that they collapsed. Indian lands for which the owners could not pay back taxes were confiscated and sold. Masses of peasants were displaced from their ancestral farms, and the Indian standard of living was brought to a new low.

British power on the Strait of Malacca began to grow with the new English East India Company settlement at Penang, on the Malayan coast, in 1786. The British presence in the Indian Ocean was also strengthened by two new settlement colonies: Australia and New Zealand. Just as Tory loyalists who emigrated from the United States rather than live outside of the British Empire founded Anglo Canada at this time, so the settlement of Australia and New Zealand also resulted from the loss of the American colonies. Britain had been solving its problem of prison maintenance by sending its convicts to the colonies. Georgia had been founded as a colony for debtors, and many of the convicts were sold to the planters as slave labor. The American Revolution deprived Britain of this outlet, leaving Britain with a need to find an alternative solution. In 1783, the British sent a load of convicts to the logging camps of Belize, but the locals refused to let them land, preferring to stick with the non-criminal black slaves brought from Jamaica. The rest of the Caribbean was already saturated with slaves. Australia and New Zealand had been discovered in the seventeenth century by Dutch explorers. James Cook, sent by the Royal Society as captain of the *Endeavor* to the South Pacific on a scientific expedition from 1768 to 1771, had claimed these lands (now ceded by the Dutch) for Britain. The new British prime minister, William Pitt the Younger, thus turned to sending convicts to Australia.

In January 1788, Sydney in New South Wales was launched as a penal colony, with wool production providing its economic base. In 1792, the second governor of the colony, John Macarthur, made large land grants to officers of the New South Wales Corps, along with awards of convict workers. The next year, the first free settlers arrived. Through the years, many convicts escaped into the interior, where they pushed back the native bushmen and squatted on the land, setting up their own wool ranches. This development passed many prison characteristics into the sporty mainstream of Australian society, including the custom of calling one another 'mate' (from cell mate). Other convicts managed to escape by boat across to New Zealand's North Island, where they fought the native Maoris to carve out an Anglo settlement in New Zealand, too. Starting in 1792, Yankee skippers from New England began to sell goods, which Sydney's market eagerly absorbed, ignoring British prohibitions against trade with the United States. The Yankees soon won a good share of the Australian market, selling American rum and Tahiti salt pork to the Australians, further interweaving the American and British societies. The Dutch support for the Americans brought Ceylon (Sri Lanka) back to the Dutch in the 1783 treaty of Versailles, but caused the British to exclude the Dutch from trading in the Bay of Bengal and the Malayan markets. In 1790, the Spanish (in the alliance shifts resulting from the initial impact of the French Revolution) opened up Manila to British and all European shipping. Thus, the French scheme to weaken the British Empire only strengthened it, in the Indian Ocean as elsewhere.

Napoleon's challenge further strengthens Britain in the Indian Ocean

The same frustrations and expectations of the French people that had pushed Louis XVI's government into challenging Britain applied a decade later under Napoleon Bonaparte. The British had used their war against the French First Republic to capture the Seychelles Islands (northeast of Madagascar) from France in 1794. When the French occupied the Netherlands in 1795 (causing the head of the house of Orange to flee to England), Britain took Dutch Cape Colony, Malacca, and coastal Sri Lanka into its 'safekeeping.' Napoleon repeatedly attempted to weaken Britain's hold on the high seas. Each effort failed in turn, due to Britain's continuing naval superiority. Every time, Britain reacted by joining in a coalition with continental enemies of Napoleon. While repeatedly losing the contest at sea, Napoleon won the great land victories that made his fame, leaving France with an ever-expanding territory under its control in Europe.

Napoleon developed a scheme to link up Russians, Indian natives, and the native Arabic-speaking Egyptians in a scheme to drive the British out of India. His agents entertained hopes of winning the Russian tsar Pavel (r. 1796–1801) over to the idea of dividing India into spheres of influence. Napoleon was to lead a French army into Egypt to champion Egyptian native Arab-speaking independence from the hated Turkish rule of the Ottoman sultan. He was then to join Pavel's Russian troops in linking up in India with the sultan of Mysore (in south central India), Tipu Sahib (whose father Haidar Ali who had fought the British in 1780). A Muslim sultan ruling over a majority Hindu population, and with only a narrow corridor from his inland realm to his port of Mangalore on the Arabian Sea, Tipu felt doubly threatened by British power. Known as the 'Tiger of Mysore,' Tipu kept pet tigers in his palace, and collected statues of the beast.

In July 1798, Napoleon defeated a Turkish army at the battle of the Pyramids. Hearing the news of this battle, Tipu Sahib declared war on Britain. In response, Sri Lanka was made a British crown colony that year, and Lord Mornington and Arthur Wellesley invaded Mysore in 1799. Tipu Sahib's stronghold at Seringapatam was overrun, and an English soldier who coveted his gold belt buckle killed the Tiger. Mornington then drove the French out of Pondicherry, this time for good. He annexed Malabar, and subordinated Hyderabad in 1800. The British occupied Perim Island off the Yemen coast in 1799, in hopes of blocking a future move of Napoleon from Egypt to India. Meanwhile, back in Egypt, Admiral Lord Nelson cut Napoleon off from France by defeating Villeneuve's navy at Aboukir Bay, east of Alexandria. The British then stopped Napoleon's move north along the Levant coast of the Mediterranean, turning him back at Acre. With Napoleon bottled up in Egypt, the British joined with continental enemies of France in the Second Coalition. Deserting his army in Egypt, Napoleon made a rush in a ship across the British-controlled Mediterranean back to France.

In 1801, Napoleon revived the plan for Russia and France to join in an attack on India. This time, Tsar Pavel cooperated. His troops were prepared to march toward India when in 1801, a group of conspirators invaded Pavel's bedroom in the middle of the night and murdered him while his wife screamed. In a plot coordinated by the British ambassador, Pavel's son was waiting down the hall to be proclaimed tsar as Alexander I. Alexander then called off the invasion of India. Warned by this close call, Lord Mornington occupied Delhi in 1803, taking charge but retaining the blind Shah Alam as a puppet emperor. By 1804, all of India but Rajputana, Sind, and the Punjab was in *de facto* British control. In 1810, Britain also conquered the island of Mauritius from the French. Napoleon never got the chance to resurrect his scheme to attack India, and in March 1814 he was deposed and exiled.

Notable creativity had accompanied the English growing trade success, from the Shakespearian age to the age of Dickens. The rise of the middle class in England as a result of the wealth derived from the Indian Ocean stimulus led to the Romantic movement running from Richardson's novel *Pamela* to the verse of Byron and Shelly. As the wealth spread downward through the social classes, a push to democratic concepts emerged, including Jeremy Bentham's utilitarianism, Robert Burns's poetry, and Mary Wollstonecraft's call for women's rights. By the early nineteenth century, concern was extended to the very lowest classes, with William Wilberforce's crusade against slavery, Robert Owens's factory reforms, and Charles Dickens's novels. Romantic England's European rivals and partners joined in the productive frenzy. Most notably, the French were provoked into making one of history's most important creative accomplishments in an outpouring that reached from the eighteenth century *philosophes* (most notably Montesquieu, Voltaire, and Rousseau) on through the nineteenth century and beyond. Parisian soul-searching as to what had gone wrong with French plans launched the four main contending political philosophies of modern times. Each of these political ideologies then span off creativity in the arts, in France as all over the Western world down to World War I. Socialism (introduced by the count of St. Simon in 1824), communism (Auguste Louis Blanqui, 1830s), and anarchism (Pierre Proudhon, 1840) inspired such pro-worker writers as Balzac, Zola and Victor Hugo, and such artists as Daumier. Auguste Comte's capitalism (1830) sparked such celebrations of worldly success and/or worldliness as are found in the writings of Baudelaire, Verlaine, Mallarmé, and Nietzsche, in the paintings of Manet, Toulouse-Lautrec, and Matisse, and in the music of Offenbach and Debussy.

Strengthening of the English in the Indian Ocean

The Napoleonic wars stimulated a continued expansion of Anglo settlement around the Indian Ocean area as around the world. Napoleon's attempt to interest Russia in making an overland conquest of India both stimulated an ongoing interest in an expansion south and southwest by the Russians, and created a determination by the British to block any such move. Napoleon's collusion with the Egyptians and his possible links with Persia elicited a subsequent British determination to control the Mediterranean–Red Sea and Persian Gulf routes.

The anchor of British control over the Indian Ocean region remained India. As the borders of British India had grown, its population had increased from 30 million to 250 million people. The Western Ghats' teakwood forests were brought under an English East India Company monopoly by 1810, destroying the native Indian shipbuilding industry. Britain gained a certain control of Nepal with the appointment of a British resident to the Nepalese court in 1816, a power base used to annex the country in 1843. The Dutch Cape Colony, occupied by the British during Napoleon's invasion of the Netherlands, was permanently retained as a result of the terms of the Treaty of Vienna in 1815. Previously Dutch Ceylon (Sri Lanka) was also kept under British rule, and its king of Kandy deposed. Malacca was briefly returned to the Dutch, only to revert to English East India Company rule in 1824.

Three freebooters helped to give Britain control of the eastern passage in and out of the Indian Ocean. Thomas Raffles, an East India Company clerk, founded Singapore in 1819 in a mangrove swamp purchased from the sultan of Johore. By 1823, this strategic site, controlling the Strait of Malacca, was a flourishing free trade center with a burgeoning Chinese population. In 1826, the East India Company bunched Singapore, Malacca, Penang Island, and Port Wellesley into a joint government known as the Straits Settlements. John Clunies-Ross similarly took control of the Cocos–Keeling islands southwest of Sumatra. In 1841, a former English East India Company army officer named James Brooke formed a paramilitary band and took advantage of a local civil war to assume control of Sarawak (northern Borneo). Installed as rajah, he launched the Brooke dynasty, which ruled in cooperation with Britain down to 1946. The western passage in and out of the Red Sea was also placed into British hands. In 1839, Britain used force to establish a protectorate over Aden at the entry of the Red Sea into the Indian Ocean, forcing the Ottoman forces to retreat into north Yemen.

Napoleon also stimulated an expansion of the zone of Anglo settlement in Australia by showing a bold interest in founding a rival French colony there. In 1802, two ships sent by Napoleon explored around the island of Tasmania, looking for the best site for a French settlement. In fast reaction, the next year Governor King of New South Wales founded the town of Hobart in the snowy woods of southeast Tasmania, populating it with forty-nine convicts from Sydney. On receiving a warning from Governor King, the British government rushed out 300 additional convicts to Hobart. In 1804, Governor King also established a colony in northern Tasmania, which in 1806 was shifted up the Tamar estuary as the start of the town of Launceston. As New South Wales aged into increasing respectability, two new colonies were established to take over its role of receiving convicts. Queensland, centered on the town of Brisbane, was founded in 1824, and Western Australia, with its main town of Perth, was begun in 1826. In 1852, Britain's dominion spread over lower Burma.

In East Africa, where the French had been carrying on a major trade monopoly in buying slaves from the ports subject to Oman, Britain convinced the iman of Oman, Sayid Sultan ibn Ahmad, to sign an anti-French treaty in 1799. At first, Oman was too weak to exclude the French merchants. However, with the fall of Napoleon, the British kept the Seychelles and the Île de France (Mauritius), which they had conquered from France, for themselves. The British, who had outlawed slave trading in 1807, after 1820 began to try to discourage the French and Arab slave traders off the East African coast, but with little success. The Muslim slave traders pointed to the Koran's sanction of slavery, and the abolitionist movement was seen as an attempt to disrupt Muslim mores. Sayid's son and successor Imam Sayid Said in the 1820s used Oman's British alliance to subordinate to his rule both the Wahabi sectarians on land and the Jawasmi pirates at sea. In 1829, the British further strengthened themselves in Arab waters by taking over control of Aden. In 1837, Sayid Said's repeated efforts to capture Mombasa, and with it control of the trade in slaves and ivory, finally met with success.

At the same time, Zanzibar in the 1830s began to grow and export cloves to Britain and the United States. Zanzibar's resulting prosperity (compared to the loss of Oman's India trade to the British and Indian Hindus) convinced Iman Sayid Said to transfer his capital there from Wahabi-ridden Oman in 1840. He ordered all remaining coconut plantations on the island to be converted to growing cloves. Arab landowners pushed the island's natives aside, and worked the plantations with slave labor. Arab and Swahili merchants obtained the slaves (both for the plantations and for export) from the interior in exchange for guns, cloth, copper wire, and beads. By the middle of the nineteenth century Zanzibar and the neighboring island of Pemba were exporting four-fifths of the world's cloves. In return for the export of cloves, ivory, coconuts, copra, and palm oil, Zanzibar imported cotton cloth, guns, brass wire, beads, and rice from Britain, the United States, and India. As in India, the inexpensive products of Britain's industrial revolution began to replace the local handicrafts, leaving East Africa dependent on and subservient to Europe.

Britain's hold on India was tightened under Governor-General Lord Bentinck (1828–1835). The English East India Company, which had lost its monopoly over Asian trade in 1813, in 1833 became a management firm for British India. British Bombay now passed up Mughal Surat as the major port on the west coast of India. Schools were set up to educate a new Indian middle class in English, creating a body of Anglicized Indians.

The British were so sure of their hold on India that Lord Bentinck dared to plan to have the Taj Mahal dismantled and its marble sold in London. Cranes for this purpose were put into position, and only when Bentinck's previous shipment of marble stripped from Fort Agra failed to bring a good profit, did he drop the plan. Thus Iberian success in the Indian Ocean had slipped away to the English; the various Dutch and French challenges to Anglo hegemony in the Indian Ocean trade in the seventeenth, eighteenth, and early nineteenth centuries had all been contained; and Britannia ruled the waves. The following century would see England moving from one challenge after another to try to maintain that position.

Further reading

On the Indian Ocean and its world contacts in this period: R.J. Barendse, *The Arabian Seas: The Indian Ocean World of the Seventeenth Century* (Armonk, New York and London: M.E. Sharpe, 2002); Ashin Das Gupta and M.N. Pearson (eds), *India and the Indian Ocean 1500–1800* (Calcutta: Oxford University Press, 1987); Denys Lombard and Jean Aubin (eds), *Asian Merchants and Businessmen in the Indian Ocean and the China Sea* (New Delhi and New York: Oxford University Press, 2000); David R. Ringrose, *Expansion and Global Interaction: 1200–1700* (New York: Longman, 2001); and Immanuel Maurice Wallerstein, *The Modern World System: Capitalist Agriculture and the Origins of the European World Economy in the Sixteenth Century* (New York: Academic Press, 1976).

On India: Sinnappah Arasaratnam, *Maritime India in the Seventeenth Century* (Delhi and New York: Oxford University Press, 1994); Bamber Gascoigne, *The Great Moghuls* (New York: Harper and Row, 1971); Sanjay Subrahmanyan, *The Political Economy of Commerce: Southern India, 1500–1650* (Cambridge: Cambridge University Press, 1990); Lawrence James, *Raj: The Making and Unmaking of British India* (New York: St. Martins Griffin, 1997); and Christopher Alan Bayley, *Indian Society and the Making of the British Empire* (Cambridge: Cambridge University Press, 1987).

On the Ottomans: Wayne S. Vucinich, *The Ottoman Empire: Its Record and Legacy* (Princeton, New Jersey: D. Van Nostrand, 1965).

On Portugal and Spain: Christopher Alan Bayly, *Imperial Meridian: The British Empire and the World, 1780–1830* (London and New York: Longman, 1989); Charles Ralph Boxer, *The Portuguese Seaborne Empire, 1415–1825* (London: Hutchinson, 1969); A.H. de Oliveira Marques, *History of Portugal* (New York: Columbia University Press, 1976); Geoffrey Parker, *Philip II* (Boston: Little, Brown, 1978); Stanley G. Payne, *A History of Spain and Portugal* (Madison: University of Wisconsin Press, 1973); Michael Naylor

Pearson, *The Portuguese in India* (Cambridge: Cambridge University Press, 1987); Nancy Rubin, *Isabella of Castile: The First Renaissance Queen* (New York: St. Martin's Press, 1991); Peter Edward Russell, *Prince Henry 'the Navigator': A Life* (New Haven, Connecticut: Yale University Press, 2000); and Sanjay Subrahmanyam, *The Career and Legend of Vasco da Gama* (Cambridge: Cambridge University Press, 1997).

On the Dutch and English East Indies: Christopher Alan Bayly, *Imperial Meridian: The British Empire and the World, 1780–1830* (London and New York: Longman, 1989); Charles Ralph Boxer, *The Dutch Seaborne Empire, 1600–1800* (New York: Knopf, 1965); Els M. Jacobs, *In Pursuit of Pepper and Tea: The Story of the Dutch East India Company* (Amsterdam: Netherlands Maritime Museum, 1991); Lawrence James, *The Rise and Fall of the British Empire* (New York: St. Martins Griffin, 1994); Om Prakash, *Precious Metals and Commerce: The Dutch East India Company in the Indian Ocean Trade* (Aldershot, Hampshire and Brookfield, Vermont: Variorum, 1994); T.O. Lloyd, *The British Empire* (Oxford: Oxford University, 1984); Alfred Thayer Mahan, *The Influence of Sea Power upon History* (New York: Hill and Wang, 1957); and P.J. Marshall (ed.), *The Cambridge Illustrated History of the British Empire* (Cambridge: Cambridge University Press, 1996).

Chapter 7

The British Raj period

With the danger from France allayed, Britain moved into direct control of India in 1858. Its hegemony in the Indian Ocean region as a whole was steadily consolidated. Justification was found in the civilizing (meaning modernizing along English lines) and humanizing (often linked to Christian missionizing) role claimed by the British. In the nine decades of the resulting British Raj, the British enjoyed a relative security in the Indian Ocean. The Indian Ocean possessions enriched Britain tremendously. In terms of purchasing British manufactures alone, India (along with the United States) was one of the two largest purchasers of British goods (each importing £21m of goods in 1867). To this were added sales to other Indian Ocean customers, including most notably Australia (importing £8m in that year) and Singapore (accounting for £2m). Muslims, who for so long had enjoyed a high profile in Indian Ocean trade, were now decisively left behind, while the principal non-Indian Ocean competitors, Russia, Germany, and Japan, would for a century challenge the British position in vain.

This chapter will deal with the first period in which ship routes and schedules were freed from the monsoon pattern thanks to the introduction of the steamship. It will examine British concerns with Russian expansionism in the mid-nineteenth century; next look at the imperialist scramble for colonies between 1871 and 1914; then review the British success and problems resulting from World War I; and end with the collapse of the British Empire as a result of the strain from World War II. The great importance of India as the jewel of the British Empire focuses much of the attention in this period on the Raj, the British colony of India.

Continued concern with Russian expansionism

As Russia's power grew, Britain began to fear for its hegemony on the high seas in general and the Indian Ocean in particular. Napoléon's encouragement of Russian expansion into India had planted a seed of aspiration in Russian hearts that haunted such leading British statesmen as Lord Palmerston. In the Russo-Persian War of 1826–1828, Tsar Nicholai I had attacked Persia with such vigor that Russia had been left as the dominant influence over Iran. This success was followed in 1828–1829 by the Russo–Turkish War, in which the Russians had come within striking distance of Constantinople. The Russian-advised shah had then tried to conquer the region of Herat in western Afghanistan in 1838. In reaction, the new Indian governor-general, Lord Aukland, had allied with Ranjit Singh, ruler of the Punjab, against Persia. A joint British and Punjabi force had invaded Afghanistan in 1839, restoring the inept Shah Shuja to the throne of Afghanistan in Kabul. However, the British had discovered that they needed to keep troops in Afghanistan to maintain Shah Shuja on the throne. In 1842, fierce guerrilla warfare had forced the British out of the country. Some 16,000 British troops had been picked off while trying to retreat over the Hindu Kush mountains into India. The anti-British Dost Muhammed had been confirmed as ruler of Afghanistan. In 1848, the marquess of Dalhousie had been appointed governor-general of India with orders to strengthen British India against Russian expansionism. Dalhousie launched the Indian railroad and telegraph systems, and annexed eight more Indian states. In 1852, because the governor of Rangoon had charged two British ship captains with murder, and held them until they had paid £920, Dalhousie declared war on Burma, and absorbed it into India.

British direct rule of India

Despite help in technological advancement, the tightening of Britain's hold on India exacerbated Indian feelings, contributing to an anti-British explosion. In 1857, revolt broke out among the sepoys, the Indian troops under British command. Lord Dalhousie's modernization program had included the replacement of the Brown Bess musket with the Enfield rifle, which efficiently combined the packets for bullet and gunpowder. The soldiers were to bite or tear off the top of the cartridge, pouring the powder down the barrel and then ramming in the bullet. Since the bullet was greased to expedite the task, the word spread that the grease used was from either pig or cow fat (the former forbidden to Muslims, the latter to Hindus), not mutton as the government maintained. Eighty-five sepoys who refused to use the new method found themselves sentenced to hard labor.

Fearing that all sepoys were to be disarmed, a mixed mob of Indian civilians and sepoys murdered some British officers and their wives at a barracks outside Delhi. The sepoys then took charge of the Red Fort and the entire city of Delhi. The revolt rapidly spread, costing the lives of 11,000 British soldiers, although it failed to win the adherence of most of the sepoys. The anti-British hatred stirred by the suppression of the revolt caused Britain to rule that henceforth the sepoys could not compose more than two-thirds of the troops of the British army in India. The main result was the crown's assumption of full responsibility for India. The increasingly fictional Mogul

Empire was abolished, and in 1858 the British East India Company was replaced by direct British rule of India through a viceroy. A British cabinet post for a secretary of state for India was created. Some of the Indian states were allowed to continue under local internal rule by their native princes. The rest were governed directly by the British viceroy. Britain reversed its earlier policy of playing off the Hindus against the Muslims in a new policy of cooperation with the largely Muslim princely elite against the average Hindu Indian. The village common land was mortgaged off to rich families, who were also favored by the tax structure. The peasants sank even further into poverty and debt, while the anglicized Indian princes enjoyed an elitist education in England. For those slightly less privileged Indians who stayed behind, the English-language universities of Calcutta, Bombay, and Madras were founded in 1857.

The establishment of the Raj was completed in 1876 by the proclamation of Queen Victoria as Empress of India in place of the deposed Mogul emperors. An attempt was made to win Indian support for the British crown by pomp and panoply. Periodic durbars (the traditional Mughal royal Indian ceremonies) were held in Delhi. Empress Victoria took pains to try to learn Hindu, and to acquaint herself with Indian affairs. Prince Edward (the later Edward VII) in 1875–1876 initiated British royal tours of India, presenting himself as a true Indian prince by his enthusiasm for polo and for tiger hunts from elephant howdas. New Delhi was laid out as a new, modern city and capital, emphasizing the neo-classical style. George V was crowned emperor of India in New Delhi in 1911, the year the new capital was inaugurated. Justification for British rule was also found in Christian missionary and 'civilizing' efforts (popularized by Rudyard Kipling's poem calling on his fellow Englishmen to 'take up the white man's burden').

British merchants and mariners benefited from a shift from sailing ships to steam ships, encouraged by the opening of the Suez Canal in 1869, with its more direct route between India and Britain, and by the development of watertight iron hulls. Dependence on the monsoon routes and seasons was finally left behind. Native sailors were left as poorly paid manual workers on European-owned ships, while trained Europeans assumed the jobs requiring engineering skills. While steamships were known in the Indian Ocean already in the 1820s, their adoption had been slowed by the introduction of the speedy clipper sailing ships. In 1856, a Scot named Mackinnon had launched a steamship line around the Indian coast. Under the name of the British India Steam Navigation Company, this company's service was now extended to the Persian Gulf and to the ports of East Africa.

The imperialist scramble for colonies

The unification of Germany in 1871 strengthened British resolve for more colonies. Colonies were now added at a dizzying rate, daunting to review.

Many of the new colonies bordered on the Indian Ocean. Burma, the Maldives, most of the Malay Peninsula, and most of southern Africa became British possessions by the 1880s. The British also occupied the Sudan, thereby gaining control over the Sudanese ports on the Red Sea. In 1871, Bechuanaland was formed from territory taken from the Boer Orange Free State after a diamond rush occurred at Kimberly in 1869. Cecil Rhodes bought up the blue-earth soil zones of the diamond rush area, and then came to dominate the gold mines in South African Transvaal. The growing importance of Cape Colony was acknowledged by its being granted responsible government in 1872. Moving up from Singapore, the British founded the colony of Malaya in 1874. In 1875, they won control of the Suez Canal.

The frenzied rate of acquisition of colonies continued in the 1880s. Bahrain's emirs signed treaties of protection with Britain in 1882, the year that Britain occupied Egypt. In 1884, Britain established the colony of New Guinea (which would be transferred to Australia in 1906), and brought British Somaliland under its protection. The following year, Britain finally conquered Burma after three wars (in 1824, 1852, and 1885). The British took over Kenya in 1885 (formalized in 1903), and established a British protectorate over the Cocos Islands. In 1887, the Arab rulers of Trucial Oman (now the United Arab Emirates) began signing treaties of protection with Britain. The same year, the Maldive Islands, southwest of the southern tip of India, became a British protectorate.

Britain's appetite for colonies in the Indian Ocean region (as elsewhere) continued unabated after 1890. The British established a protectorate over Zanzibar in 1890 (formalized in 1913). In 1896, the Federated Malay States was formed under Britain's aegis. Britain's victory in the Boer War (1899–1902) allowed it to consolidate its hold on the entirety of South Africa, crucial for the passage to India, gold, and diamonds. In 1910, Britain created the Union of South Africa as a self-governing dominion within the British Empire. Meanwhile, in 1907 Britain leased the foreshore of Kuwait from the sheik of that emirate, blocking the German and Turkish plan to use Kuwait as the eastern terminus of the planned Baghdad railway. The same year, Britain warned the Ottoman government not to take action when Abd al-Aziz Ibn Saud (the pro-British ruler of the Najd) occupied the southern coast of the Persian Gulf between Kuwait and Qatar. In 1911, Britain assumed control of Bhutan's foreign policy.

This crazed British expansionism encouraged France and Italy to join in the scramble for colonies, including in the Indian Ocean region. France, which had already been allowed to move into South Vietnam and Cambodia in 1862 and 1863 in exchange for its alliance in the Crimean War, now occupied North Vietnam in 1883 and Madagascar in 1896, as well as Djibouti (on the Red Sea) and the Comoros Islands. Italy carved its own colony of Eritrea from Ethiopia's Red Sea coast, as well as Italian Somaliland.

Few independent states remained in the Indian Ocean region. Iran and

Thailand survived by playing the European powers off against each other. This control of the Indian Ocean region, combined with the stimulus of national rivalries between the powers, lay behind Europe's creative ferment in the late nineteenth century evidenced in the fine arts, theater, opera, literature, science, and technology. The rise of the bourgeoisie, eager to prove its own fine cultural taste in the arts *vis-à-vis* the aristocracy, played its part in this phenomenon. By 1914, the main goods being exported from the Indian Ocean area were oil from the Persian Gulf, Indonesia, and Burma; cotton yarn, foodstuffs, tea, and raw materials from India and Sri Lanka; minerals, wheat, fruit, wine, and wool from Africa and Australia; sugar from the Mascarene Islands; phosphate from Christmas Island; and rubber and tin from Indonesia and Malaysia.

Inspired by Britain's imperialist success, in 1891 the Round Table Group was founded. This private organization was the creation of Lord Natty Rothschild, son of Lionel and grandson of Nathan Rothschild. Natty was a member of parliament and, since 1885, a baron, which made him the first Jewish peer in Great Britain. Natty's younger brother Alfred was director of the Bank of England. Support came from Cecil Rhodes as well. The group's aim was to pull together business and Conservative political leaders to work toward creating a new global order, resting on the British Empire as its core base. The stated hope was to avoid the misery and tragedy which war brought. The stability that such a scheme might bring to Anglo hegemony offered an additional incentive. The first step was to be the creation of a League of Nations, to be given extensive political and military powers worldwide. H. G. Wells's *Outline of History* in 1920 argued that only a rationally ordered global-state could save the world from eventual self-destruction.

The impact of World War I

The two world wars of the twentieth century weakened British power in the Indian Ocean region. In 1885, the first meeting of the Hindu-dominated Indian National Congress Party was held, in Bombay. Viceroy Lord Dufferin initially approved of the new organization, dominated as it was by pro-British Hindus. In 1906, Muslims formed a comparable organization, the Muslim League. India was promised home rule in exchange for its cooperation with Britain in World War I. This support was given, but after the war Britain showed no interest in the subject. Hindu dissatisfaction found its most famous spokesman during World War I in Mohandas *Mahatma* ('Great Soul') Gandhi, head of the Indian National Congress. Gandhi, a native of Gujarat, trained as a lawyer at London's Inns of Court. As a legal advisor to an Indian firm in Durban in South Africa, he became involved in the civil rights struggle of the local Indians. With the outbreak of World War I, Gandhi carried his campaign back to his home country.

There he condemned British Christianity as hypocritical, and called for 'godly Hinduism' to stand up to the godless British. He took on the role of a political guru, impressing the Hindu masses with his simple life style and chastity, to the complaints of Winston Churchill, who thought it all a calculated sham. Gandhi harried the British with his call for *ahimsa* ('passive resistance') based on *satyagraha* ('truth' or 'soul force'). Since distinctly non-passive riots tended to accompany Gandhi's calls for *ahimsa*, Gandhi was placed under house arrest in Bombay.

Kaiser Wilhelm II for his part tried to create an Indian revolt against the British at the end of the war. The Germans convinced the Ottoman sultan (who was also the Sunni caliph) to command all Muslims to launch a *jihad* against the British. The call was especially directed to the Indian Muslims. Indian revolutionary leaders gathered in Berlin for training and instructions. The Sikhs of the Punjab rebelled in 1914–1915 under the slogan of 'Asia for the Asians.' On Christmas day of 1915, German agents were sent to Thailand to prepare an Indian uprising. In 1917, a Hindu holy liberation war broke out in Bengal, accompanied by terrorism. Anti-terrorist laws suspended the legal process for political offenses, and allowed trial without jury, and suspended the assumption of innocence on the part of defendants. The insurrection might have been more serious had not the British prime minister David Lloyd George in 1917 promised that if India would stay loyal to Britain, it would receive 'responsible government' at the end of the war. The Germans urged the amir of Afghanistan to invade British India, but the requested invasion came too late – in 1919.

Britain's wartime position in the Indian Ocean was strengthened by Prime Minister Louis Botha of the Union of South Africa, who brought his dominion into the war on the British side despite strong opposition from the Afrikaners. Egypt was made a British protectorate in 1914. Treaties of protection signed by the ruler of Qatar with Britain in 1916 filled in British control of the south shore of the Persian Gulf. British naval control of the East African coastal waters allowed the British to drive the Germans out of East Africa by the end of 1917. The British then began to export cotton, coffee, sisal, and rubber from Tanganyika. Europeans and Asians dominated the East African trade. In 1918, the British invaded Iraq. The jubilant Kurds began to set up their own state in northern Iraq, an area that the Turks also hoped to continue to rule, but both plans were undone due to British interest in the rich oil deposits of the region. Winston Churchill as secretary of war even approved a request to use poison gas to quell the Kurds (a plan later carried out by Saddam Hussein), but this measure proved to be unnecessary. A British oil company (with France holding a quarter share) was founded to exploit these oil fields.

To judge by a political map of the world, the British Empire came out of World War I stronger than ever. It took charge of the previous German colonies in Africa, including Tanganyika on the Indian Ocean, which was officially placed under its administration by a League of Nations mandate in 1922. German Northeast New Guinea became an Australian mandate. With the final suppression of Zanzibar's slave trade, the Arabs lost their economic and social prominence in East Africa, and Zanzibar lost its importance to Mombasa, Kenya, and the new port of Dar es Salaam, Tanganyika. Nevertheless, American, Japanese, and continental European manufactures began to compete in the Indian market.

Three major British League of Nation mandates were also gained in the Middle East: Jordan, Palestine, and Iraq. The Ottoman alliance with Germany in World War I led to an invasion of the Ottoman Levant by British troops. When in 1914 the sultan-caliph of Istanbul called on all Muslims to fight the British, the British supported the emir of Mecca, the Hashimite Sharif Hussein. As hereditary lord of the holy city of Mecca, and as a descendent of the prophet Muhammed (which the Ottoman sultan-caliph was not), Hussein carried great weight. T.E. Lawrence and Emir Hussein conquered Aqaba in 1917; General Edmund Allenby led a British army from Egypt into Palestine, Lebanon, and Syria; and another British army coming from India conquered Iraq. The British promised the emir of Kuwait independence from Iraq in exchange for his help in taking Iraq in 1917. In 1919, the Paris Peace Conference established Iraq as a British mandate, with another slice of Iraq being given to Saudi Arabia. As a result of Iraqi protests against British control, in 1921 the British made Hussein's son Feisal king of Iraq (as his brother Abdullah was made king of Jordan). Full independence followed in 1932. Even at that, most Iraqis viewed the government as an imposition of the British, and resentment continued.

Sir Herbert Samuel headed the British mandate government of Palestine set up in 1920. He was the brother of Marcus Samuel who had established Shell Oil together with Rothschild financial backing, and who had developed the oil fields of Borneo in cooperation with the merged Dutch Royal Oil. Jewish immigrants were allowed to enter Palestine in large numbers in accord with the British policy of encouraging a future Jewish state in the region. When Emir Hussein of Mecca objected, the British withdrew their protection from him. As a result, Ibn Saud of Saudi Arabia and his Wahhabi reform movement took the Hejaz (the kingdom along the Red Sea coast of the Arabian Peninsula) from Hussein in 1924–1925. The British had not intended Hussein to be driven out, and their displeasure caused the Saudis in 1924 to turn to the American Rockefeller interests for oil development.

In 1922, Britain (having declared a protectorate over Egypt in 1914) granted Egypt independence under King Fuad I. The British reserved certain rights, including the overseeing of security of imperial communications, defense, protection of foreign interests and minorities, and control of the Sudan. General Edmund Allenby retained the title of high commissioner of Egypt. The French as allies received Lebanon and Syria. Iran was also held in the British sphere of interest. In 1921, a British-backed coup toppled the Qajar shah, who had shown hostility to the British during the war. Colonel Reza Khan Pahlavi led the military coup, and assumed the title of shah himself. In gratitude to the British, he encouraged British business investment and Europeanization. In 1923, work began on providing Singapore with dockyard facilities designed to make it an updated naval stronghold to continue to dominate the Strait of Malacca. (However, the space provided was too restricted to accommodate a fleet large enough for the job, as the rapid Japanese conquest in World War II would demonstrate.)

Despite this appearance of strength, Britain had been overstrained in manpower and financing by World War I, and was further weakened by the Great Depression of the 1930s. Britain lost many of its markets during the war to the United States and Japan, and at the war's end found that it could not regain them, due to its outmoded and less efficient factories. The traditional British industries of coal and iron had been losing their share of world production to up-and-coming industries like oil, steel, chemicals, machine goods, and electrical goods. The British had lagged behind the Americans in introducing standardization and mass production. Nor were the British factories brought up to date after the war, Britain being too burdened with war debts.

Eamon De Valera, prime minister of Eire, took advantage of Edward VIII's abdication of the throne 'for the woman I love' and British concern with the rise of Hitler to proclaim a fully independent republic in 1937. In 1948, Eire completed the detachment from England by seceding from the British Commonwealth. The Middle Eastern segment of the British Empire created problems as well. The Egyptian nationalist leader Saad Zaghlul of the Wafd Party pushed for Egyptian independence. Although Zaghlul was elected prime minister in 1923, he resigned in frustration the following year when Allenby banned all political demonstrations. In 1931, King Fuad suspended the Wafd government and assumed temporary dictatorial power down to 1936. By that time, the Wafd Party had grown sufficiently concerned over Mussolini's imperialist designs in the region to cooperate with both the high commissioner and the king. Stability was further served when, that same year, Fuad died and was followed by his initially popular 16-year-old son Farouk.

Challenge in India

Indian leaders also became more outspoken in their demands. Gandhi demanded that the British honor their promise of home rule, and rallied mass demonstrations in 1919. The British responded with repression, massacring 400 Sikh demonstrators at Amritsar alone. However, with a democratic system to answer to back home, the British government could no longer ignore the impact on voter opinion of such brutal actions. So, already in 1919, the secretary of state for India, Edwing Montagu, and the viceroy of India, Lord Chelmsford, announced the Montagu–Chelmsford reforms, in hopes that these measures might console Indians for not receiving home rule. These changes would have given the headship of some of the government departments to elected Indian ministers, along with an extended suffrage for native Indians, in 1922.

In rallying Indians around the call for home rule, Gandhi as head of the Indian National Congress Party developed methods designed to take advantage of Britain's democracy and its power of public opinion. He persuaded Congress Party leaders to reject their British functions, titles, and decorations. His followers removed their children from government schools, refused to acknowledge British courts, left their government jobs, and stopped voting and paying taxes.

Most effectively, Gandhi employed boycotting of British goods, turning instead to cottage industries. Gandhi's own family began spinning cloth, and soon cloth was being produced in homes all over India, creating a major loss of market for the British textile industry. In 1922, the British imprisoned Gandhi, but the *ahimsa* movement continued under Jawaharlal Nehru and other lieutenants of Gandhi. In 1924, Gandhi was released. From this point on, India ceased to float the British economy, which threw Britain into a permanent crisis that was only magnified by subsequent attempts to regain control of the Indian consumers.

During the Great Depression, Gandhi escalated his movement still further. In 1930, the 61-year-old Gandhi, wearing only the loincloth of the Indian peasant, led a march through Gujarat to the sea to obtain sea salt, circumventing the British tax on store-bought salt. Many thousands of people joined the march, which lasted twenty-four days and covered 241 miles. Gandhi was arrested soon after, along with 60,000 of his followers, including Nehru. But neither this move nor an attempt of the British viceroys to play the Muslims off against the Hindus by favoring the Muslim League under Muhammed Ali Jinnah slowed India's defiance against British control.

World War II

After Britain and Nazi Germany in September 1939 declared what grew into World War II, Hitler's rapid victories encouraged some of the German leaders to plan to challenge the British Empire for its commanding position in the Indian Ocean. A memorandum by Erich Raeder, head of the German navy, written in the summer of 1940 spoke of the United States and Britain, the two 'Anglo-Saxon powers,' as the natural enemies of the Third Reich. It stated that Germany had to become a first-class naval power to achieve its goals. In a report of June 1940, Rear Admiral Kurt Fricke outlined a plan for annexations of overseas protectorates and the formation of client states in a new German world empire. Admiral Rolf Carls, commander of Naval Group North, wrote in a memorandum in the summer of 1940 that Germany would need to establish many naval bases in the Indian Ocean and Atlantic, and take over or dominate such entry points into the Indian Ocean as South Africa, Egypt, Aden, Socotra, Iran (with its oil), Indonesia, north Borneo, and the Cocos Islands. A pro-German Indian Legion, consisting mainly of Indian prisoners of war in Germany, was formed to help the Germans conquer India from the British. Iraq joined the war on the side of Britain, despite rampant anti-British sentiment. In South Africa, one of the main control points into the Indian Ocean, the Afrikaners were pro-German, even after Hitler conquered the Netherlands. South Africa's President Herzog made a motion in his colony's House of Assembly, after the other dominions had followed Britain into declaring war on Hitler's Germany, that South Africa make peace with Germany. Only the insistence of the British elements in the House defeated the proposal. Prime Minister Jan Smuts then brought South Africa into the war on the British side, despite great protests and the interning of thousands of people for antiwar activities.

Hitler gave priority to his Operation Sea Lion (*Seelöwen*), aimed at the conquest of Britain, with the consequent absorption of its position on the high seas and colonial holdings. The strength of the British fleet meant that Hitler required control of the island's air space to carry troops for an invasion. The German air force accordingly sent its planes to sweep aside the planes of the Royal Air Force. The resulting Battle of Britain lasted from August to October 1940. However, the British, encouraged by the gifted oratory of Winston Churchill, only hardened their resolve to hold out. In October 1940, Hitler called off the air war on Britain. In the meantime, Italy had occupied British Somaliland (held to 1941).

In the spring of 1941, Hitler proposed to the Japanese a joint invasion of India. This so-called 'Operation Orient' called for German troops to advance through Egypt, Iraq, and Iran into western India, while Japan would simultaneously work its way through Southeast Asia into eastern India. Japan's main interest in the region was the oil (most particularly of Indonesia) essential to maintain the Japanese industry and war machine. Readying for the push to take Egypt, Hitler allied with Turkey, and briefly linked up with Iraqi rebels fighting against British control, assigning German officers to train Iraqi rebel troops. He then sent German forces under General Erwin Rommel, the 'Desert Fox,' to advance from Libya to the conquest of Egypt from Britain. Pro-German sentiment was strong among Egyptians. At this point, Rommel's forces were suddenly depleted by Hitler's invasion of Russia on 22 June 1941, against the advice of Japan.

Hitler's attack on the Soviet Union at a time when Germany was coming so close to its goal in Egypt, was a blunder that turned a probable victory into failure. Fear of a surprise attack by Stalin while the German forces were involved in the Middle East played a role. Britain in 1941 joined the

Soviet Union in invading Iran, and toppling the pro-German Shah Reza Khan. They replaced him with his 21-year-old son Muhammed Reza Pahlavi, who had been thoroughly westernized by his education near Lausanne, Switzerland. Hitler also managed to bring the United States into the war, by his encouragement of his ally Japan to assert its power in Asian waters. German and Japanese plans for Asia agreed on the desirability of challenging the Anglo position in the Indian Ocean, although this plan was more of a priority for the Japanese than for the Nazis.

The Japanese grab for the Indian Ocean

Germany's need for an alliance with Japan to achieve success in the Indian Ocean had been emphasized already in a 1940 memorandum by Rolf Carls. Japan's evolution over the past century had prepared it to jump at this chance to make a bid for its share of the wealth and power of the Indian Ocean. Like the Western powers before it, Japan had turned to winning new markets overseas for its burgeoning industrial production. In 1872, Japan took control of the Ryuku Islands, in 1875 the Kurile Islands, in 1894 Korea, in 1895 Taiwan, the Pescadores Islands, and southern Manchuria, in 1905 South Sakhalin and Port Arthur, and in 1918 Tsingtao and Kiaochow Bay in China, and islands won from Germany in the northern Pacific. The Great Depression motivated Japan to invade more of China, in an effort to provide adequate raw materials and consumer market to keep the Japanese economy healthy. In 1931, Japan conquered the rest of Manchuria, and occupied part of Inner Mongolia. In 1936, a military regime took power in Japan, ending popular rights and freedoms. In 1937, Japan invaded China proper, but the Chinese head of state, Chiang Kai Shek, continued to resist. By the time General Tojo took charge of the Japanese government in 1941, only rubber-stamp cabinets remained.

General Tojo concentrated on completing the Japanese occupation of Vietnam, bringing Japanese power close to the sensitive eastern entry point to the Indian Ocean through the Strait of Malacca. Convinced of the need for bringing American weight to bear on the side of the British, despite the strong mood of isolationism in his country, US President F.D. Roosevelt in July 1941 placed a total embargo on all exports to Japan. This cut oil imports into Japan to a strangling 10 percent of their previous volume. Japan was faced with the choice of either breaking the US naval hold on the route to the oil sources of the Indian Ocean and Indonesia or withdrawing from China. Tojo's offer to leave Vietnam while staying in China was not accepted.

As a result, Tojo began to prepare his air force for an attack on the American forces, to push the blockading American ships out of the way, training his pilots at Kogoshima Bay in southern Kyushu. Counting on Hitler's victories in Europe to keep the primarily Europe-oriented Americans from hitting back, Japan struck. On 7 December 1941, Japanese forces destroyed the US fleet stationed at Pearl Harbor, Hawaii. The US ambassador had warned from Tokyo that Japan might attack with dramatic suddenness. FDR had for weeks been expecting an attack somewhere, most likely in the Philippines. At Pearl Harbor, enemy submarines had been sighted, and the approaching planes had actually been detected by radar well before the attack. Yet the American forces there that Sunday morning were not put on alert. The ill-fated fleet was bunched close together, no planes were in the air, and no anti-torpedo nets were placed in the harbor. However, three aircraft carriers were safely out at sea during the attack.

Eight or nine hours later, the Japanese destroyed all the bomber and fighter planes at Manila in the Philippines. Also on that same day of 7 December 1941, a Japanese army landed in Malaya. On 17 December 1941, the Japanese began their conquest of the Dutch East Indies and its oil by landing at Sarawak and pushing on into northwest Borneo. Sumatra and the Celebes were subdued by Japan by the end of February, and Java in March 1942. The Japanese occupied Manila in January 1942, and completed the conquest of the Philippines that May. The Solomons, Ellice Island, Gilbert Island, New Guinea, and the western Aleutians were also occupied by early 1942. Moving south through Malaya, a Japanese army captured Singapore in February 1942. Thailand was allowed to keep considerable autonomy. Most of the affected areas were content to see the Japanese drive out their European colonial masters, but the Filipinos, who had been promised imminent independence by the United States, launched an anti-Japanese resistance movement.

The challenge to the British in the Indian Ocean

In response to a call from Hitler for an immediate Japanese occupation of Madagascar (then in the hands of friendly Vichy French officials) in order to block the southwestern entry into the Indian Ocean to the Anglo powers, on 26 March 1942 a Japanese fleet entered the Indian Ocean and drove the British naval forces from Sri Lanka, as a preliminary step for conquering Madagascar. The British used Diego Garcia Island in the central Indian Ocean to keep a watch out for German and Japanese destroyers and submarines. However, the stalling of German troops short of Moscow convinced the Japanese to call their surface fleet back out of the Indian Ocean for the time being. Instead, Japan and Germany sent U-boats to Madagascar. However, before they could arrive, the British were alerted to the threat by South Africa's Jan Smuts, and sent a force that took control of the island. The bomber attack on Japan in April 1942 led by James Doolittle, in response to the Japanese bombing of Pearl Harbor, turned Japanese attention away from Madagascar to focus its efforts on capturing Midway Island.

In May 1942, General Rommel pushed into Egypt, capturing three coastal towns. Happy crowds chanted Rommel's name in the streets of Cairo, and rumor had it that King Farouk was preparing to appoint a pro-German prime minister. Soon after, the Germans were halted by British troops seventy miles west of Alexandria at the first battle of El Alamein. In October 1942, a British counter-offensive under General Bernard Montgomery pushed Rommel's force back to the west at the second battle of El Alamein. Helped by the American invasion of the Maghreb, the British forces expelled Rommel's army from Egypt by 12 November 1942. Trapped between American forces moving east and British forces moving west, German forces were forced to surrender North Africa altogether in May 1943.

Germany's failure to take Egypt and Germany's problems with the war in Europe left the principal Axis role in the Indian Ocean to its ally, Japan. Some Indians urged a Japanese attack on British interests in their country. In 1939, as was his right, the British viceroy Lord Linlithgow had declared India to be at war with Germany, underscoring the lack of input by Indians regarding their own fate. However, a group of Indians now formed a 'Free India' government in Singapore, under the protection of the Japanese, and urged the Japanese to push on through Burma to free India. Between January and May 1942, the Japanese conquered Burma, with Indian volunteers of the Free India government fighting alongside the Japanese against the British. With Japanese troops occupying the eastern and southern portions of Southeast Asia, Mahatma Gandhi in July 1942 called on the British to leave India. Gandhi and the entire Indian National Congress Party leadership were arrested, and British soldiers crushed the resulting mass protests by firing into the crowds.

Despite a British campaign to reconquer Burma in August 1943, the Japanese pushed ahead with their invasion of India. In March 1944, Japanese and rebel Indian forces invaded Assam province. Gandhi prepared for a massive campaign of civil disobedience to force the British out, leading to a week of riots and attacks on the British by his followers. However, 250,000 US servicemen were sent to India to help the British hold control. The Indian Muslims, frightened by the Hindu-Japanese cooperation, generally remained loyal to Britain throughout the war, and the Sikh soldiers likewise helped the British against the rebellious Hindus. Britain again promised home rule to India after the war if the Hindus would cooperate. As a result, in June 1944, the Japanese forces and their rebel Hindu allies were defeated at the battle of Imphal and forced back out of India.

The failure of Hitler's challenge

In February 1943, the Russians began to push back the German invaders with their victory at the battle of Stalingrad (Volgograd). After General Rommel's troops in North Africa were obliged to surrender at Tunis in

May 1943, the Germans were steadily pushed back in Europe until in April 1945 the American and Russian forces met on the Elbe River.

The United States then turned its effort to completing its victory over Japan. The Japanese military push south had been halted in May 1942 by the battle of the Coral Sea and to the east at Midway. In August 1942, the Americans had prevented a renewal of the Japanese onslaught by capturing a newly built airstrip on Guadalcanal in the Solomon Islands. In the north, the Japanese were turned back from the Aleutian Islands. After that, the American and British forces steadily pushed back the Japanese. While the British reconquered Burma, the Americans asserted their control over the Solomon Islands in 1943; the Marshall Islands, the Carolinas, the Marianas, New Guinea, the Admiralties in 1944, and the Philippines by January 1945. The Ryuku Islands, centered on Okinawa and Iwo Jima, were taken by June 1945. After the atomic bomb destruction of the Japanese cities of Hiroshima and Nagasaki, on 6 and 7 August respectively, the Mikado Hirohito broadcast surrender on 2 September 1945. General Tojo was hanged in 1948.

The German and Japanese efforts had failed to bring them the wealth and power of the enchanting Indian Ocean. However, they did cause the collapse of the British Empire (although the United States and Britain maintained a strong hand indirectly around the Indian Ocean, where the oil wealth of its northwestern and northeastern corners was by now the one single most important trading commodity). Britain pulled out of Egypt in 1946 (except for keeping 80,000 men to guard the Suez Canal down to 1954), and out of Palestine, Nepal, and Sikkim in 1947. The loss of India the next year represented the main blow to the British position in the Indian Ocean. India had been promised full dominion status after World War II, if it remained loyal in the war. Prime Minister Clement Atlee followed up on this promise, setting a general election in India in 1946. Atlee was committed to withdrawing from the colonies in order to save money for his new social welfare program in Great Britain. Britain was generally tired of the empire, which had come to be more of a drain than a support. After the strain of two world wars, with aging factories unable to compete with the newer equipment of the United States and of rebuilt Germany and Japan, Britain owed £2.5 billion to its dominions, and India was one of its main creditors.

In the elections in India, Mahatma Gandhi's Congress Party won most of the Hindu vote, and Jinnah's Muslim League Party most of the Islamic vote. A constituent assembly met in July 1946, but before it could work out a new government, a bitter war erupted in August between India's Hindus and Muslims. Hindus were massacred in Bengal, where the Muslim League announced the creation of a separate Muslim nation. In 1948, the pro-Hindu admiral Lord Louis Mountbatten, George VI's cousin and commander of the Allied forces in Southeast Asia in World War II, was appointed as India's last viceroy, and assigned to find a solution. Jinnah, in the last stages of cancer, was determined to win a Muslim state before his death. Since Gandhi was for his part trying to be conciliatory, Mountbatten decided upon partition. One Hindu extremist subsequently assassinated Gandhi for his cooperation with this concession. Perhaps wanting to avoid protests, Mountbatten waited until the last minute to announce the new borders. Taken by surprise, great numbers of Muslims and Hindus flocked to rush to their respective sides of the border. Many lost their lives in the process.

In the wake of the Indian success, Burma, Sri Lanka (Ceylon), and Malaya were also given their independence (the first two in 1948, the last in 1957). Britain pulled out of Sudan in 1956. The French left Vietnam in 1954 and Madagascar in 1958. In 1960, British Somaliland was merged into an independent Somalia. Britain's ties to South Africa ended with the establishment of the Republic of South Africa in 1961. Britain withdrew from Kuwait and Tanganyika in 1961, and from Aden, Kenya and Zanzibar in 1963. In that latter year, Singapore, north Borneo, and Sarawak joined with Malaya to form Malasia (although Singapore pulled back out two years later). In 1965, the Maldives won independence. Bahrain, Qatar, and the United Arab Emirates followed in 1971. The long list of lands falling away from the British Empire was as rapid and as dizzying to recite as the similar list of lands brought into the empire a little under a century before.

In this way, Britain's period of leadership in the Indian Ocean played out, first challenged unsuccessfully by the Russians, but then fatally eroded by the rivalry of the Germans and Japanese. The heady expectation of success on the world scene had inspired one of the greatest outpourings of cultural and scientific creativity in this period from London and Paris through Berlin to St. Petersburg. The nationalism originally sparked by the French Revolution and now driven to a fever pitch by imperialism underlay such celebrations of national pride or interest as the writings of Rudyard Kipling, Ibsen, and Tolstoy, and the music of Wagner, Grieg, and Mussorgsky. The intellectual ferment spilled over to the United States and to virtually every cosmopolitan center of the Atlantic and European world. The Japanese creative genius, in contrast, was mainly channeled into catching up on Western culture. Many Britons had claimed the right to dominate the Indian Ocean region by their tutelage of the local inhabitants in democracy, rights, freedoms, and education. India, Malaysia, and Singapore most notably seemed to have emerged from the experience with such a successful transformation. The British exerted the least influence on Middle Eastern countries (most notably Iraq), but Britain's presence there was brief, and countered by a vigorous local tradition resistant to imported values. However, the continued surge of fundamentalist and authoritarian Islam and Hinduism place in question the permanence of such British reforms.

With Britain's retreat, the Indian Ocean region remained, as always, a centrally coveted prize in global power interests, and not least for its great oil deposits. Even though India lacked oil, its geographic location was still of great strategic importance, surrounded as this vast and heavily populated country was by countries that did have oil (from Indonesia in the east to Iran, Iraq, and Saudi Arabia to the west). The collapse of the British Empire left behind a struggle between two new world contestants – the United States and the Soviet Union.

Further reading

On British India: Judith M. Brown, *Gandhi: Prisoner of Hope* (New Haven, Connecticut: Yale University Press, 1989); and Lawrence James, *Raj: The Making and Unmaking of British India* (New York: St. Martin's Griffin, 1997).

On the British Empire: Lawrence James, *The Rise and Fall of the British Empire* (New York: St. Martin's Griffin, 1994); P.J. Marshall, *The Cambridge Illustrated History of the British Empire* (Cambridge: Cambridge University Press, 1996); P.J. Cain and A.G. Hopkins, *British Imperialism, 1688–2000* (Edinburgh: Longman, 2002); T.O. Lloyd, *The British Empire* (Oxford: Oxford University, 1984); and Winfried Baumgart, *Imperialism: The Idea and Reality of British and French Colonial Expansion, 1880–1914* (New York: Oxford University Press, 1982).

On the wars: Martin Gilbert, *The First World War: A Complete History* (New York: H. Holt, 1994); John Keegan (ed.), *Times Atlas of the Second World War* (New York: Harper and Row, 1989); David Reynolds, *The Creation of the Anglo-American Alliance, 1937–1941: A Study in Competitive Cooperation* (London: Europa, 1981); Charles S. Thomas, *The German Navy in the Nazi Era* (Annapolis, Maryland: Naval Institute Press, 1990); and Gerhard L. Weinberg, *A World At Arms: A Global History of World War II* (New York: Cambridge University, 1994).

Chapter 8

The Cold War period

The collapse of two of the three main challengers to Anglo hegemony in the Indian Ocean (Japan and Germany) left a bipolar struggle between Russia and the Anglo world, now dominated by the United States. Already in the interwar period, American business interests had been rapidly growing in the Indian Ocean area. American products were pouring into Malaya, which had been enriched by a rubber-growing boom during World War I. Such new imperial enterprises as Persian Gulf oil drilling depended on American capital. This fact was of special importance as the Middle East was providing the West with 70 percent of its oil by 1951.

Oil was the most crucial raw material in the Indian Ocean region in this period. Anglo prominence in the region's commerce continued, but now shifted its center of control from London to New York and Washington, DC. This chapter will review the Soviet challenge starting with the post-war Stalin era (1945–1953) and working through that of Krushchev (premier 1958–1964) and of Brezhnev (president 1977–1982) to the collapse of the Soviet Union under Gorbachev (president 1985–1991).

The rivalry between the United States and the Soviet Union was bound to focus on the Indian Ocean. At the beginning of the twentieth century, the American admiral Alfred Thayer Mahan had reminded his country that the world's future and control of Asia belonged to whatever power controlled the Indian Ocean. The oil of the lands on the northwestern edge of the Indian Ocean, upon which Western Europe and Japan depended to run their industries, was the raw material most vital to American interests. Other important regional raw materials included uranium, lithium, beryllium, zirconium, mercury, platinum, diamonds, manganese, and chromium. The Indian Ocean also provided the ideal area for firing nuclear missiles against the nations of Asia as far away as China and Russia. Furthermore, India was of crucial interest due to its location between the oil-rich Persian Gulf and Indonesian waters, and its status as the world's largest democracy and fifth largest economy. Cognizant of this state of affairs, the Indian National Congress Party that led the Indian government through the Cold War period tried to play off the Soviet Union against the United States.

It was dominated by three generations of one family, from Jawaharlal Nehru (prime minister from 1947 to 1964) through his daughter Indira Gandhi (1966–1977; 1980–1984) to Indira's son Rajiv Gandhi (1984–1989).

Jawaharlal Nehru was the son of an Anglicized Brahmin-class lawyer at Allahabad, and was schooled at Harrow, Trinity College, Cambridge, and the Middle Temple Inn of Court in London. He was opposed to a prolongation of Anglo power through American influence in and around India, and asserted his Indian identity by wearing a white native outfit with a white cotton cap. His views leaned away from Hinduism toward theosophy in religion, and away from capitalism toward socialism in political ideology. He visited the Soviet Union in the 1920s. After Mahatma Gandhi was assassinated in 1948 (by a Hindu who felt he had been too generous to Muslims), Nehru began half a century of his dynasty's leadership of the Indian government. He declared Hindi the official language, but allowed English to share that status when the Dravidian South resisted Hindi monolingualism. He brought down a hornet's nest of long-term problems on India's head by forbidding the largely Muslim Kashmiris to hold a plebiscite on whether Kashmir should return to Pakistan, with the shaky rationalization that Kashmir's ruler preferred to keep his principality as a part of India. Infusing the Congress Party with his democratic socialist ideology, Nehru abolished the social category of *untouchable*, and withdrew official recognition from the caste system. Women were allowed to inherit and own property, and to divorce, and polygamy was prohibited. The economy was rigidly controlled through a large number of regulatory and licensing laws.

Stalin's rule

As a result of Russian gains from World War II, Stalin's Russia became a major threat to Anglo dominance in the Indian Ocean. Stalin used the Russian occupation of Eastern Europe to incorporate Estonia, Latvia, and Lithuania into the Soviet Union, and to establish communist puppet states in Poland, Czechoslovakia, Hungary, Romania, Bulgaria, Albania, and East Germany. After Stalin massed troops on the Turkish border, and refused for a time to pull Russian occupying troops out of Iran, Truman blocked Russian expansion toward the Mediterranean with the Truman doctrine in March 1947, under which money and troops were sent to strengthen Turkey and Greece. Truman also launched the economic recovery of western Europe with the Marshall Plan in the same year, the administration's defenders of the plan arguing, among other reasons, that a re-strengthened free Europe could help to safeguard Middle Eastern oil supplies. With America shoring up its position in western Europe, communist expansionism focused on Asia. At the close of World War II, Stalin had been able to occupy North Korea and to set up a communist state there. Mao Tse-Tung's success in 1949 further strengthened Stalin, with whom Mao signed an alliance. The ability of the communist North Koreans, with Chinese help, to hold their own against Anglo intervention in the Korean War (1950–1953) also boosted Stalin's position.

The problems that Germany had experienced due to oil shortage in the two world wars had clearly demonstrated the importance of controlling the world oil supplies. Even the peace-time reliance of the United States and its allies on the cheap and abundant oil of the Indian Ocean area, from the Persian Gulf to Indonesia, added a new level of urgency to control of the region. Seven Anglo oil companies (five American and two British) had come to dominate the flow of oil from the Indian Ocean: Exxon, Socal or Chevron, and Mobil (all three stemming originally from Rockefeller oil holdings), Texaco (founded by Jim Hogg), Gulf (founded by Andrew Mellon), Shell Oil (formed by a merger of British Royal and Dutch Shell Oil Companies), and British Petroleum (created by Winston Churchill as a British government company). Since 1928, these companies had co-operated closely in controlling world oil prices and supplies. Gulf Oil and British Petroleum discovered oil in Bahrain in 1932 and in Kuwait in 1934. Chevron had developed Saudi Arabian oil since 1933, with Texaco joining in 1936. In 1948, Aramco was formed, when Chevron and Texaco allowed Exxon and Mobil to join them in selling Saudi Arabian oil. The French and Italians were resentful that they were left on the margins. Enrico Mattei, head of the Italian state oil company Agip, referred to the seven great Anglo oil companies sarcastically as the Seven Sisters. Under its new king, Idris, Libya (now freed from Italian colonial rule as a result of World War II) turned to making deals with American oil companies. In 1954, Mattei started buying oil from the Soviet Union, but in 1962 died in a plane crash that might have been sabotage. France, led by Jean Monnet, reacted in its own way by trying to base French energy more on coal, stressing the European Coal and Steel Community, but to little effect.

A challenge to the Anglo control of Iran's oil was evidenced in 1951, when Dr. Mohammed Mossadeq, of a wealthy landowning family, called for Iran to receive the same deal of a 50:50 split control between the government and oil companies that Venezuela had received for its oil sales in 1945. The Iranian prime minister General Razmara, who opposed Mossadeq, was shot down outside a mosque. Mossadeq then became prime minister himself, and in 1953 nationalized the Anglo-Iranian Oil Company. The British navy refused to let Iranian oil be exported, clamping a blockade on the Persian Gulf. In 1953, the Iranian army drove out Mossadeq, with the cooperation of the young Shah Muhammed Rizah Pahlevi. The Central Intelligence Agency (CIA) played a key role in the coup, and in 1954 the US oil companies were allowed to join in the British companies' extraction of Iranian petroleum. The British prime minister Winston Churchill (1951–1955) retreated from the patrolling of Anglo interests in the Mediterranean and Asia, a task now assumed by the United States.

Krushchev's challenge

Stalin's competition with the Anglo world was continued by two Russian worker leaders from the Ukraine, who had made their way up through the ranks: Nikita Krushchev and Leonid Brezhnev. Krushchev, who led the Soviet Union from 1953 to 1964, was the son of a coal miner from Kursk. He rose through the posts of mine foreman, secretary of the Moscow Communist Party, secretary of the Ukrainian Communist Party, and agricultural secretary to the Central Committee. Krushchev encouraged national liberation movements. In 1955, he traveled to India, Burma, and Afghanistan. Following up on a Soviet–Indian trade agreement made in 1953, he offered India military aid and the construction of a steel plant. Loans were also granted to Iraq, Afghanistan, and North Yemen. When Chinese and Indian forces clashed on their mutual border in 1959, Krushchev cancelled the Soviet atomic agreement with China, and offered India far larger loans than the Soviet Union had ever given China. Accepting the fiction of the British Commonwealth, Nehru invited Queen Elizabeth to visit India in 1961. However, when Portugal was obliged to evacuate Goa that same year, Nehru looked for support not to the West, but to the Soviet Union and communist China. Communist politicians were able to win office in Bengal (Calcutta) and Kerala (Calicut and Cochin). In reaction, the Americans drew closer to Pakistan, setting up military bases there and pumping in military aid. In 1955, Nehru visited Moscow again, and later that year Krushchev visited Delhi. Visits were also exchanged with China's Mao Tse-Tung. However, India's relations with communist China soured when in 1959 Chinese troops occupied Tibet, and the Dalai Lama fled to Nepal. When Nehru showed sympathy for the Tibetans, Chinese raiding parties invaded Kashmir. This development served to tighten the cooperation between India and the Soviet Union. Nehru worked to create a pro-Russian Afro-Asian block led by India.

The Soviet campaign in the Third World convinced the US government that the remaining European colonial system was no longer tenable. The Suez crisis of 1957 forced the turning point in policy. In 1955, Egypt's Gamal Abdul Nasser had begun to purchase arms from the Russians. The Eisenhower administration expressed its displeasure the next year by withdrawing its promise to build a new Aswan High Dam and holding back loans. Nasser won a Russian promise to build the dam, and grabbed the canal from the British. In reaction, British, French, and Israeli troops reoccupied the canal in the Suez War of 1957. Anxious not to drive the Arabs and Africa into the Soviet camp, Eisenhower's government obliged the British and allied troops to withdraw.

Short-term problems resulted. The Russians built the Aswan High Dam in the coming years, and gave financial aid to Egypt. In 1957, King Idris of Libya created a glut of oil in his drive for personal enrichment by making deals (as mentioned above) with smaller independent American oil companies. Regional alliances were set up by the United States to shore up its interests in the Indian Ocean area, including the Southeast Asian Treaty Organization (SEATO) in 1954, the Baghdad Pact, and the Central Treaty Organization (CENTO) (1958). Under the Eisenhower doctrine of 1957, the US Congress gave the president approval to intervene in the Middle East in response to the request of a local government for aid against communism. Arabs were alienated from the United States when in 1958 a group of Lebanese Muslims made a move for Lebanon to join the short-lived union of Syria with Egypt. President Eisenhower reacted to a call for help from Lebanon's Maronite Christian government by landing marines in Lebanon to foil the plan. Also in 1958, General Abdul Karim Qasim took power in Iraq in a bloody coup. With Kremlin encouragement, Qasim set up communist-dominated unions and professional associations. Qasim hoped to reincorporate Kuwait into Iraq, but was forced to back down by the arrival of British and Saudi Arabian forces. In 1963 Qasim and the communists would be defeated by another coup, this time headed by Baath socialists.

To preserve their control over Middle Eastern oil, the seven major oil companies rallied the leaders of the cooperating oil-producing countries to join them in 1960 at a Baghdad meeting held under the auspices of Abdullah Tariki of Iraq. There, they founded the Organization of Petroleum Exporting Countries (OPEC), as a lobby group for their collective interests. Working together in this fashion, in 1965 they won equal taxation of all oil companies by the US government, an arrangement that placed a greater burden on the independents. OPEC also proved to be a handy mechanism for the leaders of the oil-producing companies themselves to express their own interests.

Britain and France dissolved their African and Caribbean colonies in the late 1950s and early 1960s. The British prime minister Harold Macmillan, who was brought into office after the collapse of Anthony Eden's policy on the Suez Canal, committed himself to releasing the remaining colonies. As the Western powers left Africa and the Caribbean, Krushchev looked for openings to enter. Soviet encouragement was especially given to the new anti-American governments of Ghana, Mali, Guinea, and Cuba. When Eisenhower's government withheld foreign aid to Fidel Castro's Cuba, Krushchev stepped in in 1960 with credit, sugar subsidy and military equipment. After an American-encouraged invasion of Cuba by anti-Castro forces failed at the Bay of Pigs in April 1961, Khrushchev in July 1962 began sending in offensive ballistic nuclear missiles and bomber planes until President Kennedy demanded their withdrawal by threatening war, and by promising not to back another attack on Cuba. For the American part, by 1963 US Polaris submarines with missiles capable of reaching Soviet Central Asia were sailing the Indian Ocean.

Brezhnev's challenge

In 1964, a bloodless coup toppled Krushchev, and brought a return to a more overt hard-line policy in the Kremlin. Leonid Brezhnev, who was to lead the Soviet Union from 1964 to 1982, was the son of a factory worker of Dnepropetrovsk. Originally a mining engineer, he rose by bravery to be a major-general during army service in World War II. Latching on to Krushchev's star, he was made a member of the Central Committee in 1952, and president of the Politburo in 1960. The Brezhnev doctrine proclaimed that communist satellite states held only a limited sovereignty, and that the Soviet Union was obliged to intervene wherever communism was imperiled. Brezhnev escalated the war economy, spending 15 percent of the Soviet Union's gross national product on defense, compared to 5 percent in the United States at the same time. By 1976, the Soviet Union had the largest military force in the world. The Soviets were spending $70 billion a year more on weapons than were the Americans, and $3 billion a year more on weapon research. This massive Soviet military buildup was unequaled in history, and was little affected by the 1972 Russo-American SALT I agreement limiting the number of nuclear long-range missiles on both sides.

Calling for a further intensification of the struggle against the United States, Brezhnev authorized a coordination of worldwide guerrilla warfare and terrorism by a KGB (Committee of State Security) office in Paris. There Ilich Ramírez Sánchez of Venezuela maintained contact with the activities of the Uruguayan Tupamaros, the Quebec Liberation Front, the Irish Republican Army, the Baader-Meinhof gang of West Germany, the Basque separatists, and the Palestinian Liberation Organization, among others. Highjackings, bombings, and sieges were part of the activities that were planned and executed. The Soviet Union backed Muamar Qaddafi of Libya's export of revolution and terrorism. Marxist governments took control of Ethiopia, Mozambique, Guinea, the Congo, and other African nations.

In 1964, Britain announced that it would be withdrawing from the region east of Suez. In 1966, Britain and the United States agreed to share the islands of the newly-created British Indian Ocean Territory for military purposes. Then in 1968, Britain began a withdrawal from bases in the Orient, Singapore, Malaysia, New Zealand, Australia, Iran, Kuwait, Bahrain, Abu Dhabi, Saudi Arabia, Aden, the Maldives, Mauritius, East Africa, and South Africa. The American government in 1970 declared that the Indian Ocean was the third most strategic region after Europe and East Asia for American interests.

Diego Garcia, a tiny coral island in the very center of the Indian Ocean (named for its Portuguese discoverer in 1532, and bought by Britain from Mauritius in 1968), was chosen to be the pivot of American naval power in the Indian Ocean. A huge expenditure was made to develop it as a major joint British–US naval base, and it became operational in 1976. Such advanced weapons as nuclear arms came to be concentrated there for emergency use from 1981 on. Problems with the local population were obviated by Britain's evacuation of the natives from Diego Garcia to Mauritius in 1971. American missile-armed submarines began a permanent patrol of the Indian Ocean. In 1969, President Nixon arranged arms transfers, exchange of military information, and a degree of joint military planning with Australia. After the long period in which the Indian Ocean had been virtually a British sea, the region was left to American power to control.

Brezhnev vigorously attempted to counteract the new American strategic dominance in the Indian Ocean. The Soviet proposal to turn the Indian Ocean region into a nuclear-free zone, supported by a United Nations resolution in 1971, was rejected by the American government. Instead, both the United States and the Soviet Union assigned significant forces to the area, built up naval forces there, and sold arms to various local nations. The Soviet Union obtained bases in Iraq, Egypt, Sudan, Yemen, Aden, Somalia, and Tanzania. Brezhnev sent warships into the Indian Ocean from 1968 on. The Soviet Indian Ocean fleet was increased to six surface fighting ships and six submarines in 1971, and to 30 ships in 1979. By 1973, 80 percent of Soviet military supplies were being sent to the Indian Ocean region or to its immediate hinterland states. From 1975 to 1977, the Soviets stored anti-ship missiles at Berbera, Somalia. A Soviet naval base was established in Aden in 1977, and other military bases were located in Vietnam, Mogadishu (Somalia), Massawa (Ethiopia), and South Yemen, and mooring bays were developed off the Seychelles and Mauritius. However, the American naval force, with bases at Diego Garcia and Bahrain, was far greater than that of the Soviets. In the 1970s, the French also created an Indian Ocean fleet, which exceeded the size of the Soviet naval force there. Australia's naval and air presence was sophisticated, while the Israeli air force for its part frequently flew patrols over the Red Sea.

The Vietnam War might have led to the Soviet Union securing a hold on the eastern entrance into the Indian Ocean, but this danger was countered by developments in Indonesia. It is true that Russia's status was enhanced in this period by the US failure to maintain the capitalist government of South Vietnam. At the close of World War II, North Vietnam had been shaped into a communist state by Ho Chi Minh, founder of the Vietnamese Communist Party. After studying at the University of Moscow, Ho Chi Minh had joined the Kuomingtang in Canton in 1925. By fighting the Japanese occupation of Vietnam in World War II, he had become a hero, and was able to set up his own government at Hanoi. The French had tried unsuccessfully to dislodge him from power in the decade after the war. After the French withdrawal from the area in 1954, the communist-led movement pushed to reunite all of the country by attacking the corrupt government of the Catholic aristocrat Diem at Saigon in South Vietnam.

The Southeast Asia Treaty Organization (SEATO) was formed in 1954 by the United States to coordinate the military effort of America's allies in the region. SEATO members included Australia, New Zealand, the Philippines, Thailand, and Pakistan. US President Eisenhower sent some 700 US troops to South Vietnam as 'military advisors,' starting in 1955. The reactionary Catholic-flavored elitism of Diem's regime made his government unpopular with many of the Buddhist common folk of South Vietnam. The poor farmers particularly were upset over his decision to take recently distributed land back away from them, to the benefit of a few wealthy estate owners. Diem's policy brought a rural uprising under the National Liberation Front in 1960. North Vietnam used the issue to win inroads into the South by sending in aid. By 1962, Diem's hold on the country was so shaken that US President Kennedy sharply increased the number of US military advisors in South Vietnam, the number rising to 15,000 by the time of his death. By 1963, the situation was so dire that the South Vietnamese military pulled off a coup in which Diem was murdered and replaced by a series of generals.

The biggest stakes in Southeast Asia centered on control of the Strait of Malacca, the main eastern entry route into the Indian Ocean. The American position in these waters was endangered by President Sukarno's regime in oil-rich Indonesia, the dominant nation in the region, located on the southern side of the strait. Sukarno, a civil engineer who had founded the Indonesian nationalist party, had cooperated with the Japanese conquest of the Netherlands East Indies in 1942. On 17 August 1945, he had proclaimed Indonesian independence, with himself as president. The Dutch had finally accepted this loss in 1949. Sukarno challenged the Western powers with an expansionist policy that had conquered West New Guinea from the Netherlands and pressured the British-supported states of north Borneo. In 1963, West New Guinea was transferred from the Dutch to Indonesian administration, and after a 1969 plebiscite, it was be annexed into Indonesia. Ending elections in 1955, Sukarno declared himself president for life in 1963, and became increasingly close to the International Communist Party. This grew to be the third largest communist party in the world, with 3 million direct members plus 14 million members of the communist labor union and the communist youth movement. In 1964 and 1965, Sukarno turned his expansionism toward Malaysia, claiming it as a natural part of Indonesia, and launching raids against that country.

The United States thus needed to establish a strong presence in Southeast Asia, and the call for help from the corrupt but pro-Western government of South Vietnam offered the opportunity. The rationale given, along with concern to maintain democracy in South Vietnam, was the 'domino theory,' that a success or failure of anti-American forces in one country of the region could influence political developments in others. In 1964, it was claimed that the North Vietnamese fired on US navy ships in the Gulf of Tonkin.

In reaction, the US Congress gave President Johnson support for an escalation of the US involvement in Vietnam. In February 1965, Johnson accordingly ordered the bombing of military targets in North Vietnam. In March 1965, he committed 184,000 troops to fighting the Vietcong in South Vietnam, a number that grew to almost 500,000 troops by the end of 1967.

The stronger American presence in the area precipitated an attempted coup in Indonesia. On 30 September 1965, groups allegedly connected with the Indonesian communists tried to assume power, attacking top officers of the military. The army fought back under the leadership of General Suharto. On 30 October 1965, Suharto toppled President Sukarno, who subsequently retired to private life. The Indonesian Communist Party was destroyed within four months. The CIA via the US ambassador in Jakarta provided Suharto with a list of up to 5,000 names of communist party officials considered dangerous, and the Indonesian army executed them. Eventually, many – maybe a hundred – times this number of enemies of Suharto's takeover were rounded up and executed. Suharto assumed the title of president in March 1967, and restored elections, being elected and reelected over the next three decades.

The close ties between the United States and Singapore and Malaysia (along with Australia) also helped to bolster the American position in the eastern Indian Ocean. Britain's previous prime importance in Singapore's economy was assumed by the United States and Japan, which became the main provider of industrial products. Singapore's exports included petroleum products and computer parts. Britain, Japan, and the United States were the main trading partners in Malaysia's rubber, palm oil, and tin export economy. The British continued to control the bulk of the rubber production. Foodstuffs (especially rice) were important imports. From 1971, Malaysia began to export its recently discovered offshore oil, while Singapore emerged as an important oil-refining center. The profits earned were used to help make Malaysia a major exporter of light manufactured goods and electronic equipment. Both Malaysia and Indonesia continued a significant export of spices, tin, and rubber, including to Singapore. In 1967, Singapore, Malaysia, Indonesia, the Philippines, and Thailand joined in founding the pro-Western Association of Southeast Asian Nations (ASEAN) to work toward regional cooperation.

The United States thus maintained the upper hand in this region. Although a commitment to supporting the pro-Western regime in Saigon was still thought to be desirable, it was no longer crucial. The replacement under American pressure of the brash Ky as head of state in South Vietnam by the less objectionable President Thieu in 1967 brought no significant improvement of the situation. As the Vietcong continued to grow in strength, the question emerged of how the United States could withdraw its forces from South Vietnam without losing credibility. In March 1968, in the aftermath of the communist Tet Offensive and in the midst of antiwar demonstrations in the United States, President Johnson announced that he was applying the brakes to the war. In 1969, President Nixon began secret negotiations to bring the war to an end. In April 1970, he ordered US troops into Cambodia, in a last-ditch attempt to stop North Vietnamese troops from circumventing the demilitarized zone into South Vietnam by following the so-called Ho Chi Min Trail through Laos and Cambodia. When this attempt also failed, in January 1973, Nixon pulled the US troops out of Vietnam.

In this period, Nehru's daughter Indira Gandhi ruled India (1967–1984). Her husband was not related to the great Mahatma Gandhi, but gave Indira a married name whose political mystique augmented her maiden name. The ongoing cordiality of her relations with the Soviet Union (she visited Moscow in 1982), India's main arms supplier, encouraged her to act with a strong hand. In 1971, her backing of East Pakistan's revolt led to the creation of the new country of Bangladesh, weakening the Pakistani threat. Hundreds of thousands of Indians (along with Sri Lankans, Bangladeshis, and Pakistanis, all mainly Muslims) went as guest workers to the oil-producing countries of the Middle East. In 1975, her younger son Sanjay Gandhi convinced Indira to declare a state of emergency for India, and to impose a dictatorship. The press was censored, a forced sterilization program was introduced, and 10,000 people were arrested. However, democracy was soon restored when Sanjay died in a plane crash. Despite these measures, after being briefly voted out of office in 1977 and arrested for corruption, Indira was again elected prime minister in 1980. Under her drive, by the mid-1980s India developed its own nuclear device, and in 1988 would obtain a nuclear submarine from the Soviet Union. In 1984 she sent in guards to shoot down a Sikh separatist revolt centered on the Golden Mosque in Amritsar. In revenge, one of her own Sikh bodyguards assassinated her.

Brezhnev continued the Soviet defiance of China with his India policy. China, which exploded its first atomic bomb in 1964 and then rapidly went on to develop a hydrogen bomb, made its own pitch to win a Third World following. It was emphasized that the Chinese peasant-oriented brand of communism was more suitable for most of the rural Third World than was the industrial model from the Soviet Union. China joined the United States in supporting Pakistan's claims against India, and called for a build-up of American naval power in the Indian Ocean and western Pacific, as a counter to the growing Soviet presence there. The Soviet Union deployed long-range reconnaissance planes in the Indian Ocean, as well, to the concern of the United States.

Brezhnev's strategy involved moves into the eastern, central, and western sections of the Indian Ocean region. Brezhnev's greatest encroachment on the Anglo influence in the Indian Ocean area was at its western reaches. The Soviet Union found a potential position of strength on this most critical entry route into the Indian Ocean with the advent of a communist regime in Aden in 1967. The new nation was styled the People's Republic of South Yemen, and it dominated the passage into the ocean from the Red Sea. Over a century before, South Yemen had been detached from Ottoman-dominated North Yemen when in 1839 the British had occupied Aden. North Yemen had become independent as a result of the collapse of the Ottoman Empire at the end of the World War I, and it had established a pro-American republic after a civil war fought from 1962 to 1970. When the South won its own independence, expelling the British in 1967, it set up a pro-Soviet communist regime. The communist hold on South Yemen was fortified by the spread of communist regimes and rebellions to various other African countries. These included Mozambique and Angola in 1976, Guinea, the Republic of the Congo, Somalia, and Ethiopia. Cuban troops were used, under Russian officers, to train leftist forces in various parts of Africa. The Soviets aimed to interrupt the oil flow from the Middle East, as a way to blackmail the United States and its allies. Emphasis was placed on encouraging anti-Israeli Arabs to defy the United States, with its pro-Israeli policy.

In 1970, Iraq, Kuwait, and Iran (plus Algeria) were inspired by Colonel Qadaffi's successful bid for a higher cut of Libyan oil profits to demand the same arrangement for their countries. In 1973, the oil companies used OPEC to slap an oil embargo on the United States as punishment for its support of Israel. In 1971, the moderate Egyptian president Anwar Sadat foiled a KGB-backed coup plan to topple him, and formed closer ties to the United States. In Iraq in 1972 the Baath Party dictator Sadam Hussein (ruler *de facto* since 1968 and *de jure* from 1979) signed a treaty of friendship with the Soviet Union, and nationalized the British Petroleum Company's Iraqi holdings. The oil was redirected to sales to the Soviet Union for resale in western Europe. In 1973, the shah of Iran likewise nationalized 51 percent of the oil companies operating in his country, more than doubling the Iranian tax on oil, and quadrupling the price of oil in a two-month period. The Shah also sent some of his rapidly growing military forces to Oman (invited in by its sultan to crush a revolution there).

In January 1979, the shah was overthrown in what he charged as being partly a CIA-sponsored coup. If this was true, it was a miscalculation, for a strident anti-American fundamentalist Islamic regime under Ayatollah Ruhollah Khomeini replaced the shah's rule. On 4 November 1979, a mob of Muslim extremists condoned by Koumeini burst into the US embassy in Teheran, taking all of its staff hostage. US president Jimmy Carter sent a team to rescue the hostages, but the US helicopters broke down, leaving the hostage release to be slowly negotiated. Sadam's Iraq used the chaos in 1980 to temporarily take control of the oil-rich province of Kuzistan from Iran in the Iran–Iraq War.

The Soviet Union then occupied Afghanistan. Since the overthrow of the monarchy in 1973, the Afghanis had been divided between a traditionalist

Islamic faction and the secularizing and modernizing communists. A president of the Communist People's Democratic Party, Noor Muhammed Taraki, had started a program of land distribution, educational improvement, and the emancipation of women. When in September 1979, the Islamic traditionalists under Hafizullah Amin took power from Taraki, the Afghani communists called on the Soviet Union for help.

Brezhnev took advantage of the US hostage crisis in Teheran to invade Afghanistan in 1979 to help the People's Democratic Party. Amin was executed, and a new communist president, Babrak Karmal, was installed under protection of a large Soviet occupation army. Russian bombers based in Afghanistan could now endanger the Persian Gulf's oil trade. President Carter warned that Afghanistan might be a stepping-stone to Russian control over much of the world's oil supplies, and defined the Persian Gulf as being of vital interest to the United States. However, as had occurred with past Russian efforts to occupy Afghanistan, this effort ended in a stalemate. The Islamic traditionalists fought back, partly from bases in Iran, but mainly from Pakistan. They received military assistance from the United States by the mid-1980s, including the delivery of Stinger missiles. The war bogged down in an inconclusive and destructive civil war that was both costly and unpopular in Russia. As instability increased in the Persian Gulf region in 1980, President Carter in the 'Carter Doctrine' declared the area to be vital to American interests, so that an attempt to gain control of it would be fought by any means necessary. The Soviet invasion of Afghanistan induced President Carter in 1980 to inaugurate a rapid deployment force armed with atomic weapons to strike out from Diego Garcia (or Israel or Egypt) in times of emergency.

Iraq's Baath Party had moved farther from the West in 1964 by the nationalizing of heavy industry (including construction and steel), banks, insurance companies, and power production. After the Iraq Petroleum Company was nationalized in 1972, by 1975 the state-owned Iraq National Oil Company controlled the entire oil sector of the country. Iraq occupied Iran's oil-rich and Arab-speaking province of Kuzistan during the Iran–Iraq War of 1980–1989. Saudi Arabia also distanced itself somewhat from its American trading partners. King Faisal (1964–1972) stressed Islamic tradition as a balance to the growth of Western technology, and raised an oil embargo against all countries supporting Israel in the 1973 Arab–Israeli War. The Arabian American Oil Company (Aramco) became state owned under King Khalid in 1980. An effort was made to build a chemical and petrochemical industry to boost exports.

With the exception of the military stalemate in Afghanistan, the Soviet Union was riding higher than ever, when in the 1975 Helsinki Accord US President Gerald Ford in effect recognized the Soviet sphere of influence in eastern Europe. Despite serious setbacks in Indonesia and Pakistan, communism had made some major territorial gains in Yemen and Africa. Rajiv

Gandhi, India's prime minister, 1984–1989, continued his family's cordial attitude to the Kremlin. Alexander Solzhenitsyn warned that the Soviet Union was militarily stronger than ever, and was about to make a rapid move to destroy the West in a surprise attack. The British political philosopher Malcolm Muggeridge wrote that Solzhenitsyn's warning gave the United States its last chance.

The collapse of the USSR

After Brezhnev's death, Mikhail Gorbachev took charge of the Kremlin from 1985 to 1991. Born in 1931 in Stavropol, he was a graduate of the Stavropol Institute of Farm Economics and of Moscow University law school. A more sophisticated leader than any previous Kremlin boss since Lenin, Gorbachev formed close links with Western leaders, and Western ideas on international understanding met with a receptive audience in the Kremlin for the first time. Arguments for free market reforms seemed ever more appealing as the Russian economic crisis, aggravated by the Afghanistan embroglio, deepened. Confrontation with the United States around the rim of the Indian Ocean was meeting with checks at crucial points. Furthermore, American suggestions for military development (including President Jimmy Carter's proposal to develop a neutron bomb and President Ronald Reagan's plan for a Star Wars defense system to shoot down missiles from space) seemed beyond the capability of the Soviets. Reagan further increased the allocation for the US navy to about 40 percent of the annual arms budget. Space-strike weapons began to be deployed to Diego Garcia. Reagan's determination to match the Soviet nuclear build-up in Europe with new American missiles in western Europe pointed at the Soviet Union was also discouraging.

The world watched in amazement as Gorbachev dismantled the Soviet Empire in several steps. In 1985 and 1986, he replaced the blue-collar types from the Ukraine favored by Lenin and promoted by Stalin to the key positions in the state with white-collared university-trained Great Russians. The Politburo was filled with appointees drawn from the ranks of the academicians. A rapprochement with the United States came next. In 1987, Gorbachev and Reagan agreed to dismantle over 2,000 medium- and shorter-range missiles. Then in the 1988 INS Treaty, it was agreed to withdraw all medium-range missiles from western and central Europe. The next step was the policy of *glasnost* ('openness'). In 1988, Gorbachev relaxed censorship, released dissidents from prison, and encouraged free expression. Between 1988 and 1990, communist and Russian control of eastern Europe was dismantled. Soviet troops were also pulled out of Afghanistan in February 1989, and the communist president of Afghanistan Sayid Muhammad Najibullah was overthrown in 1992. The policy of *perestroika* ('restructuring') followed in 1990 and 1991, in both politics and economics.

Early in 1990, Gorbachev proposed to the Politburo that the Communist Party abandon its monopoly of power, and open the political process to genuine competition. This commitment allowed the non-communist Boris Yeltsin to be elected president of the Russian Republic. Gorbachev also advocated a free market economy.

Russo-American cooperation grew by leaps and bounds. In 1990, US President George Bush invited Russian representatives to a North Atlantic Treaty Organization (NATO) meeting, and the possibility of an eventual Russian membership in NATO was suggested. Russia was also included on guest status in the meeting of the G-7 top Western powers (the United States, Canada, Britain, France, Germany, Italy, and Japan). In June 1991, permission was granted for foreigners to buy up to 50 percent of the Russian defense industry companies. The final round of Gorbachev's dismantling of the Soviet Union began with his announcement that he planned to found a new, non-communist political party to replace communist domination in Russia. Gorbachev dissolved the Soviet Union on Christmas Day 1991. His work in Russia complete, Gorbachev became head of a prestigious new thinktank in Geneva. One of his organizations, committed to establishing a one-world government, held annual conferences in San Francisco. Another worked to create a one-world religion. Gorbachev's projects, funded by his Western capitalist backers, brought the Russian leadership to join in the latest Anglo schemes for maintaining peace. Plans were made for a new world order, in which India and other Indian Ocean nations were to thrive by contributing their vast resources and markets to a newly consolidated family of man.

Further reading

On India: Vidiadhar Surajprasad Naipaul, *India: A Wounded Civilization* (New York: Knopf, 1977); and Shashi Tharoor, *India: From Midnight to the Millennium* (New York: Little, Brown and Company, 1997).

On recent Islam: Roy R. Anderson, Robert F. Seibert, and Jon G. Wagner, *Politics and Change in the Middle East: Sources of Conflict and Accommodation* (Upper Saddle River, New Jersey: Prentice Hall, 1998); and Gabriel Kolko, *Confronting the Third World* (New York: Pantheon, 1988).

On US–Soviet relations: Robert Conquest, *Stalin: Breaker of Nations* (New York: Viking, 1991); Gale Stokes, *The Walls Came Tumbling Down: The Collapse of Communism in Eastern Europe* (New York: Oxford University, 1993); John Lewis Gaddis, *Strategies of Containment: A Critical Appraisal of Postwar American Security Policy* (New York: Oxford University, 1982); Gary R. Hess, *The United States' Emergence as a Southeast Asian Power, 1940–1950* (New York: Columbia University Press, 1987); Stephen E. Ambrose, *Rise to Globalism: American Foreign Policy Since 1938* (New York: Penguin Books, 1985); Raymond L. Garthoff, *Détente and Confrontation: American–Soviet Relations from Nixon to Reagan* (Washington, DC: Brookings Institution, 1985); Thomas E. Vadney, *The World since 1945: A Complete History of Global Change from 1945 to the Present* (New York Facts on File: 1998); Anita Bhatt, *The Strategic Role of {the} Indian Ocean in World Politics: The Case of Diego Garcia* (Delhi: Ajanta, 1992); Ilya V. Gaiduk, *The Soviet Union and the Vietnamese War* (Chicago, Illinois: Ivan R. Dee, 1996); Peter L. Hahn, *The United States, Great Britain, and Egypt, 1945–1956* (Chapel Hill: University of Northern Carolina Press, 1991); Anthony Sampson, *The Seven Sisters: The Great Oil Companies and the World They Made* (New York: Viking, 1975); Carl Solberg, *Oil Power, the Rise and Imminent Fall of an American Empire* (New York: Mentor, 1976).

Chapter 9

The latest turn of the wheel

With the United States acknowledged as the world's only remaining superpower, American leadership surged ahead in the Indian Ocean and worldwide. However, the growing American role in Indian Ocean commerce was shared with business interests native to the region. Singapore and Malaysia both enjoyed a trade surplus. Singapore especially flourished with its liberal taxes, its streamlined customs procedures, and its largely duty-free import and export policy. The United States was Singapore's largest trading partner (followed by Malaysia, Hong Kong, and Japan). Over half of Singapore's exports of electronics, computers, and machinery derived from American-owned factories located there. Singapore also exported petroleum products and chemicals. Japan was Singapore's main provider of imports (25 percent), and Singapore was a major investor in China, and was its fifth largest trading partner. Singapore was the location of the first World Trade Organization ministerial meeting, in 1996. Malaysia sought to spur the iron and steel industry, and manufactured goods rose to 77.4 percent of Malaysian exports in 1994. In 1991, prime minister Mahathir of Malaysia promoted the East Asian Economic Caucus (EAEC) as a self-protecting trading block between Southeast Asian member countries, aimed at combating an inequitable competition from Western economies. Indonesia remained a main exporter of oil, as well as of furniture, garments, shoes, machinery, and electronics.

In the 1990s, India's economy began to expand as a result of a limited deregulation and free-market reforms initiated in 1991 by Prime Minister Narasimha Rao. Even though tariff and non-tariff barriers remained high, American and other foreign private businesses were encouraged to invest, and high-technology companies set up shop in Bangalore and other cities. American manufacturing, energy, and other firms invested billions of dollars in India, and trade between India and the United States doubled in the 1990s. India's most successful industries (computers, software, and films) were precisely those that were most integrated into the world economy. Indian exports to the United States increased more than 10 percent from 1998 to 2000. The growing American exports to India included computers, aircraft, heavy machinery, fertilizer, and textbooks. The remaining high tariffs, however, set a limit to the American impact, while hampering imports from the neighboring countries of the Indian Ocean. In contrast to India's development, Pakistan's economy put in a weak performance. Two moves in 1992 and 1997 toward privatization led both to labor unrest. In East Africa, the discovery in 2001 of the Bulyanhulu mine allowed Tanzania to become an important exporter of gold, along with its traditional agricultural products. Oil continued to dominate the exports from the Middle Eastern segment of the Indian Ocean region. The bulk of oil imports went to western Europe and East Asia (led by Japan), but the health of the American economy was intimately connected with that of its western European and Asian trading partners. Oil remained the biggest single source of world energy (35 percent in 1996). Petroleum accounted for 90 percent of Saudi Arabian export earnings in 2000.

The weakening of Soviet patronage in the Middle East (described in the previous chapter) made it easier for the Americans in 1990 to take a strong stand in defense of Kuwait when Saddam Hussein's forces attacked it. Lured by its oil wealth, and claiming it as part of the Iraqi homeland, Saddam had ordered the invasion of Kuwait in the mistaken belief that the United States would not oppose him. However, the prospect of Iraq controlling 40 percent of Middle Eastern oil was a major challenge to American power. In the resulting Persian Gulf War in early 1991, sixteen countries, including the United Kingdom, Canada, Australia, and New Zealand, joined the United States in an invasion of Iraq. Victorious, they nonetheless stopped short of total occupation, thereby maintaining a united Iraq as a barrier to Iranian dominance of the Persian Gulf region. Had they carried out a total occupation, separatist Kurds in the north and Shiites in the south might have fragmented the country. All the same, the United Nations tried to monitor and deter any Iraqi development of weapons of mass destruction by Saddam Hussein's continuing defiant regime. Economic sanctions against Iraq were imposed, and the Iraqi people suffered from the shattered economy, despite a United Nations program in 1996 allowing food and medicine to be purchased in exchange for limited oil exports.

The American dream of a one world order

The age-old trend of ever more distant regions playing a prominent role in Indian Ocean trade reached its geographic limit with the involvement of the United States in the region. Reactions to the growing American presence in the Indian Ocean region came to be connected with negative attitudes about globalization (in the sense of the blending of cultural influences around the world). For Asia, globalization amounted to Westernization, and this to a significant extent meant Americanization, given the strong American impact on Western culture in general. The acceptance of globalization suggested friendliness to the United States; resistance to it implied loyalty to regional values. As China joined the rest of East Asia in embracing westernization (which had come to Africa previously), the Indian Ocean was left as the largest region of the world resisting globalization/ Westernization.

Encouragement of globalization was linked to the ideology of a 'one world order.' First espoused by Britain's Round Table Group and the League of Nations in the early twentieth century, this concept was cultivated by influential elements of American society as well. In the wake of America's success in World War I, a group of American business and political leaders had begun to investigate how to create a harmonious world society. In 1921, John D. Rockefeller, Jr., J. P. Morgan, Jr., Paul Warburg, Bernard Baruch, and others founded the Council on Foreign Relations in New York City. Its goal was to work toward worldwide integration and thus to create a peaceful future (which would hopefully also benefit US corporations). The methods to achieve this aim most centrally included the promotion of supernational controls and the creation of a harmonious global society (entailing the Americanization of other countries and the internationalization of the United States).

Between 1942 and 1946, as a result of US efforts, the International Monetary Fund, the International Bank for Reconstruction and Development (IBRD), and the General Agreement on Tariffs and Trade (GATT) were established. After the war, the trend was continued by the creation of supranational organizations like the United Nations (UN), the North Atlantic Treaty Organization (NATO), and the European Common Market. As the Round Table Group had once helped to set up the League of Nations, so the Council on Foreign Relations played a role in founding the United Nations in 1945 as an instrument for establishing coordination between nations and order in the world. President Truman appointed an advisory committee that created a Security Council made up of permanent delegates from the United States, Great Britain, France, Russia, and China, and a General Assembly with one delegate from each nation. The United Nations authorized force to handle world crises. In 1950, with the United States boycotting, it sent UN troops to resist the invasion of South Korea by North Korea. Members of the Council on Foreign Relations also helped to design the Marshall Plan and NATO. In 1954, the Bilderberger group was founded to coordinate the activities of the Council on Foreign Relations with its European counterparts. In 1972, the Trilateral Commission was founded to bring leading Japanese figures alongside their American and western European counterparts.

An important step in the direction of breaking down national barriers was made in the breaking down of national trade barriers. The supporters of international free trade launched a movement to group the world into a handful of free trade zones that could then be interconnected. This agenda was started under President Carter (1977–1981), whose national security advisor, Zbigniew Brzezinski, in his book *Between Two Ages* (1970), had stated that American national interests must now take second place to international interests in order to create a desirable future world. Free trade was given a big impetus under George Bush, president from 1989 through 1993. In 1990, Bush and Gorbachev negotiated a major arms reduction in Europe. The next year, Bush invited Gorbachev to a NATO meeting, and the Soviets declared that foreigners could buy Soviet companies, including up to fifty per cent of the defense industry. After the dismantling of the Soviet Union and its satellite empire in eastern Europe, Gorbachev retired in 1991 to Geneva to become director of a thinktank on international affairs, committed to working for a one-world government and a one-world religion (see page 166). Also under Bush, a new free trade zone of Canada and the United States was set up, in cooperation with Prime Minister Brian Mulrooney of Canada. The plan to include Mexico was formulated at a meeting in June 1990 of George Bush with Mexican president Carlos Salinas de Gortari. The addition of Mexico to the American and Canadian free trade zone was brought to realization under Bush's successor Bill Clinton, with the establishment of the North American Free Trade Association (NAFTA) on 1 January 1994.

Meanwhile, the Treaty of Maastricht restructured the European Common Market into the European Union (EU) in 1993. By 1995, the EU had expanded to fifteen member countries, and was still rapidly growing. German chancellor Helmut Kohl, in agreement with the White House, worked to involve eastern Europe in both the EU and NATO. In 1996, Canada proposed bringing together NAFTA and the EU in a proposed Trans-Atlantic Free Trade Association (TAFTA), to be expanded to all the Western Hemisphere and Europe. President George W. Bush at a conference held in Quebec in 2001 joined with the other Western Hemisphere heads of state (with the exception of Fidel Castro) in recommending a free trade zone of all the Americas. World trade agreements also worked toward the goal of universal free trade, and the G-7 organization of the heads of the seven leading industrial nations reached for international co-operation.

The growing internationalization of big business likewise promoted the idea of world integration. As each big business competed for greater profits through cheap labor, factories shifted increasingly to Third World nations. NAFTA facilitated the shift of American industry to Mexico. American, European, and Japanese industry alike moved to Third World countries of the Far East. Chinese-speaking Hong Kong, Macao, and Taiwan, largely Chinese Singapore, and South Korea, Thailand, Vietnam, the Philippines, and India were among the beneficiaries. Investment in China itself became ever more popular. Political freedom spread (140 of the nearly 200 nations of the world now hold multiparty elections). The percentage of people living in poverty decreased; the infant mortality rate dropped; and education improved.

Americanization of other countries and internationalization of the United States

The call for a blending of societies around the globe was another aspect of the program for a new world order, to be achieved by Americanization around the world and by internationalization of American/Anglo society. The internationalization of Anglo society was furthered by the immigration of ethnic groups from Third World nations, making the United States, England, Australia, and Canada all more multiracial. American stores and products (including notably McDonald's and Hollywood films) spearheaded Americanization around the globe. The spread of the internet accelerated the use of English as the international language. The Peace Corps from 1961 sent volunteer American workers to help projects in developing countries, hopefully creating good will for the United States and hastening Americanization.

As in all previous periods, religion interacted powerfully with the trends in trade and politics. Some people called for a merging of all world religions into one harmonious blend. The 'New Age' fashion for religious syncretism thus repeated what had occurred in the Hellenistic and Roman Empires, with the same motivation of avoiding social conflict. Other religions beside Judeo-Christianity were popularized in the United States, including Maharishi Mahesh Yogi's Transcendental Meditation, the Hare Krishnas, EST (Erhard Seminars Training), the Unification Church, Scientology, the Rastafarians, and the Black Muslims. Witchcraft enjoyed a revival, boosted by the popularity of J.K. Rowlings's *Harry Potter* series of books about a young warlock in training.

However, many groups both in the United States and around the world vehemently rejected globalization and either atheism or religious syncretism. The American cultural component in globalization drew special criticism. It was pointed out that, while American creativity was very impressive in science and technology (from cell phones to computers), American culture was not up to par in the arts and humanities. There are various possible explanations for this failure. The first move in this direction had come with the impact of Jacksonian anti-intellectualism in the early nineteenth century, which had been countered in brilliant but ephemeral fashion by the New England transcendentalists. The materialist culture of the Gilded Age had swept away the transcendentalist mood with a Marktwainian sneer. The growing global importance of the United States after World War I had elicited a rich harvest of writers, but many of these (including Gertrude Stein, Hemingway, and F. Scott Fitzgerald) had felt alienated from pragmatic American society, and had sought refuge in European culture. The fact that Britain smoothed the way to world prominence for the United States (as its main ally and daughter society) meant that the American rise to power was not accompanied by quite the same level of creative anxiety or excitement as had been the case with former *nouveau arrivé* societies involved with the Indian Ocean. In the second half of the twentieth century, American creativity virtually capitulated to the often moronic and vulgar standards propagated by television programming and Hollywood special-effects movies.

Widespread and extreme opposition around the globe threw the feasibility of establishing a universal order into serious question. In Japan, Mishima Yukio, author of *The Sea of Fertility*, committed suicide in 1970 in protest against the Americanization of Japan. In Germany, racists detonated bombs to drive out Turkish immigrants. In the United States, the move to globalization elicited negative reactions from both the right (including white suprematists, religious fundamentalists, and political conservatives) and from the left (including Ralph Nader and the demonstrators against the World Bank and International Monetary Fund). More extreme manifestations (coming from Americans and non-Americans alike) included the bombing by Timothy McVeigh of the Federal Building in Oklahoma City in April 1995.

The Indian Ocean reaction to globalization

The resolution of the globalist issue came to be intimately connected with the success or failure of American/Anglo leadership in the Indian Ocean area. The predominant religions of this region – Islam and Hinduism – resisted attempts to water them down by equating them with other religions or by challenging their absolute precepts and standards. The continuing strength of fundamentalist and authoritarian Shiitism, Wahhabi Sunnitism, Arab nationalism, and (in India) the Vishwa Hindu Parishad (World Hindu Council) challenged such Anglo-inspired reforms in the Indian Ocean arena. To counter these views, there was talk of nurturing a moderate form of Islam, more tolerant of popular rights and representative government. Christianity itself had undergone a similar transition in the early seventeenth century when William Ames (who received his doctorate in 1607 and subsequently taught at Christ's College, Cambridge) had posited a Christian basis for representative government by pointing to God's own willingness to make contracts ('covenants') with people. This had helped to prepare English society for John Locke's fully secular rationale for the same development by the end of the seventeenth century. The question was whether Islam and Hinduism offered a similar doctrinal base for such liberalization. If so, would Muslims and Hindus be willing to accept the many problems that had accompanied a freer (and, in its case, more secular) society in the West?

Extremists answered violently in the negative. Attempts to import Western (often especially American) mores have led to attacks on McDonald's restaurants and manifestations against the observance of Valentine's Day.

Muslim groups have raised the call of *jihad* to fight off the latest Western 'crusaders.' In 1979, Islamists (protesting the growth of Western culture as corrupting Islamic society) occupied the Grand Mosque in Mecca. Attacks on Christians were perpetrated from Pakistan and India to Indonesia. The destruction of the World Trade Center (whose wreckage, ironically, was recycled in northern India) on 11 September 2001 was carried out by suicide bombers from Egypt and Saudi Arabia, and coordinated by plotters based in Afghanistan. Al-Qaeda terrorist hideouts ringed the Indian Ocean, from Somalia and Yemen through Iraq and Iran, Afghanistan and Pakistan, to the Philippines. Using both the carrot and the stick, the American-led Western alliance in the fall of 2001 toppled the hostile Taliban government in Afghanistan, and wooed Afghani elites by giving them the hope of joining at least marginally in Western prosperity (and democracy).

In 2002 and 2003, the increasingly imperiled American position in the Indian Ocean region came to focus again on Saddam Hussein: anti-American, responsible for the cold-blooded murder of his sons-in-laws, close associates, and Iraqi minorities, and with a record of aggression against his neighbors (Iran and Kuwait). Hussein's unpredictable and extreme behavior posed a threat for the American-supported status quo in the region. President George W. Bush turned to the United Nations (the organization initially established to bring global unity behind an Anglo-spun dream of world order) to win international support for a war to topple Hussein and to eliminate any weapons of mass destruction he had stockpiled. American military installations in Diego Garcia, Saudi Arabia, Egypt, Jordan, Turkey, Kuwait, Bahrain, Qatar, the United Arab Emirates, and Oman (added to those in Europe), along with a massing of ships in the Persian Gulf, provided a source of American strength on Iraq's doorstep. However, the main traditional rivals of the Anglo powers (France, Germany, and Russia) plus China (with its age-old interest in the Indian Ocean region) joined in opposition to any United Nations approval of an American-led attack on Iraq. The arms-for-oil arrangements and other business connections between these same countries and Saddam Hussein were jeopardized by the plans for invasion. French, Russian, and Chinese companies were under contract to develop Iraqi oil fields; France, Russia, and China were due vast sums of money from unpaid Iraqi loans; and Russia was Hussein's main weapons provider, followed by China. On the other hand, the active support shown by Spanish prime minister José María Aznar for the American and British position evoked the cooperation between Iberia and England that had prevailed when the North Atlantic first rose to importance in the Indian Ocean trade in the sixteenth century.

On 19 March 2003, the leading Anglo powers of the United States, Great Britain, and Australia joined in an invasion of Iraq. Speculation that American forces might need to occupy Iraq for years in order to guarantee the founding of a Western-style capitalist democracy raised opposition cries of 'neo-imperialism.' The Bush administration emphasized its commitment to better the lives of the Iraqi masses with rights and liberties, as the British had once spoken (and acted) in their period of ascendancy over the Indian Ocean. The success of the occupation depended in part on whether the Muslim and wider world would accept it as the path to a more humanitarian and democratic Iraq as well as a safer and better world.

Final summary

One might argue that a geographic predeterminism runs through history. Geography dictated that Indian Ocean area lands would give rise to the earliest civilizations, which drew in envious barbarians, who brought down all but less exposed Egypt. Egypt's prominence encouraged its Mediterranean trading partners to get involved. At the same time, China was stimulated by the same spread of trade to reach out for a presence in the Indian Ocean. China's and the Mediterranean's distance from the Indian Ocean (and the impact of the Central Asian nomads) worked against them, and for a time Mediterranean and Chinese participation waned from the Indian Ocean trading scene. Eventually, these more distant regions recovered and reasserted their participation in the trade. However, renewed nomadic destructiveness against Asia and the Middle East (this time by the Mongols) gave Europeans a freer hand. The specific success of Venice led to a Genoese push for alternate routes that helped Portugal to enter the Indian Ocean by a hitherto unknown back door. The stronger nations of Atlantic Europe naturally elbowed their way in. England's insular position brought it to dominate for a time. However, its increasing control of the North Atlantic led to a larger overseas Anglo community on the American side of the North Atlantic, which eventually took the lead. By the start of the twenty-first century, challenges to American policy in the Indian Ocean region dominated the headlines, from terrorism in Indonesia through military occupation of Afghanistan, alliance with Qatar, embroglio in Iraq, and missiles in Yemen, to terrorism in Kenya. Some argued that the United States was becoming too involved with an attempt to control this part of the world, while others maintained that action was necessary to prevent a bigger problem in the near future. What was certain was that, if the United States wanted to maintain its position as the world's only superpower, it needed to act both decisively and wisely in the Indian Ocean area.

The wheel of world history, which had raised one power after another to the top for so long, has never been easy to control. We can study the various factors involved in its relentless motion, but its course is never certain. As it continues to move, the United States could find itself being lifted higher or hurtled back down. Whatever the outcome, the Indian Ocean region continues to form, as always, the hub of the wheel.

Further reading

On globalization and reactions to it: Karen Armstrong, *The Battle for God* (New York: Alfred A. Knopf, 2000); Benjamin R. Barber, *Jihad Vs. McWorld: How Globalism and Tribalism Are Reshaping the World* (New York: Ballantine, 1996); Martin Boothe, *The Triads: The Growing Global Threat from the Chinese Criminal Societies* (New York: St. Martin's Press, 1990); F. Gregory Gause III, *Oil Monarchies: Domestic and Security Challenges in the Arab Gulf States* (New York: Council On Foreign Relations Press, 1994); Samuel P. Huntington, *The Clash of Civilizations and the Remaking of the World Order* (New York: Simon and Schuster, 1996); and Peter N. Stearns, *Consumerism in World History: The Global Transformation of Desire* (London and New York: Routledge, 2001).

On the United States: *Problems of Sea Power As We Approach the Twenty-first Century* (Washington, DC: American Enterprise Institute for Public Policy Research, 1978); and Michael Klare, *Rogue States and Nuclear Outlaws: America's Search for a New Foreign Policy* (New York: Hill and Wang, 1995).

Index

eBooks – at www.eBookstore.tandf.co.uk

A library at your fingertips!

eBooks are electronic versions of printed books. You can store them on your PC/laptop or browse them online.

They have advantages for anyone needing rapid access to a wide variety of published, copyright information.

eBooks can help your research by enabling you to bookmark chapters, annotate text and use instant searches to find specific words or phrases. Several eBook files would fit on even a small laptop or PDA.

NEW: Save money by eSubscribing: cheap, online access to any eBook for as long as you need it.

Annual subscription packages

We now offer special low-cost bulk subscriptions to packages of eBooks in certain subject areas. These are available to libraries or to individuals.

For more information please contact webmaster.ebooks@tandf.co.uk

We're continually developing the eBook concept, so keep up to date by visiting the website.

www.eBookstore.tandf.co.uk